SILICON
SNAKE OIL

ALSO BY CLIFFORD STOLL

The Cuckoo's Egg

SILICON SNAKE OIL

Second Thoughts on the Information Highway

CLIFFORD STOLL

MACMILLAN

First published in Great Britain 1995 by Macmillan

an imprint of Macmillan General Books
Cavaye Place London SW10 9PG
and Basingstoke

Associated companies throughout the world

ISBN 0 333 64787 4

1 3 5 7 9 8 6 4 2

A CIP catalogue record for this book is available from
the British Library

Printed by Mackays of Chatham PLC, Chatham, Kent

TO ZOE ROSE

SILICON
SNAKE OIL

Me, an Internet addict? Hey—I'm leading a full life, with family, friends, and a job. Computers are a sideline, not my life.

Jupiter is rising in the east, looking down on the Connecticut farm where I'm vacationing. On one side, a forest; on the other, a cornfield. Three guys are talking about the Knicks in the next room; in the kitchen, several women are buttering popcorn. One of them just called my name. But I don't care.

Fingers on the keyboard, I'm bathed in the cold glow of my cathode-ray tube, answering e-mail. While one guy's checking the sky through binoculars, and another's stuffing himself with popcorn, I'm tapping out a letter to a stranger across the continent. My attention's directed to the Internet.

Tonight, twenty letters want replies, three people have invited me to chat over the network, there's a dozen newsgroups to read, and a volley of files to download. How can I keep up?

I see my reflection in the screen and a chill runs down my spine. Even on vacation, I can't escape the computer networks.

I take a deep breath and pull the plug.

For fifteen years, I've been online, watching as thousands of computers joined hands to form a ubiquitous global network. At first, the nascent Arpanet seemed like an academic toy, a novelty to connect inanimate computers across the continent. Later, this plaything began supplying electronic mail and an occasional data file from other astronomers.

As the Arpanet grew into the Internet, I began to depend on e-mail to keep up with colleagues and friends. The Usenet brought news from around the continent. It became a whole new way to communicate.

Then, in 1986, while managing a computer system in Berkeley, I stumbled on a group of hackers breaking into computers. No ordinary cyberpunks, these: they sold their discoveries to the Soviet KGB.

It took a year to chase them down. During that time, I realized that our networks aren't simple connections of cables and computers; they're cooperative communities.

Since then, the Internet has become a most inviting and intriguing neighborhood. E-mail and chat lines keep me in touch with friends around the world; data transfers let me exchange information with colleagues. I join in discussions over the Usenet, posting queries and answering questions. One click of the mouse and I can read the daily news or a monthly report. At once it's fun and challenging.

But what a price! Simply keeping track of this electronic neighborhood takes a couple of hours every night. I find myself pawing through internet archives or searching for novelties over the World Wide Web. I spend still more time downloading files and following newsgroups. Bit by bit, my days dribble away, trickling out my modem.

But for all this communication, little of the information is genuinely useful. The computer gets my full attention, yet either because of content or format, the network doesn't seem to satisfy.

I can't turn my back on the network. Or can I? Right now, I'm scratching my head, wondering.

Perhaps our networked world isn't a universal doorway to freedom. Might it be a distraction from reality? An ostrich hole to divert our attention and resources from social problems? A misuse of technology that encourages passive rather than active participation? I'm starting to ask questions like this, and I'm not the first.

. . . .

And so I'm writing this free-form meditation out of a sense of perplexity. Computers themselves don't bother me, it's the culture in which they're enshrined.

What follows, I suppose, shows my increasing ambivalence toward this most trendy community. As the networks evolve, so do my opinions toward them, and my divergent feelings bring out conflicting points of view. In advance, I apologize to those who expect a consistent position from me. I'm still rearranging my mental furniture.

I suspect I'll disappoint science-fiction romantics as well. Nobody can offer utopia-on-a-stick, the glowing virtual community that enhances our world through discovery and close ties while transcending the coarseness of human nature.

Oh, I care about what happens to our networked neighborhood. However, I care more about—and am affected more by—what's happening in our larger society. So do parents, professors, teachers, librarians, and, yes, even politicians.

When I put on my cone-shaped thinking cap, I wonder what I would have said fifty years ago, when the interstate highway system was first proposed. Plenty of people favored it: truckers, farmers, and shippers wanted to break the railroad monopoly. Political subdivisions, car makers, and construction unions knew it would generate money. Politicians from every state felt highways were universally good things.

Who spoke out against the superhighway system? I don't remember anyone saying, "Hey, these beltways will destroy our cities. They'll pave over pristine lands and give us hour-long commutes. They'll change our society from one of neighborhoods to that of suburbs."

In advance, then, here are my strong reservations about the wave of computer networks. They isolate us from one another and cheapen the meaning of actual experience. They work against literacy and creativity. They will undercut our schools and libraries.

Forgive me. I don't want to pontificate. But I do want people to think about the decisions they're making. It'd be fun to write about the wonderful times I've had online and the terrific people I've met through my modem, but here I'm waving a flag. A yellow flag that says, "You're entering a nonexistent universe. Consider the consequences."

It's an unreal universe, a soluble tissue of nothingness. While the Internet beckons brightly, seductively flashing an icon of knowledge-as-power, this nonplace lures us to surrender our time on earth. A poor substitute it is, this virtual reality where frustration is legion and where—in the holy names of Education and Progress—important aspects of human interactions are relentlessly devalued.

End of philippic. I don't mean to lay down an unwelcome mat. Nor do I feel that I'm entitled to technogoodies and others aren't. Quite the contrary: I look forward to the time when our Internet reaches into every town and trailer park. But the medium is being oversold, our expectations have become bloated, and there's damned little critical discussion of the implications of an online world.

ONE

A Speleological Introduction to the
Author's Ambivalence

It's some caving trip: Far below you is an active volcano from which great gouts of molten lava come surging out, cascading back down into the depths. The glowing rock fills the farthest reaches of the cavern with a blood-red glare, giving everything an eerie, macabre appearance. The air is filled with flickering sparks of ash and a heavy smell of brimstone. Embedded in the jagged roof far overhead are myriad twisted formations composed of pure white alabaster, which scatter the murky light into sinister apparitions on the walls. To one side is a deep gorge filled with a bizarre chaos of tortured rock that seems to have been crafted by the devil himself. An immense river of fire crashes out from the depths of the volcano, burns its way through the gorge, and plummets into a bottom pit far off to your left. The far right wall is aflame with an incandescence of its own, which lends an additional infernal splendor to the already hellish scene.

Yow—this is heady stuff. The year: 1976. I'd just started graduate school at the University of Arizona in Tucson. Next to me is a home-brew computer with a row of toggle switches on the front panel. I've fired up a computer game called Adventure, written by Will Crowther and Don Wood. The object is to explore a cave and find hidden treasures.

I watch this purple passage scroll across my beat-up TV monitor.

It's an early virtual-reality game, though that term, along with *Internet* and *cyberpunk*, has not yet been invented. I'm wasting time, the main occupation of grad students.

Nearly twenty years have passed. Today, nobody plays Adventure. It's been supplanted by MUDs—Multi-User Dungeons—where you not only explore programmed worlds, but interact with other users as well. These games are virtual realities over the Internet. Like their predecessor, these fantasy role-playing games are creatively programmed with tantalizing clues to solve dangerous quests.

Still, when it comes to caves, I've been swallowed up by the real thing, and it's far scarier and much muddier than anything you'll find on a computer screen.

But go back to 1976. Something didn't quite feel authentic about the words that flickered across my primitive screen. Alabaster in a lava cave? It didn't jibe with what I'd heard in my geology class. Basalt maybe. But not a carbonate rock.

So I ask the guy in the next cubicle. He's wearing a Hawaiian floral shirt, cutoff jeans, and no shoes. On his desk, a stack of physics texts, a slide rule, and a couple of stale burritos. His name is written on the side of a *Boy Scout Handbook:* Jon Gradie.

Jon looks up from a photomap of Mars. "Funny you should ask about cave formations," he replies. "I know a great cave fifty miles south of here. It makes the lunar highlands look like a parking lot. C'mon along and see for yourself."

I've hardly met this guy—do I trust him enough to lead an expedition through a maze of stalagmites, rubble, and guano? As an astronomer, he might know his way around the asteroid belt, but that doesn't mean much a hundred feet under a slab of Arizona limestone.

On the other hand, four other grad students were already planning to go, and Jon promised a side trip to the core-mantle boundary. He also mentioned bringing along several members of the opposite sex. This was during Tucson's great woman shortage, so the question was settled.

Now, real cavers bring helmets, rope, three sources of light, and an experienced leader. We had baseball caps, a ball of string, a couple of feeble flashlights, and Jon Gradie.

Cave of the Bells is two miles up a dry gulch, down the slope from the multimirror observatory. (Around Tucson, every hiking trail is downslope from some observatory.) There's barrel cactus along the way; nearby, a bird is singing.

"Just follow me," Jon tells us. "I came here with my fraternity three years ago." This explains the beer bottles near the entrance, but doesn't exactly inspire confidence. Neither does the rattlesnake, hissing by the hole in the limestone wall. Jon waves a long stick, and it slithers away.

I'm wearing a grubby T-shirt, faded jeans, and cheap sneakers— same as in class. We climb down a knotted rope into a pitch-black cavern that smells dank. The flashlights don't help much, and neither does one of the women, who's already babbling about claustrophobia. Still, we start in, trailing a string through the muddy tunnel —everything's covered with gunk, as are the six of us crawling behind Jon. Not your ordinary slimy, brown, backyard mud, either. This is the goop of inner-earth that works its way into your hair, socks, and underwear.

"This cave is easy," Jon explains as he crawls ahead of us. "It goes all the way until it quits." Through twenty feet of tunnel, all I see of him is the bottoms of his shoes.

The ball of string is patently stupid: five hundred feet into the cave, the twine runs out. Jon doesn't care—he's way ahead, yelling for us to hurry up. Slathered with mud, we follow, occasionally glancing back, wondering if we'll ever see daylight again. Time and distance have no meaning. How many turns have we made, how many rooms have we crawled through?

Ahead in the distance, echoes of Jon's voice, calling to hurry up. One of the women sits down, swearing that she won't take another step without knowing where we're going. The rest of us plead with her to continue, seeing how Jon's still way beyond us, down some tunnel in the blackness.

Two of us are limping when we finally catch up with Jon, seven million kilometers down. He's treading water in a cobalt-blue pool, flashlight beam reflecting off delicate limestone stalagmites.

"The blue's from copper salts leached out of the Bisbee vein," Jon's explaining. "The same acids that eat through this limestone are chewing at the metal ores up above."

There's Jon Gradie swimming in the nude, lecturing us on groundwater percolation. "Those marks on the wall show how the water table has dropped over the past century; probably as good of a record as exists." I peel off mud-caked jeans, wondering how this guy, who's written a dozen papers on infrared properties of asteroids, knows so much about hydrology and karst geomorphology. And so little about leading a cave trip.

Three others have a water fight while I float on my back, looking up at the shadowy ceiling. Way above, the desert might be shimmering in heat for all I know. Down here in the dark and quiet, it's a constant seventy degrees, and I'm swimming in the biggest lake south of Tucson. Probably the only lake south of Tucson.

Getting out is as bad as getting in. We're down to one flashlight, and most of us have dinged our heads on stalactites. Jon's way ahead, calling to hurry up; I'm trying to stay in sight. The knotted rope leads the way to the surface. We crawl out of the pit to find Jon toasting some burritos over a campfire. They taste muddy.

Report from the earth's core-mantle boundary: it's dark, humid, and muddy. And the only women we found were covered with mud.

You're right: this has little to do with the Internet. But every time someone mentions MUDs and virtual reality, I think of a genuine reality with muddier mud than anything a computer can deliver.

In 1986, the budding Internet linked perhaps sixty thousand people. Today, there's well beyond two million online. And a hundred thousand more join every month. What once felt like a small town is now a congested, impersonal New York City of the mind, where you no longer recognize the person who's talking to you.

I sense an insatiable demand for connectivity. Maybe all these people have discovered important uses for the Internet. Perhaps some of them feel hungry for a community that our real neighborhoods don't deliver. At least a few must wonder what the big deal is.

Being online conveys a strange type of prestige. Those with modems display their network addresses on business cards and letterheads. What was once as geeky as a pocket protector has become a status symbol. It's the ultimate revenge of the nerds.

Used to be that only scientists, engineers, and academics used e-mail . . . myself included. Networks were a part of the R and D culture—a useful tool to communicate with colleagues and exchange data. While mainly technical and academic, the traffic on the networks slowly became less formal. By the early nineties, the Internet had evolved into a self-contained, anarchistic community, with nobody in charge. At the same time, it's promoted as a legitimate conduit for governmental and public communication.

Public officials now speak of the Internet as a major resource in our nation's commercial and academic infrastructure. No longer an experiment, it's to become a part of our schools, our businesses, our homes, our lives.

Yet who knows what the proposed National Information Infrastructure will be?

Will it be a scheme for hundreds of video channels over cable? Will it become a way to bring the Internet out of the universities and into our homes and public schools? Will it be primarily a commercial endeavor or a public service? Will the government regulate its growth and content? Will it be a part of the telephone or cable-television system? Should I worry that local bulletin boards won't have access? Will the government further subsidize an industry that's making lots of money already?

The answer is yes to all of the above, and more. Authors of the National Information Infrastructure Progress Report of September 1994 expect to "reduce health care costs by some $36 billion per year, prepare our children for the knowledge-based economy of the 21st century, add more than $100 billion to our Gross Domestic Product over the next decade, and add 500,000 new jobs by 1996, while enhancing the quality of work life and forming a labor-management partnership."

Such glowing pronouncements make me wonder if some lemminglike madness has cursed our technologists. In turn, I ask myself why the networked world attracts such attention.

As I contemplate this silicon navel, I see a wide gulf between the real networks that I use daily and the promised land of the information infrastructure.

Some without a modem worry that they're missing an important part of modern living. Yet few aspects of daily life require computers, digital networks, or massive connectivity. They're irrelevant to cooking, driving, visiting, negotiating, eating, hiking, dancing, and gossiping. You don't need a keyboard to bake bread, play touch football, piece a quilt, build a stone wall, recite a poem, or say a prayer.

At the other end of the spectrum, I have friends who are online ten or twelve hours a day. They spend a substantial part of their lives answering e-mail, transferring files, playing games, reading net news, and exploring the Internet. They'd take umbrage at the suggestion that they're missing out on something important—having a rich life.

Instead, these online addicts point out the importance of networks, communications, and home computers. They see the Internet as both tool and community, essential to work and home.

I flat-out don't believe them.

Technology has become hip. I read about computer networks on the front pages of newspapers and magazines; talk-show hosts give their e-mail addresses; commercials promise a wonderful future where anything's available via computer. Lots of excitement and plenty of glitz, but little substance and even less reflection.

I'm saddened that so many accept the false promises of a hyperhyped idea. Overpromoted, the small, intimate benefits of the Internet are being destroyed by their own success.

The glamour of the Internet attracts journalists who write laudatory articles, technoburbling how this must be the wave of the future. The computer press reinforces the feeling that you must own the latest doodads—their reporters, smiling from behind laptop computers, sincerely believe that everyone needs the latest digital wonders.

It's just a short extrapolation to a society where we download the latest news and movies, where talking yellow pages show up on computer screens, and where interactive compact discs replace books.

Well, I don't believe that phone books, newspapers, magazines, or corner video stores will disappear as computer networks spread. Nor do I think that my telephone will merge with my computer, to become some sort of information appliance.

Yet the effects of this online obsession are already being felt. Elementary and high schools are being sold down the networked river. To keep up with this educational fad, school boards spend way too much on technical gimmicks that teachers don't want and students don't need. And look at the appalling state of our libraries' book-acquisition programs!

Computers and their accoutrements cost money. Big heaps of moola—whole swimming pools overflowing with bills and coins bilked from people who've paid zillions for equipment, software, and network connections, from which they may never get their money's worth.

OK, so I don't care how you spend your money. But I do care how schools, libraries, and governments spend *my* money. And much of the software and services being sold aren't worth the floppy disks they're recorded on.

I see businesses squeeze their products into computers, even when they don't fit. Books on paper work damned well, as do post offices, newspapers, and the telephone. Yet I find offerings from publishers and phone companies that leave me scratching my head. I've rarely met anyone who prefers to read digital books. I don't want my morning paper delivered over computer, or a CD-ROM stuffed with *National Geographic* photographs. Call me a troglodyte; I'd rather peruse those photos alongside my sweetheart, catch the newspaper on the way to work, and page through a real book.

I can't help but apologize for the obviousness of my comments.* Computers and online services frustrate virtually everyone. Read the computing literature to feel the aridity of the culture of computing. Or follow Usenet net news to see dolts posting utter drivel or flame wars reminiscent of the Ostrogoths and Visigoths. Watch any kid play Nintendo to sense the shallowness of computer games.

Despite the peasant mentality that's online, we're told that anyone without a modem is an inept bumpkin, hopelessly behind the times or afraid of the march of technology. Don't buy it, or the cyberbullies will bury us all.

In 1977, Ken Olson, president of Digital Equipment Corporation, proclaimed, "There is no reason for any individual to have a computer in their home."

A year earlier, I had built a dearly beloved home computer, a nifty stone-age box with 4K of memory that displayed text on a TV. Within five years, I'd connected to the predecessor to the Internet, the Arpanet. As the network grew, I wrote software and used the network for science and recreation.

But over the past few years, I've experienced something of a change of heart. What started out so various, so beautiful, so new, now appears to be less than meets the eye.

Occasionally, I yearn for the good ol' days, back when computers squatted in glass rooms and mechanical teletypes clattered. You could see the bits in a punch card, you could smell the ozone when the printer jammed.

But don't write me off as some digital Luddite, plotting to break silicon knitting frames. Like my friends on the network, I'm confident that the Internet will thrive.

I feel a bit like an axolotl who, having grown lungs and walked ashore, now wonders what happened to his gills. Yet that doesn't

. . . .

*Nor do I claim to have originated these ideas. Perceptive people galore have already discussed 'em. Thoughtful scholars have profoundly plumbed the depths of philosophical matters on which I can only back-float: semiotics, rationalism, theory of knowledge, epistemology, ethics, Neoplatonism, 'pataphysics, and radiative transfer in nongray atmospheres.

explain my nerdlike glee for the next generation of microprocessors or why my Macintosh ever itches for faster modems. Using a Unix workstation, I daily log into six networks and as many bulletin boards; every week I hear someone forecast the imminent demise of the Usenet. Death of the network predicted, film at eleven.

Still, I can't help worrying about the gross disparity between the ballyhooed electronic utopia and the mundane reality of today's networked community. It's a theme you'll hear me repeat many times. Listening to digital prophets pointing to the promised land makes me crotchety and prone to mutter.

So discount some of my comments as the grinching of an old grackle, directed to a nebulous online community. Write off others as challenges to the technicians building the next incarnation of the Internet. And dismiss the rest as misguided rant from a scoffer.

For I'm mainly speaking to people who feel mystically lured to the Internet: lotus-eaters, beware. Life in the real world is far more interesting, far more important, far richer, than anything you'll ever find on a computer screen.

"Are you some kind of sentimental reactionary?" asked a librarian friend after I'd aired my doubts. "Do you want to return to the days of postcards and card catalogs?" About the same time, several Berkeley computer jocks gave me the hairy eyeball, wondering if I was frightened of the digital frontier. On the Internet, I've read that I'm "the willing tool or unwitting dupe of the enemies of human survival."

No. I still love my networked community; the sense of belonging to a neighborhood where I recognize my friends. Daily, I'm delighted to read e-mail from strangers and acquaintances, to chat online, and to explore the growing Internet. So why do I get this vague phobic feeling as I plop down at my workstation?

Am I purposely viewing only the worrisome and distasteful parts of this pervasive medium?

Well, yes, to an extent. Technology needs no further hype these days. Open any magazine and get your fill of dithering praise and glossy full-color wonderment. Chat with a devout computer jock and you'll hear how the electronic revolution is linking all of us together through the universal Internet and how online experiences can change your life for the better.

Or simply log in—spend a week connected to the electronic world. You'll find a more complex environment than I'm letting on to here.

But remember, you're viewing a world that doesn't exist. During that week you spend online, you could have planted a tomato garden, volunteered at a hospital, spoken with your child's teacher, and taught the kid down the block how to shag fly balls.

Claim that you can do all of those things while having a rich online life? Nope. Every hour that you're behind the keyboard is sixty minutes that you're not doing something else. Throwing a vase on a potter's wheel takes the same concentration and dedication as exploring a Multi-User Dungeon. And only a little less than getting lost in a cave with Jon Gradie.

Two

An Amalgam of Popular Fictions About the Internet, Including Brief Trips to China and The City of No Illusions

"Our inventions are wont to be pretty toys, which distract our attention from serious things. They are but improved means to an unimproved end," Thoreau writes in *Walden*. "We are in great haste to construct a magnetic telegraph from Maine to Texas; but Maine and Texas, it may be, have nothing important to communicate."

That magnetic telegraph has evolved into the Internet. How will the promise of computerized communication be fulfilled?

I've listened to plenty of spoken and implied promises about computer networks. Each seems reasonable and well-grounded; most are simple extrapolations of the digital revolution that's happening over the Internet.

Yet I claim these promises are myths, grounded in dreams of an information Shangri-la that can never be realized. And were it to happen, many of us would prefer to remain behind.

Merely mention networked computers and we think of speedy communications. As digital technology develops, we can expect cheap, easy-to-use systems that quickly do our work for us. And since only bits and bytes move, the data highway will be the cheapest way to ship information around the world.

At least such is the myth. In reality, during business hours, the Internet is painfully slow. It sometimes takes a minute for each keystroke to travel from your keyboard to the target system—too slow for interactive sessions. During the daytime, it's almost always faster to fax a single-page letter than to send Internet e-mail.

A fast modem needs three days to deliver the contents of an ordinary compact disc. It's much faster to bicycle across the city or simply slide the CD into overnight mail.

Making faster communications lines and enlarging modem pools won't help—adding more users will only slow things down. The networks will be further clogged by flashy services like online audio, video, and graphical user interfaces like the World Wide Web's Mosaic.

CD-ROMs, the archive medium of the digital age, are slow. Don't be suckered in by claims of double-speed or quad-speed drives: unless a database is designed with the right kind of index, searches just poke along. And when lots of people access a CD-ROM volume over a network, everybody hangs suspended, bananalike, in lime-flavored Jell-O. My least favorite flavor.

My network friends tell me not to pan the dream because of implementation difficulties. They promise easier, more intuitive computers, with graphical interfaces, speedy interactions, and dirt-cheap hardware. Talking with the faithful, I feel like the stagecoach driver who looks across the plains and says, "Those damn trains will never work because they're too smoky."

Yet I've listened to such assurances ever since I first keypunched a Hollerith card. Yes, there's been impressive progress. My friends' extrapolations seem valid—today's gizmos make yesterday's computers seem clunky. But I don't ever remember more unabashed hyperbole than what surrounds the Internet.

We assume, too, that there's a huge population online, equivalent to a medium-sized country. As *Time* magazine puts it, we belong to "the first nation in cyberspace." Being able to reach so many people gives both a sense of power and community. The number is growing fast, doubling every year.

But nobody knows the *actual* number of networked users. Mark Lottor's "Internet Domain Survey" reported some two million network addresses in January 1994. If you assume each computer has ten users, that's around twenty million users.

Yet this is a gross exaggeration, founded on dubious assumptions. John Quarterman, editor of *The Matrix News,* surveyed the Internet in January 1994 and found a lot of empty addresses and unreachable systems.

Quarterman estimated around two and a half million users making minimal use of the Internet, and somewhere around five million people who have access to the network. These numbers are much lower than what others had touted.

Just by counting network nodes, the Internet is now doubling in size every year. This growth can't continue for long—at that rate, everyone on earth will be connected in the year 2003. Impossible.

Magazine articles tell us that the National Information Infrastructure will provide useful services for businesses and oil the wheels of commerce. Messages, services, and entertainment will reach us quickly, without waiting for the mail. Such an environment is perfect for new businesses to thrive.

After years on the Internet, I look around and see an entirely different world.

For example, electronic mail is said to give cheap, immediate communications, at once leveling barriers and reaching straight to the desk of the recipient. You don't risk missing a message because of a busy signal or a slow post office.

Yet I find e-mail to be often undependable and annoying to access; it's usually impersonal and boring. A handwritten letter is arguably cheaper, more reliable, and far more expressive. In some instances, it can even be faster.

Businesses, from the multinationals down to individual consultants, sense that it's important to be online. The Internet is supposed to be a great way to get in touch with customers, provide information, and allow for shopping at home. In turn, as the network becomes less academic and more commercialized, we'll find a wide array of products and services available online.

Shopping by modem? Hey—sounds convenient and efficient. Online catalogs, complete with color images, will let me browse from my computer. I can negotiate directly with merchants rather than driving into town.

I'd expect the fast interactions and wide customer base of networks to provide a perfect place to sell goods, especially software, computers, and high-tech toys.

But hold on. Look at the detritus, dross, and dreck sold on television home-shopping channels. Why will the computer shopping networks be much different?

Turns out they aren't. The same people who brought us the Home Shopping Channel now own the Internet Shopping Network. No surprise to learn that today's Internet offers surprisingly little merchandise. You won't find a hundredth of what you can get through mail order. There are a few florists, a half dozen bookstores, lots of computer vendors, and no liquor stores.

About the only business actually making money over the Internet is the Electronic Newsstand. You can get excerpts from several hundred magazines and, for a few dollars a month, subscribe to a magazine, to be delivered over the net.

Yet even they don't sell many subscriptions: fewer than a dozen per day. Some magazines simply get no subscribers.

Other merchants aren't having such an easy time either—*The Economist* reports that most generate one or two sales per day. Counting all online businesses, that's around twenty-five thousand dollars in sales every day. My neighborhood Safeway does more business in an afternoon.

Why so little business over the network?

Shopping over the net denies us the experience of visiting the business. There's a bookstore in Dundas, Ontario, in an old house with a water garden in the front and three resident felines. Like all real bookstores, you can browse for free and the staff won't complain. This store's atmosphere isn't available over the Internet.

Computers and networks won't let you comparison shop for anything except price—you can't pick and choose. Nor do you know that the merchant will be in business tomorrow. Your local business, right down the block, delivers more personalized service than you'll ever get on the network. There are no shop windows or even pictures —it can take ten minutes to squeeze a decent photograph through your modem.

The Internet Mall, now in its infancy, tries to sell goods and services over the modem. But no electronic shopping can compare with the variety, quality, and experiential richness of a visit to even the most mundane malls.

Did I say quality? Well, maybe I should back off. I grew up in the shadow of Buffalo's Central Park Plaza, one of those fifties turn-a-fast-buck malls. I quite recall the interminable battle of the five-and-dimes—price wars between Murphy's and Kresge's on ladies' panties; the mean, bullying clerks, who in turn were bullied by even meaner store managers; the shoddy plastic merchandise, the wobble-wheeled A & P shopping carts, the optimistically huge but badly paved parking lot that doubled as an ice rink for five months each winter. With good reason, a popular T-shirt refers to Buffalo as the City of No Illusions.

One illusion's still with me, though. It was a summer afternoon at Dewey playground, best known for its two blank concrete walls that purported to be handball courts, but since that sport was unknown, were appropriated by solo tennis players. The recreation counselor, probably a wizened eighteen-year-old about to be drafted to Vietnam, saw a bunch of us hanging around the swings. Instead of chasing us out, he called us over to organize a scavenger hunt.

I was maybe twelve—old enough to avoid kids' games. I glanced at my kid brother, Don, and we started to slink away. But this guy wasn't talking about your ordinary goody-two-shoes scavenger hunt, where you have to find popsicle sticks, lumps of coal, four-leafed clovers, and a round white stone.

Instead, we had an hour to bring back a bucket of smog, a bottle of sunlight, tomorrow's newspaper, a piece of Niagara Falls, an honest politician, and four other impossible things. The tenth on the list was a yellow yo-yo. He tossed that one in so everyone would get at least one point.

And we were off, scouring the north side of Buffalo. In an hour,

Don was carrying an old steel bucket with a paper bag over it. Another kid had a crinkled-up copy of the *Buffalo Evening News*. I was bringing the bottled sunlight.

We gathered around the sandbox, and the counselor turned to each of us, asking what we'd found. Don showed the rusty old bucket and told how he'd carried it all the way from the smog-mill. It was filled with smog—to prove it, he pulled off the cover.

Nothing happened.

"You see, there's smog everywhere," my brother said. "It's a bucket of smog."

I was up next. I'd dug around and found a quart beer bottle. My thumb was in the spout, and I showed it to everyone. "I've collected sunbeams in this Genesee beer bottle," I told 'em. "I'm gonna hold onto it until tomorrow morning, and then I'll pop the cork and there'll be sunshine."

Someone else told how she'd gotten tomorrow's newspaper—it was a bit torn in the corner, where the date's supposed to be, but "that's what happens when you travel through time," she said. "The strangest thing, though, is how it says that everything that happened yesterday is going to happen again tomorrow."

Another kid brought a squirt gun: "It's loaded with real Lake Erie water, which will soon be a piece of Niagara Falls." God knows how, but a girl pantomimed an honest politico, which took quite a bit of imagination, seeing how our mayor had just scraped by a land-fraud indictment. We got all nine impossible objects. Everything except the yellow yo-yo.

Since then, I've searched everywhere for that one true yellow yo-yo. Maybe it's hiding in some delicatessen or perhaps advertised in tomorrow's newspaper. For sure, it's not for sale on the Internet.

Whether yo-yos, books, records, or insurance, there are good reasons why business doesn't work over the Internet. As we'll see later, there's no way to send money across the network. Bit-heads talk about digital cash, but can only show experimental systems with fancy names like DigiCash and First Virtual. For a long while, it's funny money.

I'm not even certain that a transaction is valid. I don't know who's at the other end of the connection. A network address isn't associated with a physical location, so it's open turf for fraud. Hardly comforting to send your credit card number to a stranger who's only identification is bizness@nocturnal-aviation.com.

"Just technical details that can and are being fixed," says Bill Cheswick, a programmer at AT&T. "After digital cash is introduced, we'll be able to carry out business directly over the network." By implication, we'll carry out routine sales through networks, bypassing salespeople.

I disagree: network authentication software can never give the same sense of trust as a face-to-face business transaction. No computer network with pretty graphics can ever replace the salespeople that make our society work.

Then there's the myth that our computer networks will bring diversity, culture, and novelty into our classrooms and homes. I hear this alongside the rapid expansion of cable-television systems—they promise five hundred channels that will let us pick an entertaining and informative program from hundreds of offerings.

Reminds me of the pronouncement, in 1939, of David Sarnoff, the CEO of RCA: "It is probable that television drama of high caliber and produced by first-rate artists will materially raise the level of dramatic taste of the nation."*

The resultant vast wasteland thrived when there were but three television networks. A five-hundred-channel cable system will surely deliver unfathomable and boundless mediocrity. And with more channels, production values will further decline, since there will be less money spent per program.

Networks can change our social lives in many ways, introducing us to new friends and providing an outlet for our creative efforts. Interactive games come in all tastes and shapes; multimedia programs can display nifty images never seen before.

. . . .

* *Writing in* The Fabulous Future, America in 1980, *General Sarnoff also said,* "It can be taken for granted that before 1980 ships, aircraft, locomotives and even automobiles will be atomically fueled."

Yet I suspect these interactions are mostly shallow and ephemeral. Computer games develop skills without fostering friendships. Multimedia extravaganzas impress but rarely satisfy. There's no *there* there.

Since the seventies, interactive multimedia has been promoted as the future of entertainment. They'll re-create important cultural events on our desktops and let us talk back to our televisions. Video productions will truly be live, as viewers will give performers immediate feedback.

But I've never figured out what's meant by those buzzwords, *interactive multimedia.* The very things promised by interactive multimedia, namely interaction and a combination of media, seem to be present in everyday productions.

Isn't a football game interactive? Fifty thousand cheering fans in the stadium certainly stir the players on to better performance. And surely a ballet is multimedia, combining dance, music, lighting, and motion. For that matter, check out the corner tavern or coffeehouse —that's where you'll hear live local music. Interactive for sure.

Yet I doubt that a thousand viewers can genuinely influence the outcome of a video performance. And, for all the talk about interactive home entertainment, does anyone want it?

Interactive computer entertainment gives you a choice of many different outcomes, all preprogrammed. The experience is about as interactive as a candy machine.

Even the term *multimedia* is wrong, since there's only one medium employed: the computer.

Now, I'm hardly a judge of aesthetics, but of the scores of electronic multimedia productions I've seen, I don't remember any as being beautiful. These productions, designed to deliver excitement and fantasy, can't rival a live performance.

Computer games, incorporating images stored on CD-ROMs, are supposed to help with kids' homework and show that learning can be fun. Clever games and animated cartoon figures are built to challenge the brightest and respond to our every move. Uh, sure.

Expert Nintendo players are well-prepared to repel the next wave of Martian invaders. Myst wizards find clues buried within castles and caves. Many who play Where in the World Is Carmen Sandiego already know that Paris is the capital of France.

Many of these games bow to the tyranny of the right answer. You choose from a set of possible answers, and advance when you get it right.

The computer's great at developing quick eye-hand reactions, but exercises few muscles beyond those that furrow the brow or focus the eye. A neighborhood game of soccer is far healthier than any-thing on the screen. A box of crayons and a big sheet of paper provides a more expressive medium for kids (and adults waiting at restaurant tables) than computerized paint programs.

And, unlike a friendly game of chess, the computer provides no opponent across the table to award your brilliance with a wistful smile of admiration. You end up admiring yourself.

Then, too, computer games develop transient skills, which soon become mundane. Of the players who seized on Pac Man and Pong, how many still play these games today? Three-year-old Multi-User Dungeons on the Internet are passé today. Contrast these with poker, go, baseball, and Monopoly.

Consider the equipment you need. For the most modest com-puter game, you'll need a cpu, monitor, RAM, and disk. To run online, add a modem, phone line, and an account. And don't forget the software, which runs upwards of fifty dollars.

Compare this with a two-dollar pack of cards. There's a thousand games to play. You can invent new ones, change the rules, build a house, or tell a fortune. They work equally well in the backseat of a car or around a campfire. Anyone you meet can understand and join in. If you get frustrated, throw the pack out the window. Try that with your Pentium.

The Internet is said to be a great place to meet people. It's an environment to overcome shyness and find others with similar inter-ests, develop friendships, and perhaps find a mate. By comparing experiences, you can find support and advice from experts across the country.

It's true. Superficial network interactions don't carry the same risks as face-to-face conversations do. At the same time, they lack depth, commitment, and ordinary etiquette.

Perhaps that's why I once received the message, "I want your body." The commentary on my screen continued: "I want to lick you all over."

I'm logged onto America Online, where chat lines run fast and loose. I first check into a public area—the lobby. There, my screen shows one-line messages from two dozen others. Everything I type shows up on their screens. Their names range from Aztec Kong to Yetta Notha.

I'm talking with strangers, without actually meeting them. I might be communicating with a teenager down the block or a retiree across the continent.

And when you do meet someone in person, it's awkward. Perhaps reality will match your expectations, but there's far more to a relationship than can be discovered over the screen.

Electronic communication is an instantaneous and illusory contact that creates a sense of intimacy without the emotional investment that leads to close friendships.

People being people, friendships do occur online, occasionally blossoming into relationships and even marriages. Same thing happens at coffeeshops, libraries, synagogues, and football games.

No doubt, the networks are certainly great places to meet men. There are several guys online for every woman. But, like the outlook for women in Alaska, the odds are good, but the goods are odd.

San Francisco and Chicago now sport nightclubs with built-in computer terminals. You sit at a table and talk over the Internet Relay Chat, read net news, or play Netrek. What a lonely way to spend an evening—surrounded by people, yet escaping into conversations with distant strangers.

Jenny Frost is an audio producer in New York—she described how her husband got tangled up with his modem. She'd bought him the computer game Myst, and he fooled with the program every night. After getting stuck on a clue, he'd log onto America Online, looking for ways to solve the mystery.

"Inside of two months he was spending evenings on the bulletin boards, chatting with others, learning the intricacies of this computer game," she told me. "That fifty-dollar computer game ballooned into a four hundred dollar network bill.

"But that's not as bad as my friend David," Jenny continued. "He'd been doing great with his wife until he began spending three hours each night connected to the network. She's not a mean woman, but she felt him ignoring her. It became the pivotal rift in their marriage."

Is this why we promote universal connections across the country? The mental entrapment without physical interaction undermines social relationships, and the disorder seems to be gender-specific. We're fostering a wave of computer widows.

One of the more pernicious myths of the online world is that of a literary revival. Those who once used the telephone now write e-mail, post to newsgroups, and write over chat lines. Jon Carroll of the *San Francisco Chronicle* believes that "E-mail and computer conferencing is teaching an entire generation about the flexibility and utility of prose."

Plenty of schools promote this myth. California's Sonoma State University now requires all entering freshmen to own a personal computer. The college president says it's to help improve the students' writing, as well as to access material over the Internet. To make sure the effect is felt throughout, the college ordered 250 of Apple's fastest computers, giving one to every faculty member.

Al Rogers, operating the Global SchoolNet Foundation in Bonita, California, writes, "Telecomputing may be the last frontier of writing that will incite students to traditional literacy skills." He goes on to say that networks will provide an audience that will help students "become eager, conscientious writers in every content area, including science, math, geography, history, and current events."

Since the networks rely on the written word, you'd expect a rebirth of reading and writing. The Internet should be a garden for literate, well-trained users to take advantage of a new mode of communications. In addition, networks will help our schools by supplying creative software and instructional classroom materials. The result should be the honing of literary skills and a new wave of creative literature.

But instead of an Internet-inspired renaissance, mediocre writing and poorly thought-out arguments roll into my modem. E-mail and postings to network newsgroups are frequently ungrammatical, misspelled, and poorly organized. After trolling up and down the Usenet, from alt.best-of-usenet to zer.z-netz.telecom.modem, I rarely find prose that's articulate and creative.

And despite the digital paraphernalia, I've heard no evidence that student papers have improved. I visited Sonoma State University and listened to two English teachers complain about poorly written compositions. Their students, at least, hadn't become good writers after purchasing a computer.

Computers encourage specialized expertise, like running programs or connecting to networks, at the expense of general skills, like organizing coherent sentences, gathering thoughts together, developing vocabulary, or toying with ideas.

Unfortunately, learning one computer network doesn't teach you much about others. Every network depends heavily on arcane commands specific to each computer and location.

Furthermore, these commands become out-of-date quickly, as networks reconfigure and operating systems change. Unlike physics, biology, writing, or history, there's no fundamental framework that can be taught.

Mind you, some skills transcend specific networks. For instance, every computer user knows about files and commands. After using a network for a while, you know the difference between reading text and downloading a document. But these are hardly essential skills and certainly not vital to a productive life.

Long ago I learned the instruction set for Hayes modems. Today, new software releases take advantage of different modem features, requiring me to learn truly obscure commands. Instead of learning those arcane commands, I could have baked brownies or practiced the clarinet—skills that haven't become obsolete in the past five years.

Computers force us into creating with our minds and prevent us from making things with our hands. They dull the skills we use in everyday life. After years of programming, I know a dozen computer languages, but my Mandarin has fallen by the wayside.

Not that I ever knew much Chinese. My graduate school had this crazy idea that we should be able to communicate with people in other countries, so they wouldn't let me off with Fortran. I registered for Mandarin, after Jon Gradie reported that the French classes were filled with physics grad students.

Turned out that Chinese wasn't that hard—memorize ten characters per day, and pretty soon you can read a few simple stories. Within two years, I knew enough to get into trouble, but not to get out.

Which is how I found myself in Nanjing, China. Although I realized that the world didn't have much demand for planetary astronomers, I was lucky enough to stumble on the United States–China scholarly exchange program—the National Science Foundation wanted scientists to study on the mainland. It was my good fortune that they accepted me.

Mao Tse-tung wrote of the seven mountains curling around Nanjing like a sleeping dragon. Purple Mountain is the tallest of these, topped with eight telescopes, two Ming Dynasty armillary spheres, and a dual astrograph made by Zeiss-Jena. The Gang of Four were on trial when I arrived with a dozen astronomy books, a suitcase of clothes, and a portable computer . . . eight years before the uprising at Tiananmen Square.

I was to work with Professor Chen Dao Han on interactions between comets and the solar wind. Since he's a theoretician, I figured my new Hewlett Packard HP-85 computer would speed up our research—it had a plotter, printer, and tape drive, all in one sleek desktop box. At the same time, I would teach modern scientific techniques. Here was my chance to show Western technology to an appreciative audience.

Hardly. Modern instruments they may not have had, but these guys made up for it in creativity and hard work. The third week at the observatory, I met Professor Li Fang, dressed in Mao jacket and blue slacks. He'd just returned from four years of hard labor in the countryside—that's what intellectuals received during the Cultural Revolution.

He's studying star observations from the Sung and Ming dynasties. With my broken Mandarin, I ask him what can be done with a thousand-year-old set of not-too-reliable star measurements? Speaking slowly, with simplified Chinese, Dr. Li explains: "We are searching for periodic motions and may possibly get information about motions of the earth's north pole."

The wandering of the pole. These observations, culled from thousands of years, showed how the earth's axis wobbled through the ages. A sparse data set—sometimes only a couple of observations in a century, but singularly valuable.

Dr. Li hunts for periodic motions using a Fourier transform—the standard tool of astronomers everywhere. Feed in a string of numbers, turn a mathematical crank, and out pops a listing of periods and cycles.

But how he did that math! Here's Professor Li, sitting in an unlit room, before a table neatly arranged with books of data, trigonometry tables, and handwritten columns of numbers. At his side are twelve abacuses. He's doing a Fourier transform by hand.

For twenty minutes I watch over his shoulder. In pidgin Mandarin, we converse, and he shows me how he looks up sines and cosines, multiplies numbers together, and sums each coefficient on an abacus. He writes every answer into an accounting book, with a perfect script. This astronomer is crunching numbers manually, without so much as a slide rule.

I'm shaking my head as I head back to my office, where a toad's catching mosquitoes just outside the window. Remember, this is back in the early eighties, before everyone had whizbang computers. I fire up my desktop computer, scrabble through the details of a fast Fourier transform, and get the darn thing to plot graphs. I'll show him the right way to analyze data.

In a couple of days, my BASIC program is actually working, displaying all sorts of fancy graphics. I show it to Professor Li, and enter some of his pole-star data.

He'd spent five months calculating some fifty coefficients for the polar wandering curve. My program does the same job in a minute. Professor Li nods his head, looks over the printout, and compares it to his carefully handwritten table.

"*Bu tswo.*" Not bad. High praise from this astronomer. I had understood the importance of making a spectrum from this data.

Well, of course I did. But he's missing my point. This computer can save him enormous amounts of time. Instead of an abacus and trig tables, he can type in the data, wait a minute, and see the results directly. I'm dropping in and out of Mandarin with excitement.

He smiles, then speaks directly in English, with a British accent. "When I compare the computer's results to my own, I see that an error has crept in. I suspect it is from the computer's assumption that our data is perfectly sampled throughout history. Such is not the case, especially during the Sung dynasty. And so, it may be that we need to analyze the data in a slightly different manner."

At last I compare the two columns—his carefully handwritten numbers don't agree with my computer's mechanical printout. Similar, but not the same. I look at the elaborate math that Professor Li has followed. There's the answer. He hadn't spent his summer doing rote mechanical calculations. Instead, he'd developed a complex method for analyzing data that took into account the accuracy of different observers and ambiguities in the historical record. His results, literally crafted by hand, showed his meticulous care. Moreover, they were right.

I returned to my office, humbled. Having a computer, I had naturally cast the problem as simple data analysis. The calculations weren't the hard part, in the same way that learning a little Chinese wasn't so tough. The real challenge was understanding the data and finding a good way to use it.

Today, some kitchens have serious computing power: you can get microprocessor-controlled coffee brewers, microwave ovens, and bread makers. These work perfectly, yet you lose the ritual, the sense of accomplishment, the feeling of being a part of the process.

Just follow instructions on the side of the bread maker: pour in water, flour, and yeast, wait a few hours, and out pops a loaf of bread. It'll taste fine.

Still, you've missed the best parts: the feeling of flour between your fingers, kneading the dough, punching down air bubbles, finding a warm place for it to rise; you're connected to your meal, as well as to generations of bakers before you. Your friends' grins at the dinner table compliment you, not a machine.

Just as computing is supposed to make our home a better place, it should also make our workdays more efficient. By passing documents over the Ethernet, we'll save paper and speed up communication. Also, network connections can give us fast-breaking news and let us ask others for specialized help. Supposedly, we can concentrate on our problems with fewer distractions.

That's not my experience. I spend almost as much time figuring out what's wrong with my computer as I do actually using it. Networked software, especially, requires frequent updates and maintenance, which gets in the way of doing routine work.

I haven't heard talk of the paperless office in a while, so I guess everyone's conceded that computers generate more paperwork than the systems they replaced. I remember the Paperwork Reduction Act —its main effect was to add a few paragraphs to every governmental form, explaining why this document was necessary. If you include the square inches of paper wasted by these notices, it has probably increased paperwork.

Now, I've heard that e-mail and networks will make our workplace more efficient and let us get more work done every day. Like the paperless office, I feel this is a falsehood.

E-mail takes time to read, even when it's junk e-mail. Other network services, like net news, can eat hours from each workday. And the fast response of computers and networks causes us to repeatedly refine what once might have been good enough. Since it's so easy to revise documents, well, we go ahead and revise 'em.

Networks hold out the promise of telecommuting. One day, many of us will be able to work at home, any hour of the day or night. We'll save gas, have closer family ties, and have a happier workplace.

Oh? I doubt our offices will be replaced by minions working from home. The lack of meetings and personal interaction isolates workers and reduces loyalty. Nor is a house necessarily an efficient place to work, what with the constant interruptions and lack of office fixtures. Perhaps it'll work for jobs where one never has to meet anyone else, like data entry or telephone sales. What a way to turn a home into a prison.

Indeed, the most common jobs require a workplace. Can a supermarket checkout clerk work from home? How about an auto mechanic, dentist, or police officer?

And where would country music be without old-fashioned jobs —trucker, miner, cowboy, teacher, farmer, waitress, bartender? These are the people that turn the cranks of every nation. Computers can never take their places.

Nor can a computer replace boogie-woogie music. Lately, my radio, cassette deck, and gramophone just won't stop playing Meade Lux Lewis, Art Tatum, Fats Waller, and Albert Ammons. Lately, I'm even typing at eight beats to the bar, hitting tabs on the syncopation.

The first boogie that ever was woogied? It was December 29, 1926, when Pinetop Smith first uttered the immortal words, "I wanalla y'all to know Pinetop's Boogie Woogie!" Three months later, Pinetop was shot dead in a barroom brawl, the first man to lay down his life for his boogie.

The myth holds that our networks are the ultimate in democracy —all voices can be heard. Bytes have no race, gender, age, or religion. What effects will we see when the government comes online?

Computer access will let us send messages to government officials, and get quick responses from them. We'll know what's happening in the back rooms of our legislatures. We could read committees' reports the same day they're written, and get fast responses to our queries.

The myth grows: elections will change, too. Politicians will be available through electronic forums, with less emphasis on expensive television ads. They'll upload position papers to the net, and reply to e-mail from their constituents.

Eventually, we'll see electronic voting—a way to further democratic participation, with polls giving near-instant feedback for representatives.

The reality? Anyone can post messages to the net. Practically everyone does. The resulting cacophony drowns out serious discussion.

Online debates of tough issues are often polarized by messages taking extreme positions. It's a great medium for trivia and hobbies, but not the place for reasoned, reflective judgment. Surprisingly often, discussions degenerate into acrimony, insults, and flames.

And although the Internet is growing fast, it will be a long time before computer terminals are as widely available as newspapers and televisions. Until then, only the technoliterati will be enfranchised with network access.

The electronic constituency is certainly unrepresentative. Across the continent, fewer than one voter in fifty has access to the network, and those who are connected come from the highest income groups. Even among those with modems, few will read political statements —they're as boring over the computer as they are on paper. The vast majority of people don't own computers, so they're excluded from the online democracy.

Norm Jacknis set up a bulletin board for Andy Spano, a candidate running for county executive in Westchester County, New York. Part of his platform was that government should take advantage of the Internet—for example, he proposed diverting highway funds into telecommuting. He put every press release and position paper on the forum, answered every piece of e-mail, and printed the bulletin board number on all the printed literature.

Westchester is an affluent county of almost a million people, the headquarters for companies like IBM and Prodigy, and computers are in more than half the homes. How many people do you think dialed in?

A couple dozen.

That bulletin board did help organize and energize grassroots workers. But it wasn't enough to elect Mr. Spano—he lost to a traditional state assemblyman in a tight election. Norm Jacknis concludes, "Despite what they teach in universities, knowledge—and technology—is not always power."

Since readers often skip arguments that take up more than a screenful, electronic meetings simplify complex issues. This encourages short, simple questions, and equally concise replies. Just as television gives us sound bites, the online interview provides one-line answers.

And suppose there is a vast online constituency, able to speak its collective voice via modem. This electronic town hall removes valid reasons for representative government. What's the purpose of a representative when each of us can vote immediately on every issue?

Electronic referenda on current events would further shorten the event horizon for public policy. Instead of political changes every few years, policies would be voted on every few months. This is hardly the path to long-term planning. The electronic constituency would be a most fickle electorate.

Mr. Jacknis's and Mr. Spano's experience aside, few busy officials can read even a tiny fraction of their e-mail. I sure don't expect the president to answer his e-mail. Easier to ignore it or let a staff member sample a few messages.

Such sampling of e-mail isn't a good dipstick for the electorate's opinions. Not only is e-mail unrepresentative, but it's easy to pad a petition campaign with thousands of duplicate e-mail messages. Someone can just program a computer to send in multiple copies. Handwritten letters, which require dedication and reflection, are far more serious vehicles of grassroots opinions.

I once watched California Governor Pete Wilson answer questions over an online interview. He wasn't adept at typing, since in half an hour, he hardly answered five questions. Seeing his text intermittently scroll across my screen, I realized that I had no way of knowing if hizzonor himself was at the keyboard or merely one of his minions.

The digital networks promise a more open government. State legislatures are already placing bills, amendments, and laws on the

Internet. Administrative decisions, too, can be made available through archives and bulletin boards. Soon, we should have fast access to a good fraction of the government's regulations.

Hey—these reports and regulations have always been printed and distributed. Once online, that paper trail may partially disappear, replaced by a digital archive. There's a feeling that computer access may save money and release governments from the responsibility of printing hard copies.

But there's a serious trade-off here: this could jeopardize our right to free and open access to government information. As we'll see later, there's good reason to keep records on paper—it's the one medium that never goes out of style. And as governments provide their information online, those who are wired to the net will continue to become more powerful, those without modems will become even more disenfranchised.

For these reasons, let's hope that federal and state governments don't succumb to the temptation to abandon printed publications.

Closely related to this, I hear about the national performance review. It's a way to electronically evaluate objectives of government and see if they're being met. In theory, this will grade how services are being delivered, reward those doing a good job, and show which areas need attention. It's supposed to streamline a hidebound, unresponsive bureaucracy.

I have serious doubts about this proposal. Centralized planning and standard-setting create internal paranoia and rampant opportunism; at least it has in every organization I've ever belonged to, including the Cub Scouts.

I've also noticed that the computer cognoscenti hang on to their jobs by creating systems where they are at the choke points of the organizations. Workers who don't know computers get trampled, discounted, or pushed to the side. And honestly, would you prefer park rangers to be computer-literate or know their wildlife?

Privacy's a serious concern of network activists—they know how easy it is for institutions to collect massive amounts of data about each of us. Not just Big Brother, either. Businesses, junk mailers, and politicians all want that information.

What's collected about us? Our political party affiliation is public record. Some grocery stores keep tabs on what we purchase. Mail-order businesses often save records of phone calls—incoming caller-ID tells them who's on the line even before they pick up the phone. To speed up highway traffic, states are introducing automated car identification systems—a computer remembers every time a car crosses a toll bridge and sends a monthly bill.

Individually, each of these droplets of data isn't much of a threat. Collectively, though, the entire ocean becomes a serious threat to anonymity and privacy within our society.

Privacy advocates—who seem to be especially vocal online—often want the best of both worlds. They appreciate the speed of automated checkouts, automated teller machines, and automated toll booths. At the same time, they want strict laws prohibiting governments from using this information.

When every transaction leaves electronic footprints, pretty soon a computer knows things about us that we may want to keep hidden. I'm not talking about illegal things here, but simple stuff: a computer may know how much someone spent on liquor last week. How often I traveled to San Francisco. What phone calls I've made.

Many people are uneasy about having such data collected and downright concerned that it may be stored and shared. You may have nothing to hide, but even then some of these details could be used in ways that are annoying, if not intrusive. Out of this worry grows an absolutist position: don't let Big Brother collect information about me.

While I listen to privacy advocates, I also realize that we constantly move between openness and seclusion—between community and privacy. When I walk to a café, I'm engaged with my friends and neighbors. At one extreme end of this spectrum if I run for public office, I'll find my life reviewed on television.

At the other end of the spectrum, the solitary hermit seldom interacts with others, he pays all his bills in cash, and he is hardly recognized on the street. He leaves few traces behind, yet doesn't avail himself of the comforts of society.

Most of us move between the private and public throughout the day. We're disturbed when our digital shadows don't follow. Even though nobody followed me to the store, a computer knows that I bought a quart of tomato juice. Its sister computer, however, doesn't believe that my check is valid, and requires two pieces of ID.

The Internet certainly will let different computers compare their data faster, and will bring more databases online. Special programs can traverse the networks, ferreting out public information about any of us. A chilling discomfort.

I'm not so worried. Today, we're protected against this kind of database correlation by deep incompatibilities between different computer systems. It's darned difficult to compare information from multiple sources, because databases are laid out in bizarre ways. Since each data structure is hard to understand, cross-comparisons require programming expertise.

Also, plenty of information out there is simply stale. Databases about people quickly go out-of-date unless someone keeps them current. Commercial information sources aren't trustworthy—when I check friends' addresses in online directories, I routinely find serious mistakes. And the public Internet is downright unreliable—several e-mail addresses listed for me are wrong.

Who keeps these databases up-to-date? Typing in names and addresses is grunt work, given to minimum-wage clerical staff. Of all jobs, theirs are the most sterile, seldom recognized and rarely appreciated. They have the least incentive to get things right, yet everything down the line hinges on their accuracy. Their mistakes and slow response gum up high-tech surveillance efforts.

So I suspect Big Brother won't have an easy time tracing us. Many important computers will forever be off-net. Most have such weird data structures that it's just not worth the effort to correlate with other databases. And untrustworthy data pervades the system. Our privacy will be protected, as it always has been, by simple obscurity and the high cost of uncovering information about us.

The Great Wall Vegi and Seafood Restaurant is a hole-in-the-wall restaurant a few blocks from my home. Mr. Tho always grins when I walk in the front door, knowing that I'll mangle his native language. Patiently, he corrects my speaking—"Chieu, not Chow," he'll tell me. Lately, he refuses to serve me until I pronounce the words right.

He knows, as I do, that speaking Chinese is easy compared to writing the language. One glance around his restaurant shows why. Every wall has beautiful artworks, mixing poetry, painting, and calligraphy.

While showing a group of visiting mainland scholars around Berkeley, I introduced them to my hometown restaurant. Mr. Tho exchanged a few honorifics, served a pot of green tea, then left us with a pen and a sheet of paper.

My five visitors looked at each other for a pensive moment, then nodded to the oldest. A decision had just taken place, silent yet important.

I understood: the group had to decide on who would write the order. Now, all of them can write perfectly and clearly. The unspoken discussion was about which of them had the most *expressive* handwriting. It's an honor to write.

Fine penmanship is held in high esteem throughout the Orient, where writing's an art form. Every sage, scientist, and scholar has practiced a virtuous script. Any philosopher without elegant handwriting was scorned.

Those poems in calligraphy on the wall don't just sound beautiful, they look beautiful.

For almost a century, the Palmer Method was taught in America —it was invented to promote legible writing. Today, you find people who go out of their way to scribble, perhaps as a way of scoffing at such handwriting training. Instead of penmanship, we teach word processing.

Nothing wrong with that—clerks with copperplate hands went out of style with bloomers and celluloid collars. Handwritten letters lean toward conversation; processed words toward communication.

Don't get me wrong: word processing is great stuff, one of this millennium's great inventions. Rather than penmanship, our culture values communications. We need to get the right words across.

Myth: computers don't just free us from handwriting and let us revise letters on the fly. They also give each of us a printing press. Coupled with a modem and an Internet account, any file can be uploaded to the network. Once placed on a file server, archive, or a Usenet newsgroup, anyone's words are open for others to read.

This electronic publishing is said to give each of us a potential audience of millions. The future Internet promises more than just the written word—we'll be able to send sounds, images, even videos across the network. There's probably a collection of Chinese calligraphy out there.

Network junkies excitedly tell me that self-publishing leapfrogs over publishers, editors, and broadcasters. The network passes messages from your keyboard to a thousand other monitors. It's not one-to-one communications like the telephone or one-to-many broadcasting like radio. Rather, it's a many-to-many medium, a garden where freedom of speech blossoms.

But the reality is that with millions of users posting messages to the network, the valuable gets lost in the dross. There are no pointers to the good stuff—you don't know which messages are worth reading. You can select by subject area, but there's no way to pick only the interesting comments.

With everyone able to upload their works to the network, the Internet begins to resemble publishers' slush piles. It's up to the reader to separate out the dregs. What's missing from the network are genuine editors.

Ah, editors! The bane of writers, reporters, and publishers, editors yet serve as barometers of literary quality and advocates for the reader. Without them on the nets, you simply have no way to tell what's worth reading.

By eliminating editors, our networks demonstrate their importance. There are plenty of writers on the Usenet, but few editors. It shows.

Indeed, the best newsgroups rely on voluntary moderators, serving as unpaid filters. Rec.humor.funny, news.announce.newusers, comp.risks . . . behind each of these is an unthanked and rarely seen volunteer who filters out the noise. Their attempts to impose order on the chaos generate resentment, accusations of censorship, and occasional subversion; but it's the moderators who give shape and direction to the newsgroups. There are so few moderated newsgroups only because nobody's willing to put in the long, unpaid hours.

Want to impress this net news lurker? Offer a few hours of your time to filter traffic on a newsgroup. After approving or rejecting dozens of messages a day, unraveling bounced traffic, and replying to a constant stream of inquiries, you'll understand why there are so few network moderators.

Plenty of places need moderators, reviewers, and editors, including online magazines and mailing lists. These offer fast ways to get the word out, whether for science fiction buffs, feminists, or astronomers. There's probably a mailing list that covers all three groups.

Even so, network magazines haven't attracted many first-rate writers, perhaps because online publishing is considered trivial. It's self-publishing that doesn't pay—Internet writers are freebie freelancers.

Researchers naturally save their best work to publish in journals and books, realizing that the review process ensures that better papers make it into print. They're unlikely to post good, original stuff to the network first; somebody might swipe their material.

It's the not-so-good stuff that gets onto the network. Pat Berger, former president of the American Library Association, points out that the Internet was created as a tool for researchers, not as an archive. Starting with the cold-fusion debacle in 1988, scientists began exchanging messages that would have been published as letters to the editor in technical journals.

As a result, quite a bit of scientific research never makes it into print, especially the minor results and dead ends. You'd think this stuff doesn't matter, but good researchers need to know what areas aren't worth looking into.

But messages passing across the Internet aren't cataloged, the way magazines and journals are. Some of them are saved on disk, but these don't get checked into libraries and cross-referenced. It's hard to retrieve a message posted to the Usenet from a year ago, and virtually impossible to search for it.

These same problems extend to the Internet program archives. They're stuffed with terabytes of data. Some specialize in public-domain programs for Windows, others in governmental records, still others keep track of weather-satellite pictures. You'll find literary archives as well, places where you can download a science fiction manuscript or a thesis reviewing Shakespeare's *Othello*.

Which of these are well-written? Which are worth your time to read? In short, which have any value? You don't know until you download, decompress, and read 'em. Without reviews, simple ways to skim information, and a Dewey decimal system to direct your attention, you will waste gobs of time.

With no way to browse, documents appear out of context. You not only don't have a reviewer to help select the good stuff, you don't know what related information might help you. The Internet supplies almost random facts, unchecked and unfiltered.

The Internet archives include thousands of high-quality, public-domain, and shareware programs. Many are far better than you can buy, some represent years of development by amateur and professional programmers alike.

Sad to say, far more programs are buggy or obsolete; they're not worth the space on my disk drive. In hunting for a good calendar program, I downloaded and tested twenty shareware versions. In one sense, these were free: I didn't pay for them. On the other hand, it was expensive: the exercise wasted a full day of my time. So I sigh, reach into my pocket, and buy commercial software.

How about electronic books? You can now download computer versions of classical works, including Shakespeare, Milton, and Voltaire. Modern works, too—witness the panic of publishers to bring out the latest fiction formatted for portable computers. I scoffed, until I got this note from a friend:

Hey Cliff,
     Check out the hypercard version of The Time Machine by H. G. Wells. It's cool how you can jump from page to page. You can see

where all the great science fiction books came from. Try reading it on your Powerbook tonight.

—Carl

It's e-mail over the Internet. Carl has just discovered a science fiction classic, this time as a computer program. He's so pumped-up about it that he wants me to read it in bed. I shake my head, reread his mail, and shrug. Might as well try.

I dig through the archives, download the program, and charge up my battery. Might as well do it right, so I butter up some popcorn, stretch out on my futon, and give it a try.

Ugh. Can't lie the laptop on my chest. A paperback might weigh ten ounces—a pound at most—but this thing weighs five pounds. So I lean it on the pillow, turn off the lights, and crank up the backlit screen.

Report from the online bedroom: yes, you can read an electronic book in bed. The backlighting is perfect when you don't want to awaken your companion. And despite the crick in your neck, you eventually get used to paging with the keyboard.

But your every suspicion is correct: it's cumbersome, clunky, ghastly slow, and mechanical. The text isn't hard to read, it just feels unfriendly. The butter from my fingers got on the keyboard and trackball. Next morning, I woke up with the computer smooshed against my cheek.

There are no pages to turn. No dust cover to touch. The hyper-text has things called virtual bookmarks—commands to return to a paragraph. They're not as good as the real bookmarks from my book-store.

Maybe I haven't discovered the right novel—a real screen-scrol-ler—but I feel computers just aren't a friendly way to read a book. Save your money: buy a real book and a flashlight.

Come to think of it, I can't read an electronic book in the bath-tub, on the beach, or on the subway. Book publishers have nothing to worry about.

THREE

*Further Explorations into the Culture of
Computing, Leading to Questions About the Isolation
of Networks, the Nature of Tools, the Utility of
Sewers, and the Author's Continuing Ambivalence;
with a Sidetrack into a Four-Wheeled Discussion of
Maintaining the National Infrastructure*

I just saw a video from Pacific Bell—I mean the Pacific Telesis
Group—showing an imaginary couple buying a coat from Mongolia.
We listen to them chat with a yak dealer; a computer interprets on
the fly. In the background, children happily play with a three-dimensional game that teaches math.

The phone company wants me to believe that they'll invent
automatic translation and worldwide video-phones. And that virtual
reality will be primarily used for teaching.

They might equally well show us a less benign future: boring
corporate conferences held via satellite and big-screen music videos.
Junk mail brought to us at the speed of light. Children avoiding
their homework by playing shoot-'em-down, slash-'em-up games.
Pornography downloaded into home computers. Credit companies
sending dunning letters to a young couple via e-mail.

Now, I've also seen plenty of encouraging things over the networks: seventh-grade students exchanging poetry with friends. A shy
woman who met her husband-to-be through the Usenet. International collaborations in sciences and humanities. Specialized mailings
for nonprofit groups. Friendly support for a man whose child has
leukemia. A family that used the Internet to get the latest research

results on a disease. A retarded twenty-five-year-old woman who used a children's math program to practice addition.

Those aren't eye-popping uses like computerized translators or three-dimensional virtual realities, but they're the blossoms in today's garden—much more real than the dreamland painted by network futurists.

In 1986, while managing a cluster of Unix workstations, I viewed networks mechanistically, as a collection of cables, connectors, and computers. After all, my job was to keep the system running, and the main ingredients are hardware. It hadn't occurred to me that the Internet, then so young, formed a community.

Experience dealing with people—not computers—changed my point of view. Other system operators and government agents went out of their way to help me out of a bind. Cooperating together—not only to link our computers, but to track down a renegade—showed me that a computer network is, indeed, a community.

But what an impoverished community! One without a church, café, art gallery, theater, or tavern. Plenty of human contact, but no humanity. Cybersex, cybersluts, and cybersleaze, but no genuine, lusty, roll-in-the-hay sex.

And no birds sing.

Even ignoring everything palpable—children's laughter, plum jam, my sister Rosalie's green sports car—what's missing from this ersatz neighborhood? A feeling of permanence and belonging, a sense of location, a warmth from the local history. Gone is the very essence of a neighborhood: friendly relations and a sense of being in it together.

Oh—I hear you: It's only a metaphorical community. Much of what happens over the networks is a metaphor—we chat without speaking, smile without grinning, and hug without touching.

On my screen, I see several icons—a mailbox, a theater, a newspaper. These represent incoming messages, an entertainment video, and a news wire. But they're not the real thing. The mailbox doesn't clunk, the movie theater doesn't serve popcorn, and the newspaper doesn't come with a cup of coffee at the corner café.

How sad—to dwell in a metaphor without living the experience.

The only sensations are a glowing screen, the touch of a keyboard, and the sound of an occasional bleep. All synthetic.

There's something else missing from this networked world. My bamboo flyswatter. In Nanjing, next to the Drum Tower building, I visited a small shop beneath a giant poster of Mao Tse-tung; I was hunting for a flyswatter.

"Honorable Sir," I addressed the shopkeeper in my ramshackle Mandarin, "kindly tell me if your virtuous store might sell a single wide flat machine to hit small flying animals." They don't teach you that one in language lab.

To which he responded something about not being able to understand the honorable foreign guest from across the seas. Except he added a little bow. It took a short pantomime of buzzing and swatting, but yep, there's my bamboo flyswatter. Ten cents.

And a bargain at that. Today, that flyswatter sits alongside my monitor, ready for any small flying animals that might buzz this way. No icons, batteries, or network connection, and it seldom misses.

The common claim is that networks, like computers, are tools—utensils to get work done. I've heard this so often that I'm beginning to doubt it.

"A tool for what?" I ask my friends. Their replies are telling: it's a tool for thinking.

Ouch. We need a tool to spare us the effort of thinking? Is reasoning so painful that we require a labor-saving device? What is it we're trying to avoid?

Maybe we're obsessed with computers as tools because, as Thomas Carlyle wrote, man is a tool-using animal . . . without tools he is nothing, with tools he is all.

And so everything within our scope becomes a tool. Advertisements promote pens, dictionaries, and word processors as writing tools. I search in vain for something that isn't a tool: my shoes are personal-transportation tools, chewing gum is a relaxation tool, and the moon is a tool for telling time and illuminating the evening.

But I've never heard of a typewriter user's group, or schools spending thousands of dollars to put a radial-arm saw on every student's desk. Nor do I know of any screwdriver that inspires the same slavish infatuation as the Internet. The computer is a remarkably different kind of tool—one which can turn kids into reactive zombies, adults into frustrated bumblers.

Calling a computer a tool gives us a warm feeling that we're craftsmen, burgeoning with physical skills and manual dexterity. It imparts none of these.

Rather, the computer requires almost no physical interaction or dexterity, beyond the ability to type. And unlike a chisel, drill, or shovel, the computer demands rote memorization of nonobvious rules. You subjugate your own thinking patterns to those of the computer.

Using this tool alters our thinking processes. When Gutenberg invented the printing press, the prevailing style of writing changed, and again when the typewriter became common. Telegraphs, too, influenced literature. Stop. Think of the terseness of Hemingway. In turn, word processors change not just how but what we write. The handwritten bread-and-butter note gives way to an e-mail greeting.

Databases aren't just computer programs—there are other ways to organize information, like Rolodexes, address books, and manila folders in filing cabinets. These mechanical filing systems are intuitive, easy to use, and simple to set up. Yet the person deeply committed to a relational database system won't recognize opportunities where these physical devices might work better.

Nor is the computer the only tool for doing mathematics—analytic equations, calculus, approximations, and trigonometry have worked for centuries, if not millennia.

Simply by turning to a computer when confronted with a problem, you limit your ability to recognize other solutions. When the only tool you know is a hammer, everything looks like a nail.

Which is the tool: the computer or the user?

This leads to some important questions that I'm not smart enough to frame. When your thinking is strictly logical—when you're constrained to a digital mode of work—you lose the ability to leapfrog over conceptual walls.

The stiff-walled logic of computers rewards those who can rigorously follow strict-thought rules. These incentives include prestige and employment . . . our software and networks nourish drones.

At the same time, computers punish the imaginative and inventive by constraining them to prescribed channels of thought and action.

For example, we think that painting and drawing programs open up new vistas to graphic artists. But they strongly limit the artist's choices of colors, sizes, shapes, and textures. Moreover, the artist must strictly follow the program's rules. The artist working at a computer never lays a hand on media like origami, textiles, or alabaster.

When we find dance and music on computers, it seems so refreshingly delightful simply because the nature of computing is antithetical to flights of fancy.

And what of the person who can't follow instructions? Often he's the one who comes up with original solutions to problems. Yet this is the guy who cannot boot up without a snag. He has constant troubles with computers, simply because his thoughts are out of sync with the conventions of software designers. In a Darwinian manner, creative people are ill-adapted for survival around computers.

In short, the medium in which we communicate changes how we organize our thoughts. We program computers, but the computers also program us.

Marshall McLuhan divided media into hot and cool—movies and radio were hot, television and the telephone were cool. Hot media are low in participation; cool ones high in it. I'm not sure what he means, but on that scale the Internet, especially the Usenet, is certainly cool.

Think of these media as social interactions. Movies can be participatory, even if you don't get to choose who's on-screen. Get a group of friends together to watch *Casablanca* at a campus cinema some weekend. There's gossip while waiting in line, along with the smell of popcorn, and the anticipation of seeing a classic film. You nudge each other during the good scenes, or perhaps put an arm around your sweetie. Or head over to the *Rocky Horror Picture Show,* and don't forget the toast.

Compare this to an intense night surfing the Internet—you have nobody to compare notes with, nobody to harmonize as you hum "As Time Goes By," nobody to spill popcorn on your favorite blanket. Your community disappears when your modem disconnects.

What's the nature of this networked community? It runs in all directions. Professorial, technocratic, punk. Sparks of intellect scattered across electronic fields, without coherent direction.

Listening to traffic crossing the Usenet, I hear a distinct libertarian political leaning: stay off my back and let me do whatever I please.

It attracts extreme political positions and long-standing international feuds. They spill out of newsgroups frequented by Turks and Armenians, by Israelis and Palestinians, and by Serbs and Croats.

And so far, I know of only two serious petition drives over the Internet, both surrounding privacy issues. The first convinced Lotus not to sell a CD-ROM with individualized shopper preferences. The second opposed the government's proposed Clipper encryption standard. Each generated well over fifty thousand electronic signatures.

Curiously, neither of these are major public-policy issues. That is, technologists speak to their own concerns. The single overriding common interest among network users is the medium itself.

Thousands of Internet users will tell you that I'm giving but one side of a complex story. They'll point to hundreds of self-help groups that work as effectively as any neighborhood counseling organization. They'll show you the comp.risks forum, where anyone can read about the social implications of computing. They'll talk about the World Wide Web, where a click of a mouse will bring the latest news from London, Tokyo, or Berlin.

They're right. The Usenet is a community where hundreds of thousands engage in friendly banter. From across the net and across the ocean, I hear the latest jokes on rec.humor.funny, reports on travel adventures on rec.travel, and listings of jobs on misc.jobs.offered. Before checking out an old Dracula film, I check into rec.arts.movies.

If I were being fair to the Usenet, I'd have to mention the experts who thanklessly help newcomers on such forums as comp.unix.questions, news.answers, and news.newusers.questions. I'd probably have to include some of the lesser-known watering holes, like rec.arts.books, where book-folk congregate, and alt.best-of-usenet, where every day I read gaffes by newcomers as well as exceptionally creative flames.

Don't get me wrong: there's lots of good things happening on-line. I've seen bulletin boards for cancer survivors, bagpipers, and cave explorers. A carpenter's union in New York State gets the news out over a bulletin board.

Another way to spread the word is through electronic mailing lists. These lists let exclusive groups thrive over the networks, whether medieval English scholars, feminist authors, or Japanese animation addicts.

Mailing lists are universally available over e-mail. To get on the mailing list for postcard collectors, just send mail to postcard-request@bit.listserv.postcard, with the subject line of *subscribe*. They're simple, too: a user sends mail to one site, and everyone down the line gets a copy.

The neatness of these mailing lists extends beyond their simplicity and wide availability. It's a great way to make a closed discussion, say for sensitive topics like gender issues or recovery groups. There's a place for folk dancers to compare steps and accordion players to exchange notes. Around San Francisco, book fanatics send mail to ead@netcom.com to get the latest scoop on bookstore happenings.

But mailing lists almost guarantee mailbox overflow. When the comet crashed into Jupiter, I picked up fifty messages from the net; another hundred fell into the bitbucket. And mailing-list traffic, like Usenet newsgroups, often has little content.

Virtually everything is debated on the Usenet: whether computers are best left on at night, if cats can be fed a vegetarian diet, if abortion should be legal.

Predictable replies—maybe, maybe, and maybe, but each with more stridency. Plenty of opinions, but not much informed dialogue, and even less consensus.

Of course, since there are no easy answers, arguments over the Usenet are seldom resolved. They'll degenerate into name-calling; eventually one of the participants figuratively walks away, and a new debate begins.

Now, recurrent debates aren't bad—they're just circular and tedious. Next time I have to spend a week in traction, I'll check into the Usenet. One of the joys of computers is how they're great at wasting time that might otherwise be difficult to waste.

Imagine driving from Yankee Stadium in the Bronx to Jones Beach on Long Island. You'd likely take the Cross Bronx Expressway, the Throgs Neck Bridge, the Cross Island Parkway, the Long Island Expressway, and the Meadowbrook State Parkway. Say thanks to Robert Moses—he created these public works.

From 1930 to 1970, Robert Moses built roads, bridges, parks, and housing projects. Nothing stopped him—not politicians, community leaders, urban planners, neighborhoods. Quite the contrary: he bribed politicians, intimidated community leaders, hired the urban planners, and plowed under the neighborhoods. Anyways, in 1955 only a reactionary Luddite would possibly oppose highway construction. The automobile was clearly the key to the future.

Your imaginary trip across the Cross Bronx Expressway won't show you the thousands of people evicted from their homes, the old brownstone apartments paved over, the diverse neighborhoods cleaved by noisy traffic arteries. Robert Moses did more to destroy New York City than any one individual.

Moses disdained anyone who couldn't afford a car, so he built parkways with low overpasses that blocked buses. No walkways or bike paths, either. Computer mavens shun the technophobes, so they write manuals that can't be understood by novices. Internet merchants want government subsidies to build ever faster links, but they won't offer lower connect rates for the poor.

Today's Internet hustlers invade our communities with computers, not concrete. By pushing the Internet as a universal panacea, they offer a tempting escape from this all-too-mundane world. They tell us that we need not get along with our neighbors—heck, we needn't even interact with them. Won't need to travel to a library either; those books will come right to my desk. Interactive multimedia will solve classroom problems. Fat pay checks and lifelong employment await those who master computers.

They're well-meaning, of course. They truly believe in virtual communities and electronic classrooms. They'll tell you how the computer is a tool to be used, not abused. Because clearly, the computer is the key to the future.

The key ingredient of their silicon snake oil is a technocratic belief that computers and networks will make a better society. Access to information, better communications, and electronic programs can cure social problems.

I don't believe them. There are no simple technological solutions to social problems. There's plenty of distrust and animosity between people who communicate perfectly well. Access to a universe of information cannot solve our problems: we will forever struggle to understand one another. The most important interactions in life happen between people, not between computers.

While snaking a plugged bathroom drain, I yearned for a virtual-drainpipe program—a computer that would siphon out the muck and unclog my pipes. Just double-click on the cute icon of a clean pipe, and my problems would disappear.

Watching the snake dredge glop from the drain, I wondered if the Internet might better be described as a pipeline rather than a highway. After all, it delivers a stream of data on demand. In this sense, the modem's a faucet, letting information flow into the computer.

Or perhaps a sewer pipe. Don't snicker—good sewers are way more important to public health than highways or communications. On second thought, this is a poor metaphor: I can live quite well without the Internet, but not without operative drains.

. . . .

The federal government's National Information Initiative promotes universal access. Like universal health care, this means something different to each person.

At one extreme, universal access means that every citizen will be trained in the use of the network, given a workstation, a modem, and an account.

At the other extreme, universal access may mean that everyone is welcome online, as long as they pay the fare. That's pretty much the way things are today—commercial providers like CompuServe, PSI, and UUNET charge for service.

At the last turn of the century, the Bell System also advertised universal service. At the time, they meant that any telephone could connect to any other—if they both used AT&T. Complete technical compatibility, a major monopolistic advantage.

And so evolved today's phone system: billed by the mile and by the minute. Local calls are cheap; long-distance costs more. An hour-long conversation costs twice that of a thirty-minute call.

In North America, after you pay a monthly service charge, local calls generally don't cost extra. You can spend five hours a day on your phone and never pay over thirty dollars. It's flat-rate service.

Most phone companies also offer measured service, where you are billed for every local call. Even though this system would save many people money, most of us prefer flat-rate billing. You enjoy a sense that local calls are free, even though you pay for them on your flat-rate monthly bill. In turn, you've got no incentive to cut down on local calls.

The interstate highway system is also universal—anyone with a car can use it. It's strictly a usage-based service—you pay by the mile. Gasoline taxes supposedly pave the roads; the more you drive, the more you pay. You don't have a sense of these costs, since you think you're paying for gas.

Today's Internet has flat-rate billing. Or maybe it's no billing. Its designers never figured on charging for service, so packets sent across town or across the ocean are all charged the same—nothing. Later, I'll talk about the effects of this free ride, but for now, realize that users aren't paying for the infrastructure—it's heavily subsidized.

Like the post office, the phone system, and the highway system, most of the cost of the Internet is in infrastructure. The incremental cost of sending one more file is nearly zero.

Almost, but not exactly zero. E-mail isn't free. Someone must pay to transfer those bytes across the network. Even ignoring the infrastructure—the cables, satellite links, routers, and packet switches—there's a significant overhead to manage the system. Someone's got to set everything up, keep it running as hardware changes, update the software, and answer questions from frantic users. On the Internet, the users aren't paying. This can't continue for long.

In the same way, someone has to pay for road repairs. Nationwide, bridges and road surfaces show signs of wear. Nobody wants to pay for maintenance and improvements to the infrastructure.

Well, almost nobody. I know a guy who single-handedly took action to rebuild the national infrastructure. Andy Odell's name is synonymous with non-radial oscillations in stars and protoplanets. While a grad student at the University of Wisconsin, he noticed the sorry state of the nation's railroad system. Decades of neglect had left Wisconsin crisscrossed with abandoned train tracks. With a scruffy red beard, scruffy blue jeans, and scruffy black sneakers, Andy set out to capitalize on this situation.

Working late nights in the astronomy department's workshop, he liberated an eight-foot sheet of plywood, four rubber wagon-wheels, a couple of four-and-a-half-foot axles, and a lawn-mower engine.

Andy built a go-cart for railroad tracks.

"You gotta make the tires out of rubber," Andy explains. "Otherwise, they'll conduct electricity and you'll set off the lights along the way."

To keep the cart on the tracks, he welded steel plates alongside the wheels. The rubber sits on the rail, and the plates slide along the inside edge. Makes a wonderful swishing sound as you roll down the track.

I mention these construction details not to encourage duplication of Andy's experiment, but rather to show that working on any national-infrastructure project requires both planning and understanding. Oh, Andy says to keep the center of gravity low, since the ride's plenty bumpy.

Now, you probably figure that anyone who understands how stars pulsate must also be aware of the Pauli exclusion principle: no two objects can occupy the same space at the same time. Probably Andy had a theoretical grasp of this law of physics, but he didn't allow it to get in the way of his experimental work.

For it's clearly insane to drive a go-cart down a track with an oncoming train. That's why Andy always brought another grad student along—one of them faced forward, one looked back. As soon as they saw a train, they'd cut the engine, hop off, and pull the cart off the tracks. A simple method of sidetracking that the railroads only discover during wrecks.

The guy in front also had another job—to watch for trees. The old passenger trains used to flush the toilets right onto the tracks, which made for great fertilizer. Consequently, these abandoned lines often have lush vegetation growing alongside—and sometimes between—the rails. When you're scooting along at twenty miles an hour, even a small cedar can mightily impede your travel. So the forward observer, hand on the throttle, would slow down, nudge up to the sapling, hack it down with a handsaw, and the twosome would continue on their way. In this fashion, Andy helped maintain clear access to essential roadways, and measurably improved our nation's transportation infrastructure.

It worked great: looping from Madison to Monroe in around a day. With the path cleared of trees, Andy was dreaming of opening up his own commuter line on the old Illinois Central line. The Odell Cannonball.

To become a railroad baron, however, Andy needed a western expansion, toward the Continental Divide and, ultimately, the Pacific Ocean. So he scouted along the Milwaukee Railroad lines as far as the town of Darlington.

There's maybe six thousand people in this Wisconsin county

seat, along with twenty saloons, a couple of gas stations, and one sheriff. Andy hadn't visited before, or he'd have realized that the tracks go straight across Main Street, right in front of the bars, gas stations, and the sheriff's office.

Grinning like fools, Andy and his companion coasted into town around eleven on a Saturday night. Doing ten miles an hour, they got most of the way through town, past streets named Lucy, Minerva, Harriet, Ann, Alice, and Louisa. It was someplace around the last three streets that they looked up to notice a police car ambling alongside.

They killed the engine as Darlington's sheriff caught up with them, as did many of the citizens from the bars. "You're traveling on railroad property," the sheriff told Andy. "If the Milwaukee Road complains, I'm going to have to arrest you on charges of trespass."

Andy came prepared. In his backpack, along with a six-pack of Huber, he'd brought a suit and tie, so as to be properly attired if he were hauled before a judge. Rebuilding our national infrastructure requires foresight and ingenuity.

Now, Saturday night's not the best time to reach the legal department of the Milwaukee Railroad, but the sheriff did his best. The closest he got was a dispatcher in Milwaukee, who asked if the cart was setting off the switches and lights. Andy explained how the rubber wheels worked as insulation, and the dispatcher was satisfied that the cart didn't set off the lights. "Talk to the legal department on Monday," he said. "Leave me out of it."

Without the railroad's help, the sheriff couldn't find any reason to detain the two adventurers; Andy, however, still worried about spending the night in the clink.

As the bars closed at 1 A.M., the crowd grew restive, unsure how to celebrate the town's railroad revival. The atmosphere became friendlier when Andy offered trips to the onlookers. The sheriff went first.

"He was pretty nice after we gave him a ride," Andy reports. "Instead of arresting us, he dropped us off in a park and made sure nobody bothered us."

Meanwhile, Andy had figured his way out of his bind. If the

Milwaukee Road pressed charges, he'd publish plans on how to build your own railroad go-cart in the underground press. Every dope-smoking hippie that could hammer together a few sheets of plywood would soon be tripping the light rail fantastic from coast to coast. Should the railroad choose to ignore the incident, Andy would keep his experimental technology to himself.

Which is what happened. Andy never told a soul, and thanks to his dedicated clearing of almost a half dozen trees, the Milwaukee Railroad stayed in business for the betterment of Western civilization.

Today, you can't duplicate Andy's work—someone uprooted the tracks, leaving behind a few rotted ties and a bicycle path. Andy's contribution to the national infrastructure lives on.

Andy's now a professor of astronomy at Northern Arizona University, in Flagstaff, where the nearest abandoned railroad line is an hour away. He absolutely denies running from the town of Williams up to the Grand Canyon on the old Santa Fe tracks.

I, too, have hopes of helping our national transportation system in the same way as Professor Odell. I've searched the Internet, hunting for plans on how to replicate Andy's motorized railroad cart, as well as for an atlas of abandoned railroad tracks. The closest I've come is a newsgroup devoted to rail fans and a diagram of the New York subway. Suggestive, but not exactly what I'm looking for. For the while, I'll stick to a less-visible infrastructure, the Internet itself.

For a year, I lived with a 110-baud teletype next to my bed. A terrific machine—I could watch relays and cams convert pulses of electricity into type on the page. Slow, but satisfying. I dreamed of a 1200-baud modem—no reason to go faster since that's about how fast I read.

Today, I can't find teletypes or 1200-baud modems; 14,400 is the norm. Not that people read faster: they're downloading files, running interactive games, and watching images on their screens. When text scrolls across the screen at this speed, you might catch one word in ten.

This obsession with speed is made painfully clear in how we treat messages over computer networks. E-mail may take a minute to traverse the continent; we somehow feel obligated to reply just as quickly.

Virtually every computer has a spell-checking program. And there's no need for an eraser with delete keys and full-screen editors. So how come so much of the e-mail I receive has spelling errors and grammatical mistakes?

Why not spend more time composing replies and polishing our communications? Maybe it's the online charges—when I'm paying ten dollars an hour, I don't want to recast a paragraph or start a spell-checker. But even when logged into a network that doesn't charge by the hour—like the Internet—few users double-check their letters before sending them.

So perhaps it's the clunky nature of most online editing programs—they have truly obscure syntaxes. Or do we send out uncorrected e-mail because of the informality of the network? We expect our mail to be read, but then either filed or discarded.

I suspect one reason is the implicit speed of computing. We strive to keep up with the network and the river of text flowing onto our screen.

The ephemeral nature of network connections also encourages fast replies. Because it's so easy to edit text, we think that revising isn't important. I compose a screenful, hit enter, and it's in the ether. Quick, informal, and direct.

We're accustomed to deliberating over the written word. In reading a book, I may stand up, pace the floor, and return to the same place. But I can't easily disengage from this cathode-ray tube. I might slow down the scroll rate, or interrupt a file transfer, but I rarely sit back and contemplate what's on my screen. It's too immediate, too demanding, and the next file is pressing.

America Online, CompuServe, and public Free-nets, by making the networks easily accessible, have brought lots of newbies online. It's a young, mostly male population . . . informal surveys suggest that fewer than a quarter of all users are female.

Logged in, it's hard to tell who's who—some hide behind pseudonyms, others advertise their names directly. The Jane Fonda that's listed in a return address may well belong to some guy; another may simply be listed as K8366.

Since there's no identification required on the Internet, you can be as anonymous as you wish. You can change your name and identity as you please, and your location may be little more than a node.

You can invent a more confident persona, freed from shyness and physical limitations. A housewife in Boise, Idaho, gives herself the name Amazon Gal; a New York City teenager becomes Ranchhand. At this masquerade party, you truly don't know who you're associating with.

Anonymity and untraceability seem to bring out the worst in people. I'm hardly surprised to see online chat rooms labeled "Want MF for Affair" and "Teenage Confessional."

As my computer screen scrolls before me, I see each person with the same font, style, and packaging. In person, we'd sense a difference in clothing, facial expression, accent, and sex. All these disappear online.

Meet a bigot on the street who's shouting obscenities, and you get away from him fast. Should the same person post to net news, you'll read most of his message before going on to the next. Access to the network gives both audience and credibility to extreme opinions.

MUDs—Multi-User Dungeons—are interactive role games, played across the Internet. People connect to a distant computer, create their own characters, and interact with others by typing commands and comments. Nobody knows anybody else's identity; online persona is everything. We can step outside of traditional boundaries of social constraint, confide in strangers, and become intimate with utterly fictional characters.

Both in role-playing games and in chat rooms, the network presents an unreal world where you can appear to be anyone you wish. Adopt a friendly persona or that of a grinch. But you aren't who you pretend to be. Inside, you're still you.

Participants at this masked ball are free to talk about otherwise uncomfortable or verboten subjects. Popular discussion groups revolve around sex, bondage, and pornographic images.

All this from a decidedly unsexy medium. There's no possibility of physical intimacy; at best, only a hope that a correspondent might turn out to be as you imagine. Yet you may well be chatting with someone masquerading as a different sex and different age.

Tailoring a persona is an experience of otherness, a way to escape the here and now. I'll bet some bearded philosopher—Martin Buber, maybe—discussed how the authenticity of experience can diffuse alienation from our true selves. The separation between us, once imposed by circumstance, is now chosen by network addicts.

Yet for all these network creations, you have nothing physical invested. No matter where you appear to be, you are always in the same place. No matter how dangerous the situation seems, you're always safe. No matter how sensual the conversation feels, you cannot consummate the relationship. And no matter what persona you adopt, inside you're still you.

Computer networks isolate us from one another, rather than bring us together. We need only deal with one side of an individual over the net. And if we don't like what we see, we just pull the plug. Or flame them. There's no need to tolerate the imperfections of real people. It's the same intolerance found on the highway, where motorists direct intense anger at one another.

By logging on to the networks, we lose the ability to enter into spontaneous interactions with real people. Evening time is now spent watching a television or a computer terminal—safe havens in which to hide. Sitting around a porch and talking is becoming extinct, as is reading aloud to children.

The Internet puts me in touch with thousands of people across the country. But it's more important to spend time with my friends and neighbors. Karen Anderson, the penguin keeper at San Francisco's Steinhart Aquarium, puts it this way: "The people who are right close to me are the most important ones in my life. Why should I get excited about personal relationships on some computer network?"

Karen told me of the work of Dr. Luis Baptista, the curator of ornithology at the California Academy of Sciences. This guy knows his birds—he can whistle the songs of doves and sparrows. Jeez, he did his dissertation on the dialects of these birds.

Well, to see how birds learn songs, he raised white-crowned sparrows. When they left the nest, Dr. Baptista placed single fledglings in a special cage where they could see and hear an Asian strawberry finch. The young birds could also hear several dialects of their own sparrow songs in the same room, but they couldn't see those sparrows.

The fledgling sparrows didn't learn their own songs. Instead, they matured, singing the songs of the Asian finches with whom they socially interacted. And later, as parents, these sparrows taught their young to sing Chinese songs, too. Sparrows learn from living teachers, not from machines.

In the same way, the isolation of computers and online networks causes us to sing others' songs. Children, raised with less social interaction, adopt the ways of the first people they come in close contact with. It encourages a divorce from parental values and the dominance of peer culture. Kids that interact with computers rather than their parents miss out on the most important part of growing: being close to their families.

Think I'm exaggerating? One teenager in Berkeley began using a computer when he was three years old; today, he's utterly fluent in getting around the Internet, but can't converse with an adult. I know several computer wizards who can tell you details of their computer's disk cache, but don't know when their family immigrated to America. And I've met dozens of high school students who can proficiently use a word processor, but have never written a thank-you letter.

Four

So what's special about computers? Why's it so difficult to adjust the margins? How come my Mom, who illustrated complex aircraft parts during World War II, is frustrated when she tries to compose a letter? Why do we associate words like *wizard* and *guru* and *swami* with those who know computer systems?

It's the exclusionary nature of technocratic culture. For all the talk of friendly, open systems, there's no warm welcome for novices. It's up to the user to figure out a new terminology, heavy with jargon and acronyms; up to the user to figure out which system is best; up to the user to install and maintain the software.

In the same way, the networked community is an exclusive club for the initiated. Too often, there's an established hazing ritual to get online. First you try the system, make mistakes, and walk away frustrated. Then you hunt for the documentation, and hope that the manuals match the current software.

Or perhaps there's an online help file—it scrolls off your screen when you leave its menuspace. Software designers feel that online help is a great way to answer questions. As a result, we find balloon help on the Macintosh, function key 1 on Windows, and online help files for networks. All these assume that I'm having a problem with a command. But often, I'm floundering, not knowing what command to use. The only way to get an answer is to ask someone.

So I grovel before a technician or pay a long-distance telephone fee to get lost in a thicket of automated help messages. Or I watch an expert quickly type a few symbols and rush off without an explanation. I repeat this rite for a month, and I'm in.

I've spent uncounted hours listening to music while on hold, feeling the deep frustration of a simple question being unanswered. There's a sense that any question is a stupid one. After all, the computer is logical, the commands are documented online, and the lord-high-fixer is too busy to hold my hand.

Maybe the frustration of computers comes from their complexity. With so many parts and such a variety of interactions, naturally they're hard to use.

But wait. What's the most complex device in your house? I'd say it's the television. Within it, you'll find an amazing variety of circuits: radio, audio, digital, and analog. There's a millivolt detector next to a 20,000-volt flyback transformer; magnetic deflection coils surround a triple-gun vacuum tube; phase-locked loops that latch on to weak signals; amplifiers, buffers, and oscillators running upward of 800 MHz. All this connects to a dozen high-bandwidth networks. Coupled with the electromechanical wonders of a VCR, I'd expect only a trained expert to be able to operate such a system.

Despite this complexity, every child can operate a TV and a VCR. The documentation is less than twenty pages; even then, it's rarely read. Sure, every VCR has plenty of unused features—like setting the clock and programming the recorder—but we don't hear of people frightened of using their televisions.

Well, not entirely. Try figuring out computerized TV sets. The day after an airplane crashed near Pittsburgh, Don Alvarez listened as three friends discussed the news coverage. A fourth sat silent, and finally explained that her television couldn't tune the local news channel. Her TV was programmed to scan her favorite stations, and she couldn't find the reprogramming instructions. Her job was made no easier by the fad of unlabeled black push-buttons hidden under black panels.

It's not necessary to hide the controls of a television; this just creates difficulties. In the same vein, must computers be hard to use?

Every year, computer interfaces become conceptually easier: command-line interfaces gave way to multiple-choice menus, then pulldown and tear-off menus, then later to palettes. Yet after every improvement, I'm lost in an overload of choices.

Yesterday, I used Turbocad, a computer-aided design system that populates my screen with five palettes and fifty icons, each an unlabeled picture. And online systems are worse still: each level presents hundreds of choices. I'm literally navigating through a maze of twisty passages, all different, without signposts or maps.

In sympathy to the manufacturers, user interfaces are damned hard to build, and nobody knows how to do it. The more degrees of freedom available, the tougher the job, since commands often affect one another. Yet software makers concentrate on adding features to programs rather than making programs more intuitive.

Result: the computing elite claim that theirs is an open, accessible world, while barring outsiders through a liturgy of technology. It's the culture of exclusion.

In the October 1994 *Byte* magazine, novelist Craig Nova tells how he wants to use the Internet, but finds a thinly disguised hostility to those who are less than adept with computers. "In many ways, I feel that I am a barbarian at the gate," he writes. "I can smell the sweet perfume of paradise, and yet I am condemned to fiddling with the lock. There are a lot of people like me, imperfectly hooked up to the Internet, impatient, waiting for what we know to be there, just beyond our reach: easy, complete access to information."

He's right about the hostility. As we'll see later, that sweet perfume of paradise is an olfactory hallucination, the fragrance of a unicorn. There is no easy, complete access to information. Never was. Never will be.

In March 1949, *Popular Mechanics* described the latest number cruncher: "Where a calculator like the Eniac is equipped with 18,000 vacuum tubes and weighs 30 tons, computers in the future may have only 1,000 tubes and perhaps only weigh one and a half tons."

Toadlike, that mechanical brain of the future now crouches on your desk.

Hardware has long been built without thought for the user. On/off switches hide in the back, among cables and connectors. The control key on my PC is below the shift key; on my Macintosh, that site is occupied by the option key; my Sun workstation places a different key there. The rarely used caps-lock key always gets prime real estate, where it's easily struck by accident. Meanwhile the commonly punched delete key is way off in the corner. Come to think of it, wasn't the keyboard designed to slow down typists by placing the most commonly used keys farthest from our fingers?*

My modem has lights labeled CTS, DTR, CD, RX, TX, and AA. Now I know these mean "clear to send," "data terminal ready," "carrier detect," and stuff like that. But I'm furious that engineers routinely use cryptic labels that mystify the technology and deny access to ordinary people.

Anyways, what does "clear to send" really mean? Why not have a light labeled "computer's disconnected" or "modem has a problem" or even "connection is working fine"?

I hear a satisfying plunk when I strike a key on my Sears typewriter. If the paper jams or the ribbon tears, it makes a different sound. Most drivers can tell the health of their cars simply by listening to the engine. And a mechanic can often diagnose an engine's problem from its noises alone.

But my computer always sounds the same. Whether the program's working or not, I hear the whine of the disk drive and white noise from the fan blades. The fan doesn't speed up when it's crunching through a spreadsheet, nor does the disk stop whining when the system is hung. Happily, my disk does make a subtle clunk whenever I save a file—a pleasant confirmation that the computer is actually working.

. . . .

*Yep. In Milwaukee, C. Latham Sholes and James Densmore built the first typewriter in 1868. It was easy to type too fast and jam the roller; to end that annoyance, Densmore asked his son-in-law, a school superintendent, which letters appeared most often in English. So, in 1872, they created a keyboard with the most-used characters as far apart as possible. Thus, the horror of qwerty.

Plenty of bleeps, pings, and zings announce when my computer demands input, as do dialogue boxes and fancy cursors. But these aren't continuous feedback.

I long for more subtle sounds that, like the sound of a car's engine, tell me what's going on: a change in the sound when the system crashes, or soft noises that vary as operations progress normally.

Such hardware is trivial: most computers have sound blaster boards and stereo outputs. Yet it's rare to find sounds intelligently integrated into the user environment.

Software is hardly better: commands aren't intuitive, there's little standardization, and many functions hide behind special function keys. Naturally, this leads to mistakes and steep learning curves. Lives there a computer user who hasn't accidentally erased a file?

When you install a new program, likely some system file will get modified, risking interference with other software. These changes are hidden, often undocumented, and make it hard to remove software. Worse, program files get stashed all around the disk, labeled with utterly mystical names like WP1422.INI.

Am I asking too much that commercial software be tested and bug-free upon shipping? Apparently so, because I've never received such a product. Never? Well, hardly ever.

On my home computer, these bugs don't just hang the application I'm running . . . they cause my whole machine to crash. Often, I'll run four applications at once—a word processor, database, spreadsheet, and communications program. Should my phone line hiccup, the online program halts and everything freezes. The only remedy is to reboot, thereby losing any changes I've made since I last saved my data.

Someday such interdependencies will be solved with quality operating systems and better-tested software. Uh, right.

Throughout computing, I sense an obsession with power. This, in turn, is equated with speed. It's easy to compare how fast two computers run; anyone can understand what this means.

Far more difficult to measure are simplicity, ease of use, and cost to learn. Yet these yardsticks affect how most people get along with their systems. Much of the time, our high-speed cpu's sit idle, waiting for us to do something. Or else they're displaying screen-saver animations.

But is a program more powerful because it has more functions, supports a built-in programming language, or runs quickly? Is one language more powerful than another? Compare, for example, English with Yiddish. Sure, it's hard to describe a carburetor in Yiddish, but try describing a schlemiel in English.

In the same sense, I'm beginning to feel that power in computing is the same as in physics: the ability to get work done. A complex online system may have many capabilities, but its complexity hampers doing work. I spend more time learning the damn commands than getting the information I need.

Computers and networks don't just get in the way of work. They also separate us from the pleasures of daily life. I've met a programmer who balanced his junk food by popping vitamins through the day. And most every campus has stories of students who move out of their dorms to spend more time in the terminal rooms.

Makes me wonder: these guys eat at the keyboard, consuming calories without the sensuality of dining. Their eyes fix on one place for hours. They exercise only their fingers. No wonder there's an epidemic of carpal tunnel syndrome.

Hey—why not require computer jocks to walk on treadmills while they work, in the interest of preventive health care?

For that matter, to promote mental health, anyone who works with computers should be required to say hello to five real people before they log on in the morning. Insist on sixty minutes of conversation for every hour online. And each computer manual should be followed by an evening with a novel.

I reserve more sympathy for people with the opposite problem. They're so frustrated with computers that they use them only when required.

Maybe their difficulties come from having to mold their ways of thinking to the demands of a program. They know where they want the margins, but the software can't understand. Or perhaps it's the isolation of using a computer that accounts for their stress: when they need help, there's nobody to turn to.

For these people, I prescribe sixty minutes of gardening for every hour online. As a further encouragement, they get to walk in a meadow whenever they call a help line and are put on hold.

These people dread plowing through documentation and must force themselves to learn enough to perform minimal tasks. They're the ones with a phobic reaction to high-technology.

Can't blame 'em. They're treated with condescension or curt hostility by technicians and help lines. Look at the titles of introductory computer manuals: *DOS for Dummies* or *The Complete Idiot's Guide to the Internet.* Intelligent readers pass for morons because they aren't nimble on the keyboard.

Paging through even elementary computer manuals, I find pages crammed with acronyms. Like other net hacks, I'm accustomed to them—*ftp, tcp/ip, telnet,* and *biff,* the last being the name of a programmer's dog. But I understand why others can't get into them. The vocabulary of computing is so arid and lacking in adjectives that the very language is diminished. No wonder novices hate reading manuals.

Even keeping the vocabulary limitation in mind, consider the abysmal quality of software documentation. Unless you own Microsoft Word, you'd never pick up the documentation. It weighs five pounds. That's more than many laptop computers.

Microsoft needs a thousand pages to describe a popular program, written for ordinary people? Am I expected to know all this just to write a letter to my friend Gloria? Are computers so complex that they cannot be described simply?

An automobile is more costly, complex, and dangerous than any word processor. Yet you don't find a thousand-page operating manual, nor must you check with a friend to figure out how to close the window, parallel park, or wash the hood.

"Oh, but a word processor can do more," reply my keyboard-tapping friends. "It can set tab stops, count words, and even correct your spelling." But can it make left turns and coast down hills?

Oh, but for the most astonishingly inept documentation, check into Unix. It's entirely online—just enter *man* to read the manual. If you want to know how to search for a phrase, type *man grep*. To learn how to type out a document, enter *man cat*. To find out how to set margins, uh, well, I haven't found that yet.

In response, Unix will tell you that "Patterns used by grep are limited regular expressions in the style of *ex(1)*; it uses a compact, non-deterministic algorithm . . ."

Wondering about *ex?* It's a text editor for Unix—the online help recommends that you avoid it.

And what if you don't know the name of a Unix command? Typing *help* won't do any good. You need to enter the Unix command, *apropos*. (That word means "appropriate," not "help.")

"Unfair," retorts Bill Cheswick of AT&T Bell Laboratories. "Unix was designed as a power tool for the professional user. It's more like a locomotive or an aircraft than a car. It's a bear to set up and a nightmare to administer. It wasn't meant for Granny."

But guess what Granny finds when she logs onto the Internet?

"I see and interact with a user interface designed by adolescents and constructed deliberately so as to make access as difficult as possible for the novice," says Rachael Padman, a British astronomer who's no grandmother. "Mnemosyne, goddess of memory, must be rolling in her grave."

She's exaggerating, of course. No mere operating system would disturb the mother of the Muses, wife of Zeus, and daughter of Uranus and Gaea.

Still, Dr. Padman points out that Unix was widely adopted because it's free. This allows computer makers to concentrate on making zippy hardware. In a world that believes speed is the only indicator of computer power, Gresham's law holds—as long as it's fast, bad software drives out the good.

Unix documentation, like much of computing, treats novices with contempt . . . it's assumed that anyone reading about *grep* already knows the *ex* editor. No doubt that it's internally elegant, a fine software tool. But for all its internal elegance, Unix offers no sympathy to the beginner. It's programmer-friendly, not user-friendly.

Contrast this with my Sears mechanical typewriter. It came with a dustcover, a spare ribbon, and a cute bottle of oil. For a hundred and fifty dollars, it's entirely adequate for many business applications. It delivers instant hard copy, never crashes, handles envelopes with ease, and anyone can adjust the margins. The sixteen-page instruction booklet includes diagrams of where to place your fingers, how to tab, and a drawing of correct posture. The carrying case even has handles.

FIVE

*A Short Chapter About the Short Lives
of Digital Things*

I buy my clothes at Goodwill. A good place for housewares as well—dinnerware and cooking pots. Whenever I visit, I see rows of bun warmers, hot dog cookers, and electric can openers. These are the sublimate of three decades of electronic gizmos.

The electric can opener—the perfect time saver, as well as a device to modernize your kitchen. It's especially good for the arthritic and disabled. Guess you might say the same for hot dog cookers and bun warmers.

So why do I find so many electric can openers at Goodwill? And why can't I spot them in my friends' homes?

Because old, manual devices actually work. Fairly efficiently, too. Unless you open a lot of cans and cook a lot of wieners, an electric can opener and its cousins won't save you much time, and will clutter up your counter.

Despite having few moving parts and little to wear out, these devices have short life spans. They're discarded before they break.

Sounds like a personal computer. An original IBM PC, now over ten years old, is fully obsolete. Likely, it will still work perfectly and do everything it was built for; after all, the silicon and copper haven't deteriorated. But you can't get software for it any longer. Who could run a computer without a hard disk? What word processor can squeeze into 64 Kbytes?

Within two years, the value of a computer drops in half. Within five years, it's pretty much been superseded. And within a decade, you find them at Goodwill. I know—they're over in aisle B, not far from the bun warmers.

At some thrift stores, computers aren't even welcome. One manager told me that he's inundated with obsolete systems that simply won't sell. "We just dump 'em," he said, then added, "People overvalue their own junk, and computer owners are among the worst. They think that a ten-year-old computer is still valuable. Crazy."

Contrast this with an automobile. For three times the cost of a computer, you purchase a durable machine that will function for well over a decade. *Yowsa*—they're even guaranteed for five years. When something goes wrong with your car, you know where to take it for repair. Some people have been known to drive cars for years without a single crash or hang-up.

Makes me wonder: what are the Edsels of computing? Was it IBM's PC Jr, with a keyboard that felt like a row of Chiclets? Or was it Apple's Newton, the personal assistant that could almost recognize handwriting? Maybe it's the giant fifth-generation computers that were supposed to let robots interact with humans. Is anyone compiling a history of these digital duds?

Even good computers have a brief useful life; this makes computer hardware an expensive investment. Ironically, for online interactions, faster computers make little difference. The bottleneck is your modem or network connection. While Intel and Motorola fight to make faster microprocessors, Internet users await faster modems.

With this fast obsolescence, it's curious that all computers look the same. I keep waiting for a Danish modern keyboard, a solid walnut mouse, or a monitor with Victorian filigrees. Weren't early televisions available in fine wood cabinets?

Not only computers have short lives. The network infrastructure is in constant need of upgrades. Communications lines don't wear out, but their users demand faster speeds. As a result, these links become obsolete almost as quickly as computers.

When I hear of schools being wired for network access and interactive video, I think of the Space Telescope Science Institute in Baltimore, built in 1983. The architects decided on a high-tech building, with a built-in local area network. They placed a computer connector on the wall of each office, and routed these to a central point. Using serial lines, each astronomer connected to the central computer, at speeds of 9600 baud.

Within five years, this modern system was obsolete, replaced by thick-wire Ethernet. Pulling new coaxial cables into each office cost the better part of a million dollars. Speed: 10 megabits per second.

Seven years later, Ethernet is considered slow for local area networks. Better to replace it with FDDI, a fiber-optic communications system that runs ten times faster. On the horizon is another still faster system, ATM.

Our experience with ordinary house wiring misleads us into thinking that communications cables are permanent. After all, the electric company doesn't change its voltage every decade. Yet nobody figures on this short lifetime of communications lines when talking about the free information on the Internet. Nor do school districts budget for upgrading these cables. Wires don't wear out, they think.

And if hardware has a short life span, consider software. Unlike mechanical and electronic things, software can't physically deteriorate. So why does its value drop to zero after you break the shrink-wrap?

The program doesn't change, but its environment sure does. I upgrade my computer, printer, and operating system. Cooperating software changes. Competitors announce better products.

Aah, software upgrades! You don't have much choice but to buy the latest update, since it corrects bugs of the current release. If you're lucky, you don't have to convert your old data files.

A word processor may last two years before the next version. These upgrades likely add as many new bugs as are patched, and result in a bigger, more complex program. One that's less and less compatible with old files. And one that requires me to learn new commands, functions, and menu locations.

These upgrades convert simple programs into giant software

monoliths; each an operating system unto itself. It's as if my eggbeater mutated into a cyclotron.

Curiously, as computer hardware gets faster, programs run slower. Microsoft Word version 1 took about twenty-five seconds to start on my antique Macintosh Plus. Eight years and five releases later, I wait the same length of time to fire up this program on my much zippier Macintosh Quadra.

What does this latest upgrade do for my word-processing needs? Oh, it lets me include video clips and voice announcements within my documents. Now, don't ask me why I'd include a movie in a letter I'm writing. I can't print it out, can't mail it over the Internet, can't even view it on the computer down the hallway, which doesn't have the right hardware.

Were these useless features simply add-on whistles, I'd shrug. But I've paid someone to develop and test this code. And it's wasting space on my disk drive, not to mention slowing down my computer. Trivial complaints, perhaps. But multiply such silliness by the number of programs on each system, and they begin to add up. I'm happy to sacrifice functionality for simplicity, reliability, and, especially, ease of learning.

Lately, I notice more and more people ignoring upgrades. Instead of carefully following every improvement, they simply use their programs. Makes sense to me—no time wasted reinstalling software. Maybe the software market is maturing, after fifteen years of frenzy.

Upgraded or not, old software doesn't wear out. Yet there's essentially no market for used software. At least I can't find any at Goodwill.

Computers change quickly, but our learning can't keep pace. Computer jocks pride themselves on knowing several operating systems and dozens of applications. Should we expect everyone to become a digital polyglot?

St. Joseph's hospital in Paterson, New Jersey, spent twenty-five million dollars on a computer network to tie all its physicians together. The system is supposed to replace handwritten orders and verbal commands. The administration gave the usual rationales: it'll improve efficiency, reduce errors, and save money in the long run.

The old-guard doctors screamed and hollered. Naturally—before they could use the system, they'd have to learn it.

Suppose you're an overworked doctor: you want to spend time with your patients, your medical committee wants you to study the latest techniques (and prove it on an exam), and your department wants you to publish papers. Now the hospital asks you to learn some obscure command-line operating system. How do you react?

Those doctors, along with countless secretaries, salespeople, and astronomers, want to pitch the dumb beasts out the window. We've all listened to people seething with frustration as they tackle what should be a simple task on the computer. These aren't dolts—they're capable people who can't figure out a program.

The cult of computing emphasizes hardware speed and software capabilities, while generally ignoring the difficulties of learning. In sales talks and meetings, experts will show how much these systems can do. It's hard to stand your ground against such a juggernaut—if you admit it sounds difficult, you're greeted with condescension, disbelief, or sarcasm.

An Apple employee demonstrated a version of Unix at a Berkeley Macintosh User's Group meeting. The demo went fine—he showed all sorts of commands like *grep, awk,* and *yacc.* A strange thing to do, convert an easy-to-use computer like the Mac into a hard to understand system running Unix.

At the end of display, there were plenty of technical questions about speed and communications. Finally, a woman timidly spoke up: "I need to write a term paper. Can this computer help me?"

It's the obvious question. She had been told that the Macintosh was easy to use, so she sat in on the talk. Instead of a warm welcome, she was confronted with a wall of jargon and a description of one of the most difficult operating systems around. She wanted to attend driver's ed, but wound up in a mechanic's school.

It's not just operating systems. Learning a new program takes many hours, often several days. To become fluent may require a month of patiently figuring out commands and reading manuals.

This cost of learning dwarfs the price of the software and hardware. We each have a major investment in the systems that we already know. A new program must offer substantial benefits to make up for the time I'll spend figuring it out and memorizing its commands.

Computer jocks plead with me to get rid of my shopworn programs and replace them with faster, more efficient software. They promise tighter integration, more capabilities, and speedier communications. From experience, I know my real cost: hours of frustration.

Past generations of millwrights, blacksmiths, and machinists are almost gone. Theirs was a real workplace, of forges, lathes, and anvils. Nothing virtual about a diesel engine or hydraulic press. They built iron horses with muscles of steam, skyscrapers with brick and rivet and lime.

We're fast replacing their hard mechanical world with a gossamer network of fibers. Ours is one of artificial reality, software tools, and expert systems. There's nothing to touch; no inner workings to admire. The pendulum clock from sixty years ago attracts more attention than today's more accurate quartz watch.

Makes me wonder what history we're leaving behind. Footprints across an artificial reality are as evanescent as data on the Ethernet.

Today, gone is craft, replaced by career. Instead of workers on our feet, we've become sedentary professionals, entering data into computers.

As the analog world of our parents gives way to the digital universe of our children, I compare the tools of these two environments. Handwriting is replaced by word processing, mail by e-mail, accounting books by spreadsheets, rotary dials by Touch-Tones, drafting by CAD.

Efficient improvements, yes, but one thing saddens me. I sense little love for this technology, and even less appreciation for the wonders of this digital age.

Once, kids read of Tom Swift's adventures in electric cars and high-speed aeroplanes. Today, there's a blasé acceptance of instant global communications and microelectronic wizardry. These are impressive accomplishments, deserving of curiosity, awe, and praise.

For all my ambivalence about the barrenness of technoculture,

I'm blown away by the devices themselves. Once, you brought a six-transistor radio to the beach. Now, there's a half million transistors in every cellular phone. Johann Kepler needed six years to analyze the motion of Mars; my pocket calculator can do this in a minute.

Yet despite the footsore cliché of an information revolution, I rarely hear genuine esteem for the internal workings of today's technologies. Hardly anyone takes apart a computer just to admire the designers' work. Kids don't disassemble VCRs to figure out how they work—I wish they would! There are no Heathkits to let you solder your own modem. Indeed, it's a rare hobbyist that wires his PC into an experiment.

I guess today's experimenters build things in software, without ever touching a soldering iron. The hocus-pocus is inside the program. It's cleaner this way—nothing to burn or zap, and you don't need a voltmeter.

What happened to home-brewed and breadboarded circuitry? Where's the joy of mechanics and electricity, the creation of real things? Who are the tinkerers with a lust for electronics?

We've become a nation of appliance operators, who take pride in what we own, rather than what we build. Reminds me, in an odd way, of my fortune cookie from The Great Wall Chinese Restaurant: "Work to become, not to acquire."

SIX

Comparing the Digital Tools of Computing, Such as Image Manipulation, with the Physical Tools We're Leaving Behind; This Chapter is Heavily Biased by the Author's Astronomical Bent

Paging through catalogs, I find programs like Pagemaker, Fontographer, Powerpoint, and Persuasion. Each does a splendid job of formatting text and creating dazzling graphics. Indeed, the last generation of typographers and layout artists could never manage such special effects.

These programs let anyone generate multicolor graphs with nifty backgrounds for "powerful, compelling presentations." You see these projected at business meetings, scientific conferences, and sales seminars. Or look behind the evening news announcer—that zippy line drawing was probably made with this kind of software.

Most any computer can make these charts. And most every one does. I understand the temptation: pretty graphics create a sense of professionalism and order. Besides, it's fun to play with color blends and shadowed fonts; collecting more data or analyzing a proposal is drudgery.

Yet I've never seen a memorable computer-generated chart. The speakers who have amazed me scribbled their displays by hand, using blackboard or overhead projector. Of course: they knew their subjects, wanted to tell me about them, and could rattle off their main points impromptu. Their ideas carried me along, not their graphics.

Ever watch technoids speak with computerized projectors? They connect their laptop shows to an audience. They're always nervous ahead of time, because there are so many ways to screw up. So, before their talks, they have to double-check their electronics. Contrast this with an ordinary blackboard: you can keep going even if the chalk breaks.

Pagemaker and its cousins make it easy to lay out newsletters, signs, even greeting cards. You see these everywhere, complete with clip art, multiple fonts, and flashy headlines. Coupled with high-resolution laser printers, every résumé now looks striking.

Why, then, am I disappointed when looking for a qualified research assistant? Before me, a stack of sixty résumés, each a sterile, word-processed summary of someone's life. Not a smudge or fingerprint in the lot. The only sign of humanity are signatures at the bottom of cover letters; several of those are computer-generated as well.

It's so easy to manipulate the appearance of a message that people spend inordinate amounts of time trying to get it perfect.

I want to hire a human being, a living person who can handle the job, one who will latch on to a problem with verve. Judging from these résumés, I'm presented with a row of automatons, each with a different set of fonts and page-layout routines. No life here—just dry compilations of administrivia.

And why don't those nifty newsletters impress me? They're certainly laid out well, what with their multiple columns, pullout quotes, and drop-shadowed headlines.

Fancy backgrounds and multicolor borders pull my eye away from the text. Special fonts and classy paper emphasize the designer's message. Pullout quotes and inset headlines flash the editor's point of view.

Such eye candy gets in the way of the author's message. It prevents me from searching out fallacies in his logic. The typography dilutes the presentation.

It's grand rounds at the University of California Medical Center. I'm watching a nervous resident stand before fifty physicians, presenting a case study of a patient with renal failure. Interspersed with microscopic pictures of kidney biopsies, I see elegant charts of text and graphics.

This doctor is being judged on the scientific merit of her medicine, yet she's worried that her presentation might not be technically elegant enough.

Result? She spent three weeks learning Persuasion and formatting two dozen Kodachrome slides of text, time which could have been spent further researching glomerulopathy.

You know, I'd rather listen to her stammer through a talk with handwritten charts and scribbled notes. Professional slides add the veneer of glib certainty, yet they obscure the substance of her talk—the patient.

A resident physician has a hell of a lot to learn about basic science, clinical medicine, and human interactions. Why add the pressure of a complex computer program?

Because the mastery of complex computer programs soon becomes baseline. After a few physicians give talks with flashy graphics, others follow suit, and rapidly, these graphics become expected in every presentation.

If I have renal failure, I don't want a doctor who's adept at page layout. I want her to treat me. Ideally, she'll be compassionate and spend her time by my bedside, attending my kidney instead of a keyboard.

Computers hide mistakes in logic while sanctifying information with an aura of truth. Dan Sack, a lighting specialist in Buffalo, regularly helps architects prepare bids. "I put everything into a database and spreadsheet," he says. "Makes it easy to organize and change, as well as giving a nice-looking product. The architects love it.

"But in my last bid, I had two simple errors in my spreadsheet formulas. Only by sheer luck, they pretty much offset each other, and didn't much affect the bottom line."

The architects didn't review his work because of the professional gloss of the spreadsheet. "If I'd used pencil and paper, they'd have combed through it, and the mistakes would have popped right out."

Style shouldn't overshadow content. But at the other extreme, I find messages from computer networks with no formatting at all. Daily, e-mail rolls across my screen with a uniform color, font, and spacing. Their content is expressed in raw ASCII—the simple alphabet of every computer's keyboard.

Ha! That answers all my complaints about slick productions and fancy layouts. Here's a medium that's gritty and direct. There's virtually no emphasis on form.

So why am I still not satisfied? Is it the lack of warmth, the distance between the writer and myself? Or is simple ASCII text too intimate, too close for comfort? Is it my own inconsistency?

Maybe it's that I miss the closeness of a real letter or the warmth of a voice across the telephone line. My electronic screen just isn't as friendly.

Networks, bulletin boards, and file servers are amazingly efficient at duplicating and distributing information—it's easy to copy files. As a result, I find the same files in lots of archives.

Copying and modifying—that's the computer's strong suit. As a result, I find drawings made from replicated graphics. They have a *USA Today* feel: simple montages made from circles, squares, and random geometric shapes. Stick people instead of hand-drawn illustrations. Repetition rather than creativity.

Check out Photoshop, the widely acclaimed program to retouch photos, process images, and create color separations. Spend a week learning this program and you can lighten or darken pictures, sharpen or smudge sections, feather in collages, or perhaps tint and texture a whole page.

Once this was the domain of photographers in darkrooms, augmented by airbrushes, scissors, and paste jars. What then took an hour at an enlarger now takes a few moments behind the cathode-ray tube.

Anyone can create a new image by importing sections of other pictures. Grab a door from one file, a window from another, and a roof from a third. Duplicate the window four times and blend these components to make a house.

It won't look right because each section has a different vanishing point. The colors and texture aren't matched; there's no design integrity.

So spend a few hours manipulating the image parts, twisting the geometry until the shapes fit properly, and getting the colors right. By the end of the day, an image of a house has been created.

Yet this synthetic house never existed. A modern door may have been mixed with Georgian windows under a Victorian gingerbread roofline. The Photoshop program, for all its power, cannot confer unity on mismatched components.

These jarring images rattle my eyes as I page through glossy magazines—evidence of powerful tools in the hands of the unskilled. Everything is collaged, dimmed, tinted, overlaid, and formatted.

But nothing's original—we're simply treated to new ways of viewing shopworn images. Pictures without creativity.

I watched a ten-year-old write a story on a computer. Using cut and paste, he called up a picture of a boat and plunked it into his document. His paper was now illustrated, and his teacher was impressed.

I'd much rather this kid tell me what's in his imagination, rather than in someone else's. This might mean a penciled drawing in the margins or a crayon picture on the backside. It won't look professional, but hey—what do you want from a ten-year-old?

Well, OK, image processing and synthesis are creative tools. No way can you say that of prepackaged computer images. At the Seybold Publishing Conference, rows of vendors sell clip art and stock photos. Once published in stapled booklets, they're now distributed by CD-ROM and online networks.

Much like the canned laugh tracks of sitcoms, these techniques create the illusion of creative work while gnawing at the very meaning of originality.

Sure, clip art is cheap—a CD-ROM of a hundred images might cost thirty dollars. For that, you can't hire even a hack artist to draw one cartoon. And a library of a thousand photographs is cheaper than an afternoon of a professional photographer.

But look at the corrosive effect on our creative community. We reward designers rather than illustrators. Magazines, for instance, have become playgrounds for fonts, photomontages, and color bleeds. These are easy to generate on any computer. Drawings and hand-shaded cartoons, well, they're more challenging. So we find our literature littered with giant letters and italicized pullout quotes, but few illustrations or cartoons.

In turn, artists become computer jocks. And computer jocks pass themselves off as artists.

Yet for all the typographical sophistication, pages look uglier than in the days of hand-set type. Leaf through any of the computer magazines, say *Wired* or *Mondo 2000.* You'll find mixed fonts, colors, graphics, and noisy backgrounds. Typographical impact—the easy stuff—counts more than readability and beauty.

I showed a copy of *Wired* magazine to Drew Kingston, a chain-smoking reactionary printer who was weaned on a Linotype. He shook his head and stubbed out a cigarette.

"Now that every kid can set type," he said. " I'm embarrassed to have anything to do with the trade."

Why draw cartoons when you're competing with a collection of a hundred CD-ROMs? For that matter, why hire a photographer when you can grab a stock photo?

In response, commercial photographers are switching to digital systems. When an advertiser wants a specialized photo for fast publication, it's more convenient to shoot with a computerized camera. These have electronic detectors rather than film and can output directly into Photoshop or FrameMaker files.

Not everyone swims with the current. Kim Nibblett, a twenty-five-year-old photographer in Chicago, uses chemicals instead of a computer: "In the darkroom, I carry the exposed paper from the enlarger to the developer. While I agitate the tray, I can see the image slowly come up. It's ghostlike at first, then coalesces and gains weight and gravity. It's a real image before me. You can't get that from a computer screen.

"With tongs, I slip the paper into the stop bath. I've physically moved the print. I've touched that image and I can smell the pungent acid. And when it's in the fixer, I know that the silver grains are now permanent."

Listening to her, I think of Ansel Adams, carrying a view camera out to the desert. He'd spend a day exposing a single sheet of film, then hours in the darkroom. The process won't allow a mistake, so he had to get it right.

"On the computer," she continued, "the image is only a glow. You can't make marginal notes, or put stars on the sides, or circle mistakes with a red pen. It's not real until you make a paper copy. You don't get the satisfaction of crumbling up your mistakes and throwing them into the trash. Instead, you type *delete* or *undo*. Your mistakes don't teach you as well.

"The computer lets you be sloppy. You try vast numbers of images before settling on one. Using film, I get one try.

"The romance and mystery is gone. Computer-processed images have no delicacy, no craftsmanship, no substance, and no soul. No love."

That's the effect of computing on the creative arts. Technical perfection without soul. No love.

In the same way, computers work against musicians. There's no need to create new music when existing sounds can be sampled and recycled. A drum machine lays down an unvarying rhythm track while a MIDI system creates an unimaginable range of tones.

That electronic drum can't change the beat to follow the bass guitar; the synthesizer doesn't respond to dancers on the floor. Music without a soul.

What's the purpose of the audience in a live performance? Ask any of the thousands of Deadheads who follow the Grateful Dead from concert to concert. All the shows are available on tapes; many of the performances repeat songs played decades ago. So why camp out for a week, waiting for tickets?

Better yet, ask the performers if they could put on such superb shows playing to an isolated video camera, hooked up to the Internet. The finest music happens when the audience cheers on the performer; the best teaching happens when students' faces encourage the teacher.

Cheap, ubiquitous electronic music is driving out live orchestral music. Across the country, symphonies are closing their doors, and it's hard times for chamber music groups. A cultural Gresham's law.

Yet there are counter-currents. Hollywood producers have found that they prefer live musicians. *Variety* magazine reports that it's often cheaper to hire a hundred-piece orchestra than to run some of the sophisticated synthesizer programs now in use. Film and TV producers like hearing a show's entire score all at once, without waiting for electronic layering.

As a side effect, the musicians understand the producer: "Try that again, with more warmth!" or "Make it feel more solemn during the funeral scene . . ." No waiting while the synthesizer is reprogrammed, and no excuses that the computer has crashed.

Suppose I said that Mount Everest is fifty miles high. Is it a lie or a statistical exaggeration? Your own experience tells you that the earth has no such mountains.

NASA's Jet Propulsion Lab produced images of the planet Venus showing a thirteen-mile-high volcano, complete with bright-orange lava flows. You can download these pictures from their archive and display them on your screen. A wonderful application of networks, well-suited to teach high school students about planets.

But the image is phony. Since the planet is covered with clouds, nobody can tell what color it is. Analyzing pictures from a Russian lander suggests an orange, but in direct sunlight the planet would likely appear gray or brown.

With geometric manipulation, Jet Propulsion Lab stretched radar data to make the volcano appear extremely tall. Then they computationally placed the viewer at the base of the volcano, so we're looking up at the caldera. Then they associated radar reflectivity with hue. A spectacular effect, though scientifically unsupported.

The picture looks like a cartoon volcano, with pointed mountaintop and deep caldera. It brings to mind one rugged mountain, like Mount Vesuvius or Fujiyama.

The reality is much more subtle. The Venusian volcano has a gentle slope, much more like the Hawaiian shield volcanos. In turn, this suggests a low-viscosity lava, probably a basaltic flow, once up-welled from the planet's mantle.

But I can't tell that from the downloaded image. It comes with this one sentence of documentation: "8000-meter-high Maat Mons on Venus, from NASA's Magellan Spacecraft, courtesy of Jet Propulsion Lab."

Image processing stretches contrast, saturates colors, sharpens edges, and distorts geometry. These are the tools in trade of both scientist and photo editor. One uses these techniques to search out elusive details, the other creates a more memorable image. By emphasizing different aspects, they make truly impressive pictures, which contain enough truth that they cannot be called lies.

Now consider the June 27, 1994, issues of *Time* and *Newsweek*. Both show the same mugshot of O. J. Simpson, taken by the Los Angeles Police when he was arrested. *Newsweek* ran the image straight, without digital finagling.

Time hired Matt Mahurin, a photo-illustrator who retouched the mug shot with a computer. Working fast, he smoothed and shaped Simpson's face into what *Time*'s editor called "an icon of tragedy." He also darkened OJ's skin color.

Had *Newsweek* not run the unmodified picture, few would have noticed the changes. Viewing the two covers side-by-side immediately showed the difference. *Time* walked into a firestorm: major news organizations and black journalists charged that *Time* had intentionally darkened Simpson's face, a prejudicial attempt to make him look more sinister.

Photo retouching isn't new. Digital image processing, however, can be so extensive yet undetectable that it undermines the foundation of photojournalism—that seeing is believing.

Those images try to convey facts. Try looking at online art—paintings digitized by galleries and uploaded to networks. At first glance, it's wonderful—the Internet is bringing me a painting of Jan Vermeer from 1665.

My color monitor shows a Dutch maiden holding a pitcher, opening a stained glass window with her other hand. A simple painting done by a master.

Yet the image on my screen is a far cry from the actual painting. When I look closely at the monitor, all the details disappear into pixels. Her eyes, so mysterious from afar, become blurs up close. Vermeer's palette, famous for subtle hues, is now rendered by 256 discrete colors.

This isn't even close to the continuum of colors that you see in the painting hanging at the Met. And the quarter million pixels on my screen are nowhere near the resolution that Vermeer used. A picture postcard shows more detail.

Bill Gates of Microsoft is said to be buying electronic rights to artworks, with the intention of becoming the dominant purveyor of electronic art.

At the same time, the National Gallery in London lets visitors browse parts of their collections on terminals. Alongside the art are a few paragraphs about the artist. For eighty dollars I can buy a CD-ROM from Microsoft that includes selected paintings along with animation and audio tracks. For the same money, I can get two hefty coffee-table books with great photographs and superb commentary.

After seeing Vermeer's maiden, I decided I don't want this CD-ROM. I'm not worried about Bill Gates taking over the art world, either. Aside from the technical inaccuracies of reproducing art on a computer, I find it disconcerting to view a work of art in the same place that I read nasty arguments on the Usenet. Going to a museum is an escape from daily tasks and a trip into another world.

I dream of visiting the Rijksmuseum in Amsterdam to look at Rembrandt paintings and surreptitiously glancing at the museum staff as they go about their business. Rembrandt painted real people —their facial features and mannerisms live on today in the Dutch population. Dressed in period costumes, I'll bet the security guard with his war medals and the young woman tour guide would look as if they stepped out of one of those incredibly detailed paintings.

It's as difficult to contemplate and appreciate art on the screen as it is to appreciate a magic show on television. What astounds in person feels flat over the screen. Flashing fifty great works of art across my monitor in two minutes cheapens the work. A part of the value of art is its rarity.

. . . . .

In another window, my computer shows a close-up picture of Jupiter, photographed by NASA's Infrared Research Telescope Facility in Hawaii. It's a gaudy mix of purple, green, and red—I recognize that someone's been having fun with the color lookup tables. All the hues are false, since infrared images have no color.

Not only are these colors fictional, but they're misleading as well. When my computer shows green, does that represent more or less infrared emission?

Any subtlety has been stretched out of the image, leaving a garish, contrasty picture. I've spent many nights behind a telescope, watching this planet—Jupiter is a beautiful world, with delicate shades of pinks, browns, and satiny yellows. But my computer image shows ribald rouge, licentious lipstick, and mawkish mascara.

Oh, I know that computers can't render accurate colors—the phosphors in the cathode-ray tube limit both the brightness range and color saturation. Like that doctored cover of *Time*, you can't see the changes without a comparison. And false colors do have a certain utility: they show details that might otherwise be obscured.

Yet any high school kid worth his sneakers, upon comparing two downloaded images, ought to wonder why Jupiter's red spot is glowing purple in one picture and shows up orange in another.

Better yet, that high school kid ought to see for himself. Take the kid up to a telescope and look at Jupiter—it's a kicker to watch the moons orbit the planet and see the real colors of the red spot. Experts will show pictures with purples and oranges, but I know better. I've seen it.

So has Guy Consolmagno, who'll tell you the evolution of Jupiter and its moons, as well as its temperature, composition, density, and, yes, colors. As grad students, we learned how to color maps without computers. In 1978, colored pencils were cheaper than color monitors.

Guy did theoretical work about Jupiter—"The icy moons actually," he added. "I know their compositions and work out how they evolved. My trusty computer program tells all." He patted the side of a deck of punch cards.

Two thousand cards of Fortran IV—he'd been writing his code for two years; every time he'd find a bug, he'd revise his estimate of Europa's composition.

But Guy's not a purely theoretical astronomer. "Hey, I get my fingers dirty," he tells me. "Right now I'm working on the microprobe. Its name is from the Latin: *micro*, meaning very little. And *probe*, meaning research. Which accurately describes what I'm doing."

Guy uses this microprobe—actually a complicated electron microscope—to analyze crystals in moon rocks and meteorites. He reaches into a drawer and pulls out a carbonaceous chondrite* and a couple of stony-iron meteorites, and settles into work. Around the back, there's the usual laboratory impedimenta: computers, vacuum pumps, and a sign on the wall: DO NOT LOOK INTO LASER BEAM WITH REMAINING EYEBALL.

This is a part of planetary astronomy. Repackage earth sciences and apply it to the other planets. Do the same for geochemistry, geophysics, geomagnetism, and geomorphology. It's not quite astronomy, but not geology, either. For that matter, we're not really astronomers or geologists. Something in between.

Now, none of this should concern us here, seeing how the Internet hadn't yet been invented, and image processing wasn't especially common. I'd have forgotten about it too, except that Guy and Jon Gradie showed me how to make false color images.

It was part of our lunar geology course, taught by one of the masters, Bob Strom. He wouldn't tell us the answer to a question. Instead, he'd make us figure it out ourselves. Early on, he aimed us at age-dating the lunar craters.

You'd think that all the moon's craters look the same, until you

. . . .

* *Carbonaceous chondrites are the class of meteorites closest to the makeup of the original solar system—they're unchanged from 4.6 billion years ago. They're made of hard chondrules and inclusions in a loose organic matrix.*

You can model their composition in a computer, but I simulate them by creaming together 1/4 cup white sugar, 1/3 cup brown sugar, 1/2 cup butter or margarine, and beating in 2 eggs with a tablespoon of vanilla, and 1/3 cup cocoa, 3/4 cup flour, and 1/2 tsp. baking powder, and a double handful of white chocolate-chip chondrules. Chopped walnuts make good inclusions. Bake in a 7-by-11-inch pan at 350°F for 20 to 30 minutes.

study them on a photograph. Most of these impacts date from the early solar system, back when the Cubs won pennants. Some, however, are much more modern, perhaps only five or ten million years old.

You figure out their relative ages by comparing craters. The younger ones sit on top of the older craters, all overlaid by rocks and ejecta from the youngest impacts—clues to relative ages.

With a magnifying glass, you study lunar photographs, hunting for secondary craters, interrupted hillocks, and broken fault lines. With every clue, you color in a composite map, keying a different color for each geological epoch.

I spent that semester coloring moon maps.

No, not with an image-processing computer. Not even with films, filters, and a darkroom. We used crayons. Crayolas.

One crater's the same as the next? Naw—every one has a name. Here's the crater Theophilas, almost right on top of Cyrillus. Ejecta from the Copernicus impact is strewn all over the floor of Reinhold. Jon and Guy and I would argue about each clue, decide on the most likely answer, then color in the map. It was sorta like a paint-by-number map, except we didn't know the right colors.

Turns out that a billion years after it was formed, lava flowed to the moon's surface, filling in the biggest craters and forming what we now call the seas.

Guy, sharpie that he is, latched this on to his study of meteorites. Some of those samples went clear back to the beginning of the solar system, others had been melted around the time when the moon's lavas were formed.

"Probably the same thing melted 'em both," he said. "Most likely a radioactive element with a billion-year half-life." Which was one of the answers, though it's a long trip to connect that to the flatlands of the moon. Those meteorites I'd been toying with have seen a lot of history.

OK, real scientists had figured all this out years before we did. But there's nothing like going through the evidence yourself. And at the end of the semester, the prof showed us a real chart of lunar history. We'd missed plenty, all right; but we'd nailed down the main parts.

And that moon map—the one with the garish reds and greens? The colors don't mean much without having done the work. The real moon only shows shades of gray, but these colors told us which parts were oldest.

Combining our map with evidence from meteorites and samples of moonrocks, we could see the evolution of the moon's surface. It's true: meteors just aren't as common as they were four billion years ago. I've got a crayoned map that shows it.

That high-tech microprobe, complete with vacuum pumps, computer, electron beam, and X ray analyzer, didn't tell as much as six weeks spent with a magnifying glass and a box of crayons. Bringing them all together, well, that's science.

False color photographs and maps have plenty of uses. I sure understand why astronomers use them to show infrared maps of Jupiter. Still, they mean a bit more when you do the coloring yourself.

SEVEN

Much Business, Some Computing, Precious Little Astronomy

"Tomorrow's businessman will have the information necessary to do his job, right at his fingertips, due to the growing acceptance of microfilm as the solution to the information explosion." So wrote Walter Steel in 1974.

Two decades later, I stumble over similar statements every day: how electronic networks will help manage the same information explosion. Where's all the promised productivity of computers? Will the Internet actually be useful in commerce?

A business that only reads microfilm or e-mail isn't doing much. You have to make something, service a need, produce a product, or deliver the goods. I claim that computer networks only indirectly enhance this type of productivity—that the main tools for business are good ideas, capable machinery, and smart, hardworking people.

Yep, computers are essential for counting supplies in the warehouse, adding and subtracting dollars, drawing up schedules, and writing reports. Networks, too, help pass along decisions and follow changing markets.

All these are predicated on a business *doing* something. There's gotta be a product in the warehouse to be counted, or a service to be provided. It's a rare business, indeed, that survives on reading e-mail, fishing through archives, and following net news.

Expensive corporate seminars spout about the Internet's broad e-mail capabilities, vast online resources, and cost-effective commercial benefits. I scratch my head, wondering just what those benefits might be. Would I want my employees to read net news during business hours? Would I pay my engineers to play interactive "Star Trek" games against challengers in Japan?

Well, maybe—there's a hot game of Netrek going on right now, with forty players on my side of the universe and fifty-seven on the other. You know, on second thought, sure, give 'em network access. It'll even out the sides.

There are hundreds of games designed for teams of people, each on his own personal computer. Since nobody has ten PCs at home, people naturally play these games at work or school. If I saw an architect at work while dealing a deck of cards for poker, I'd have serious doubts about the business. Yet we're hardly surprised to find just such a program next to his Autocad window.

I'll bet most academics check on to the net daily. With most every campus wired, plenty of undergrads sure do. Plenty of programmers and office workers have the Usenet piped to their desktops over Ethernet and fiber. Does it make their work more efficient?

More and more journals are reviewed and published electronically, giving faster turnaround and quicker feedback. I can reach a researcher directly, and perhaps get an answer within an hour. Instead of retyping lists of numbers, I can transfer data straight from the collector into my analysis program. Networks are terrific.

On the other hand, I've watched researchers waste morning after morning, reading irrelevant net news, plowing through e-mail, and fine-tuning their screen savers. I've seen a particle physicist panic when his dissertation evaporated in a disk crash. I grinned to learn of a friend who spent a month building an elaborate puzzle room in a Multi-User Dungeon—I stopped grinning when I heard of his three missed midterms.

It's easy to spend hours reading the news from the network. With more and more newspapers and magazines coming online, you can burn up your mornings reading *Newsweek, The Atlantic Monthly,* and the *New York Times.* But what kind of work lets you read magazines and newspapers on the job?

Come to think of it, I hardly know anyone who subscribes to popular newspapers and magazines at work—maybe doctors and dentists? Why the sudden demand for online news services?

Aren't networks the most efficient way to trade? After all, financial exchanges depend on computers, readouts, and terminals. Fifty years ago, stock prices were displayed on chalkboards; today networks instantly relay quotes around the world.

Yep, computers deliver fast updates—the big board shows each trade. Every exchange has dozens of displays, hovering just above the trading floor. But fundamentally, trades happen by people haggling over prices.

Check out the Chicago Mercantile Exchange, where speculators and risk managers trade commodity and financial futures. They trade in pork bellies and feeder cattle, as well as Eurodollar deposits and Japanese Yen.

Looking down from the visitor's gallery, you'll see hundreds of traders in yellow jackets hustling around floor pits, buying and selling futures contracts. Using a frenzy of hand signals, each trader is trying to get the best possible deal. The trading floor is nuts—shouts, waving hands, and flying paper. Capitalism on steroids.

It's an open-outcry auction—every broker is trying to buy cheap and sell dear. Each is risking lots of money along the way. Deals happen by traders waving to each other; the moment buyer and seller agree, they scribble the price on cards. Messengers pass these slips of paper to the exchange, where the trades are typed into a terminal. That computer only reports trades, it doesn't arrange them.

What a perfect system to automate—create a computer system that arranges deals. To sell a three-month Eurodollar contract, just type in your asking price. When someone else bids, the computer matches the two of you and handles the mechanics of the deal. No more shouting and hand waving.

So the Merc collaborated with Reuters to create Globex, an electronic trading system. A broker types in a buy order on the terminal, the computer matches it with a corresponding sell order, and the transaction automatically clears. Fast, direct, and convenient.

Globex runs all night and it's available worldwide. That's important for the Chicago Mercantile Exchange: they fear competition from trading floors in Tokyo, Hong Kong, and London.

Before Globex went into operation, floor traders worried that brokers would abandon the open-outcry market and flock to the computer. Trading would turn into a computer game, and the value of seats on the exchange might plummet.

After several years of operations, their fears proved unfounded. Every day, the Merc handles some eight hundred thousand contracts on the floor, worth well over a trillion dollars. Only four thousand contracts go through the Globex computer.

Other exchanges report similar experiences. At the London International Financial Futures Exchange, traders deal in Euromark futures contracts by open-outcry auction. They could just as well trade on the computerized German Deutsche Terminbörse, since both handle the same contracts. After four years of competition, three quarters of the deals take place on London's LIFFE floor; the German DTB network handles the rest.

One study suggests that the spread between bid and asked prices is slightly tighter on the computerized DTB market, which would mean it costs less to do business there. Despite this, you'll see far more trades at London's open-outcry auction.

So why do brokers prefer exchange floors to computerized trading? Partly it's inertia—for all their risk taking, traders are a conservative lot who change habits slowly.

Then there's a cost to run a twenty-four-hour market—every member firm must keep someone at the terminal, even if few trades are happening. And the traders behind the screen aren't happy at 2 A.M.—they'd rather spend their waking hours in a hot market, where there's more excitement, not to mention more money to be made.

It's not just comfort, either. Centuries of experience with open-outcry markets give traders a deep trust in floor trades. Trades take place in the open—floor auctions are completely transparent—so brokers get a better feel for the market. At a glance, traders see which players are trading and which are standing aside. They immediately know the size of the deals and whether the market's hopping.

From this trust, traders are willing to commit themselves to handling bigger contracts—to take on more risk. And this willingness to carry risk gives the market greater liquidity: the price won't change as much when big trades happen, and the spread between bid and asked remains small. Such liquidity makes the market efficient.

Someday, computers may take over commodities exchanges. But that's decades into the future. So don't hurry over to see the Chicago Mercantile Exchange—you've got plenty of time before computers replace their trading pits.

On September 15, 1842, the British Astronomer Royal, Sir George Biddell Airy, K.C.B., M.A., LL.D., D.C.L., F.R.S., F.R.A.S., responded to a query from the Chancellor of the Exchequer. The government was considering funding an invention of one Charles Babbage. Should Parliament support the construction of the analytical engine—the first mechanical calculator and predecessor to digital computers? What would be the value of such a device?

The learned astronomer's one-word reply: "Worthless."

Until the 1950s the future of computing was generally underestimated. After its first successes, things swung the opposite way, with the artificial-intelligence researchers at the cutting edge of grand predictions.

One of the earliest AI programs was immodestly (and inaccurately) named the Generalized Problem Solver. Such excesses grew into the eighties' race for fifth-generation computers. Japanese scientists, with the Americans close behind, would build superfast parallel-processing computers.

Claims of the AI pioneers appear to be about as accurate as Professor Airy's. Having swallowed billions of yen and dollars, fifth-generation projects today lie beached on both sides of the Pacific. In a scene reminiscent of the Cretaceous-Tertiary extinction, lots of little computers have taken over where once giant mainframes roamed. With this background, the artificial intelligentsia now present intelligent agents.

Agents will help you do your work. For example, if you want to find someone, your agent sends messages out over the network to search the relevant databases. These work well enough to be available today as General Magic's nifty personal communicator. For around a thousand dollars, it'll keep track of your addresses, send faxes and e-mail, and log on to networks.

Carnegie-Mellon University developed the Calendar Apprentice, which learns its users' scheduling preferences. Computer people often seek ways to help me keep track of my time, little suspecting that my friends give me calendars every December.

Can't make up your mind about new music? *"Ringo* is a personalized music-recommendation system," Professor Pattie Maes of MIT's Media Laboratory writes in the July 1994 *Communications of the ACM.*

Of all the software agents she's considered, "This one might have the best potential to become the next 'killer application.' " Along with other entertainment-selection agents, it will help you select movies, books, and television shows, by correlating your tastes with other intelligent agents.

Now, I don't need a computer program to tell me what books or music I'll like. Friends, reviews, and browsing work just fine, thank you.

Intelligent agents are a fantasy sprouted in the tomorrowland of MIT's media laboratory. They're believable enough to generate heavy grants for big-name researchers. But I wonder if Professor Airy's prediction may now be coming true, a century and a half late.

I remember predictions of giant mechanical brains . . . robots that would collect information, then monitor and control workers. With vacuum tubes and coils of wire, they'd keep us enslaved. The perfect tool for Big Brother.

A far cry from today's networked systems, which decentralize and distribute computing power. Yes, the boss can monitor what's going on, but it's hard to be certain what an office worker is doing with her computer. Maybe she's correlating data, preparing some financial report, replying to a love letter, or playing Tetris.

So the snooping technology escalates—computers lend themselves to being used as management tools. They can keep track of idle time, number of words typed, number of errors made. Telephone operators must handle a certain number of calls per minute. Secretarial staff face a quota of typing a certain number of insurance claims every hour. A digital dungeon.

Workplace monitoring creates mistrust. Viewing the computer as a ball and chain, people understandably are glad to escape at day's end.

Networks bring a flood of both useful and useless information to our desktops. They help me work more efficiently yet still are counterproductive—they're equally great for working and goofing off.

Every budding cybernaut and net-hack will eagerly tell you plenty of ways that the networks make your workplace more efficient. Such universally accepted dogma makes me wonder: would my work suffer if I tossed out my modem?

For that matter, does a corporation really need e-mail? It's a direct path between the executive suite, employees, and the outside world. Maybe this beeline access isn't such a good thing.

In *The Wall Street Journal,* G. Pascal Zachary reports that executives feel an open e-mail address is similar to a published phone number. It's an invitation to irksome contact with the electronic masses.

After Bill Gates's e-mail address showed up in *The New Yorker,* the chairman of Microsoft received thousands of letters, from across the Internet. They ranged from congratulatory notes to letters suggesting worthwhile charities, and even one that said, "I fervently believe that the key to immortality is living a life worth remembering."

Mike Godwin, an attorney with the Electronic Frontier Foundation, plows through a daily queue of a hundred letters. "Maybe a quarter are carbon copies mainly for someone else," he reports. "Another twenty-five are from mailing lists. That means I only have to reply to fifty."

He answers fifty letters a day? "I forward some to people who can better answer the questions. Other mail I reply to with a form letter.

The hard part is deciding what stuff you can't answer. I want to reply and I have something to say, but I just don't have the time."

Over time, unanswered e-mail stacks up. "I probably have three hundred letters waiting for a reply," Mike says. "Eventually, I flush them out—there's a certain relief to filing them away."

Bozo filters let you cut down on unwanted e-mail; they're programs that scan your mail and only let the good stuff through. Net news addicts use killfiles to filter out the sediment. Before showing you the latest postings, the news software checks this file and doesn't bother you with messages from those already flagged.

These filters might be nice, except that few computer systems give you such abilities. I've long heard promises that expert systems can solve this problem. By watching my actions, an intelligent agent will learn my preferences and needs.

Hardly. I can't imagine someone whose daily tasks and preferences are so simple that they could be predicted by software. The most advanced software might serve as the crudest of gatekeepers, but I doubt these can tell me which letters I'll find most interesting.

Just as no publisher can find an electronic substitute for an editor, mechanical systems will never replace common sense and a feeling for what's important.

And no automatic system can do your work. As an attorney, Mike Godwin sees his job as both helping people and handing out information. "As a result, I'm afraid of mail filters," he says. "They might screen out important mail."

Right now, Mike handles his mail with prewritten answers. "When a sysop asks a general question about legal issues surrounding online obscenity, I'll upload an article I've written on the subject. If nothing else, it lets her think about the subject and ask a more specific question."

Computer Associates makes business software, including a custom e-mail system. But the chairman, Charles Wang, doesn't use it. Indeed, he shuts down the company's e-mail system for five hours a day, so that his business gets work done.

Why this backlash against e-mail? Partly, the content is trivial.

Mitch Kertzman, chairman of Powersoft Corporation, receives hundreds of messages a week; one of them, addressed to all employees, came from a worker selling a dog.

More than an annoyance, the impersonality of e-mail may communicate an aloof attitude. The president of a company can send e-mail to all employees, but it hasn't the effect of a visit to their offices or a heartfelt congratulation. I'd rather taste a scoop of homecooked fudge than be nineteenth on the list of recipients of some form letter.

Network communication feels like it's cheap—there are no postage stamps or envelopes to buy. Sounds like an easy choice.

To connect, you need a computer, modem, telephone, and network account. This hardware alone costs well over a thousand dollars; hookup fees typically run ten dollars a month, plus online charges of five or ten dollars an hour. In the extreme case, for specialized data searches—say, NEXIS or Westlaw—plan to spend two hundred dollars an hour.

True, colleges often provide subsidized connections—students get free accounts. It feels like free communications and a wonderfully cheap playground, yet it's paid through tuition, fees, and overhead.

Across the Internet, I find heavy subsidies from direct and indirect government grants, often made through universities and research groups. This keeps costs lower than they'd be if users paid their own way.

For example, the University of California's Internet links cost well over ten million dollars a year. Students and faculty shrug at the costs—they aren't billed.

Internal business networks don't enjoy so many subsidies, yet still hide the costs from the ultimate users. These nets aren't cheap, and the obvious costs may be the smallest part of the price. The visible part of the iceberg—wiring, connection fees, hardware, and software—hides a major investment below. Teaching everyone how to use the network, hiring a technician to keep the connections running, periodic software and hardware updates, security systems, and time wasted because of disk backups and downtime . . . it all adds up. You won't find these concealed expenses mentioned when a bright-eyed manager calculates the cost of networks.

Online systems are brittle: they work when everything's normal, but are exquisitely sensitive to software, hardware, and communications problems. A stream of data can't wait for the computer—if it's not decoded immediately, bits fall onto the floor. Thus, we hear of commodity-exchange programs that pass all their tests, yet fail just when the computers slow down from a heavy load.

A squirrel burrowed through a telephone line in December 1987, disabling the NASDAQ stock exchange. On July 15, 1994, the same exchange ground to a halt when upgrading their transaction system. Two weeks later, they were again shut down by another squirrel, this one near Trumbull, Connecticut. Their fail-safe power switch-over system failed, switching the system into a blackout.

Why's a world center of capitalism at the mercy of a couple of rodents? Because it's tough to make communications systems robust, reliable, expandable, and usable. Squirrels—self-propelled short circuits—don't conform to network guidelines.

Other problems are data-dependent—they only show up when the right string of characters passes through a router. Try sending to your modem three pluses in a row, followed by a carriage return. Typed without a delay, almost every modem will pass it perfectly, except those made with the TIES chip set. These modems drop into the command mode and won't pass the data. Built this way to avoid infringing on someone's patent, they're hidden snags to the smooth flow of data.

Just who is responsible for a business's networked system? The computer maker doesn't know what modem you're using. The modem maker is unfamiliar with the communications software. The phone-company technician doesn't know what noise level causes data dropouts on a 9600-baud trellis-encoded modem link. Multiple vendors means delays, finger-pointing, and widespread frustration.

In short, data communication is expensive and semireliable.

When it works, we grow to depend on it; when it fails, we're high and dry with nobody to turn to.

Connecting to the Internet may take a few simple computer commands. Just as likely, it can become a week-long, frustrating ordeal.

First, you need a service provider. Some are set up for individuals —America Online, CompuServe, GEnie. They give access to their own services and limited Internet connections. This is how most people get online . . . it's easy.

A different story for the small business that wants a full Internet link, with a separate Internet domain. This enables them to create public libraries for others to read, and give each employee a network account. For this, a business goes to an Internet service provider.

OK, so you lease a phone line, register your business with the network information center, buy a computer to handle network traffic, string a local area net, figure out exactly how mail will be forwarded, assign accounts, make a net news spooler, and maybe create some public file space. Don't forget to build a security fire wall, so hackers can't mess with your system.

Now try debugging your Internet link. If you think the gauntlet of software support is tough, hoo-ha! You'll be calling technicians at the service provider, your local phone company, the business that sold you a modem, the company that wrote the communications software, and the people who installed your mail reader. All point their fingers at each other.

All this is easy for networking wizards, who know the magic incantations. But for a novice, well, good luck.

Wide bandwidth is one of the holy grails of the online community. How about a three-million-bit-per-second communications channel, connecting your desktop to the latest news? Hey, it's already here, in the guise of broadcast television.

If you must keep abreast of the latest events at work, put a television on your work desk. Tune it to the Cable News Network. A TV is cheaper than a modem, easier to operate, and you'll get a wide bandwidth, channelized news, with an occasional commentary tossed in.

Of course, it's absurd to put a TV on your work desk. Yet the Internet, with its wide access to games, newsgroups, and chat lines, is considered desirable for the office. Go figure.

Interactive video links are promoted as money-saving systems to allow wide-area collaborations. We're supposed to work with colleagues across the country and divvy up tasks without leaving our offices. It'll save time and travel. Seems perfect to exchange information, reports, programs, and schedules.

Such is the dream. When I've been in these hookups, I've felt isolated and on the spot. There's not the warmth or excitement of a real meeting. Since I'm not hanging around with my teammates, it's hard to get pumped up about the project.

I'm on a virtual team, one that seldom meets and never parties. I'm truly a cog in some invisible machine.

Probably, you can find a job where you never meet anyone. Perhaps you'd be a fire spotter on a New Mexico mountaintop or the lookout for an Aleutian military base. One of the promises of the Internet is short-term collaborations without meetings. Sounds as lonesome as that lookout.

Businesses depend on cooperation. It's the essence of the corporation. I wonder if networks help or hinder this process.

Academics talk about how the Internet has become an indispensable part of their work. They routinely compare notes over e-mail and send programs and files to one another. Yet sciences and humanities, like businesses, require face-to-face contact to succeed.

Lisa Kadonaga called me from Yellowknife, Northwest Territories. She's a Canadian researcher attending a meeting on climatic change. "There's hundreds of researchers here, all working on different facets of the same problem," she says. "At coffee break, people are exchanging names and addresses, and when the bell rings, nobody wants to go back to the lectures. This is where the best stuff is happening. If I ever end up organizing a conference, I'll supply lots of comfortable chairs and make the breaks twice as long."

Maybe not all collaborations are helped by personal meetings. Gilbert and Sullivan come to mind as a partnership that probably would have worked better if a computer network had separated the two. Arthur S. Sullivan, the gregarious musical composer, rubbed shoulders with the titled nobility. Cranky William S. Gilbert, however, had no use for pomp. He'd write his librettos, send them to Sullivan, and head back to the theater. They hated each other.

Individually, neither did much worth remembering. Sullivan thought of himself as a serious musician, but all that remains is *Onward Christian Soldiers.* Gilbert, the great dramatist, wrote *Engaged,* which gets performed every few decades.

Oh, but together . . . the beauty of their creations rings across a century. *The Mikado, H.M.S. Pinafore, Iolanthe,* and, especially, *The Pirates of Penzance.* These bosom enemies would have loved the Internet, a way to work together without ever having to deal with each other. But never having to confront their difficulties, would they have made such great operettas?

Don't computers streamline officework? Maybe. Maybe not.

Word processors can drive up the cost of doing business. For example, consider boilerplate sales contracts.

When you buy a house, you'll likely use a preprinted form: standard paragraphs of legalese with places to fill in your name, address, sales price, closing date, and any special terms. You can buy these boilerplate contracts at stationery stores, where they're called Blumberg forms.

These standardized contracts let businesses run efficiently—they direct your eyes to the important points. Any changes stand out immediately, so you don't waste time reading inconsequential notes.

Today's businesses and attorneys have computers, so they no longer need those preprinted forms. Instead, they copy the boilerplate text from word processor files, edit the contract, and dump it to a laser printer. Seems like a good idea—after all, it saves on stationery costs. Looks professional, too.

But now you can't recognize the boilerplate from the special conditions! That contract to buy a house has no blank spaces to fill in . . . everything's in the same typeface with the same spacing. You have no clue as to which paragraphs are vanilla legalese and which have been modified for this particular deal.

You don't know if some shyster has slipped a ringer into the contract—adding an obscure sentence that changes the entire meaning of the document. Your only choice is to read every word alongside a standard agreement.

In turn, businesspeople have to waste time checking through details where they once would trust the preprinted form. Lawyers have the same problem—they can no longer skim the boilerplate, but must carefully read every sentence, watching for deviations. What used to take minutes now wastes hours.

Lawyers—think of the troubles that computers have brought to their offices. Since it's easy to collect citations from online services, attorneys build legal reports by copying and pasting text—not really creative work, but a great way to slow down the system. The result is a long brief—a most expensive oxymoron, since another lawyer will eventually have to read all those words.

No spreadsheet can create data where there is none. No word processor can help me write better. No online database can answer the tough questions . . . those which do not yet have answers.

When I'm doing astronomy, I spend much of my time thinking and writing. Double the speed of my computer and I won't think or write any faster. I can't communicate over the Internet any faster either.

Yes, there are plenty of places where a faster computer will let me explore alternatives. In science, as in economics, we model complex systems within a program. Yet these calculations seldom give deep insight. Analytical solutions—equations—are far more powerful and trustworthy tools.

The hard part of my job isn't formatting text or sending things off over the network. A faster computer may let me build more models, but fundamentally, it won't give me a deeper understanding of Jupiter's atmosphere. No, the hard part is understanding the data before me; thinking hard about my observations and drawing conclusions.

No doubt, the Internet's a cheap way to reach lots of people. This trendy medium seems perfectly suited to deliver to the young and technically adept who have scorch marks on their wallets.

Some networks, such as Prodigy service, have always promoted advertising; others, like the Usenet, try their best to discourage it. For years, the Internet was free of commercial promotions; that's changing now.

Some advertising methods simply don't work. Unwanted junk e-mail angers enough people that it's self-defeating. Same with broadcasting messages across the network, as two Phoenix lawyers learned.

On April 18, 1994, I logged in, fired up the Usenet software, and discovered dozens of messages telling how I could get an immigration green card—just contact a legal firm in Arizona. A couple of lawyers had spammed the net—they posted a crass message to some five thousand Usenet newsgroups, around the world.

There's no law against such things, although this kind of commercial use of the anarchistic Usenet is frowned upon by most everyone. And most everyone expressed their disapproval, with e-mail and faxes. Within a day, these jerks received their comeuppance: thousands of letters protested their action, including insults, threats, and suggestions of where they could place their modem. Enough nasty e-mail arrived to repeatedly crash the computers of their service provider, Internet Direct, who promptly disabled their account.

This didn't faze the two legal cybernauts. In a *New York Times* interview, they threw down the gauntlet—they'd sue Internet Direct for cutting off service. Moreover, they'd continue to advertise on the network.

Netnerds responded in kind. Within a day, hundreds of faxes arrived at the lawyers' office—enough to exhaust their paper supply. They found bogus magazine subscriptions on their doorstep. But the final word came from Arnt Gulbrandsen of Norway: he created a cancelbot, a program that automatically erased every message the couple sent out. The attorneys posted a message; twenty seconds later, the Norwegian program deleted it. Electronic frontier justice.

These lawyers, so happy to threaten suits against American firms, were powerless against this Norwegian. A technical knockout.

So how do you advertise over the network? If the future of the data highway is advertising, then the Prodigy network got there first. Every couple of minutes, an ad pops on screen, pushing everything from Allstate Insurance to IBM computers.

Probably the most useful method for businesses to advertise over the network is to simply post factual information about products. Increasingly, computer vendors create illustrated documents available for browsing with Mosaic. The information is available only to those who seek it out, so this technique isn't invasive. Anyone can stop by, page through your catalog, and examine specification sheets.

Works fine for industrial ads, but it's a long way from mass-marketing cola. Until someone invents a way to insert commercials into the Internet that doesn't offend the purists, the network won't be awash in sweet brown syrup.

With the great power, high speed, and vast reach of the Internet, why isn't commercial software sold over the net? Why can't I log into CompuServe, find essentially any commercial software product, pay for it by credit card, and download it immediately?

It can't be the inability to handle online transactions—I can pass my credit card number through e-mail. I don't have to wait for a delivery—just download the software immediately.

Maybe it's the nonphysical nature of software. But advertisers and businesses have long confronted the problem of selling the nonphysical—insurance, stocks, health-care plans. Politicians have been doing it for centuries.

When I buy something, I want to see it, touch it, and feel it. I know the software I purchase is made of nothingness. The packaging, manuals, and shrink-wrap give it heft, substance, and newness. They make it real.

Given the choice, I want to visit a store to buy software. I'll be able to compare different products and get advice from a real person. Trite as it sounds, the business and the salespeople stand behind their products.

And that's what's missing from sales over a network. Even though the medium is perfect for distributing software, it lacks a real person who will respond to my needs.

There's another message here: many who work in computing think that salespeople can be replaced by catalogs and product listings. The network mavens feel that a business need only get its message onto the computer screens of potential customers. The salesperson is so much overhead.

To think that a salesperson is only selling merchandise is to belittle a most important individual in society. A good salesperson does far more than simply show and tell. He keeps the business aware of the customer's needs. After handling an account for a few months, it's a moot point whether he works for the customer or his employer—there's a tacit agreement of mutual advantage. It's a relationship as old as capitalism and as young as your favorite restaurant.

The salesperson is an essential part of every business—one who can never be replaced by listings of goods to sell. No pretty network graphics will make this job obsolete.

Plenty of businesses are hot to exploit cybersales. I'll bet that most lose their shirts. Today, about the only ones making money are the communications and computer companies. There is no magic way to make a fortune from the Internet.

On the other hand, I'd have thought it'd be hard to sell cars by computer until I saw a hypertext commercial for Buicks. I figured it'd show the same shiny views that appear in television ads. To my amazement, it displayed product specifications, measurements, and prices. This I like—prices without the fuzziness of haggling! If my bicycle ever throws a rod, I'll buy a Buick.

What about security on the Internet? After chasing hackers across the nets, I've wondered if computer people would cork up the obvious holes in systems. Sure enough, most of the obvious flaws have been fixed—hardly anyone sells networked systems with default passwords or built-in guest accounts. The average computer is tighter.

But there are a lot more systems on the net, so there are plenty of insecure computers. Most have no system manager . . . one person may handle dozens or hundreds of systems. Hard enough to keep the software current and users happy, let alone watch for intruders breaking in or grabbing passwords.

There are a dozen ways to steal passwords—Trojan horses, password crackers, and file scavengers. Among the slimy set, the latest fad is password sniffers, software that captures packets that pass across the Internet. Such software records the first hundred bytes of a remote interactive session . . . when I *telnet* to a distant site, my keystrokes pass through many other computers. Should one of these sites be compromised, the magic program will save my account name and password to its own special file. A few days later, the hacker logs in, prints out the stolen password, and there's the key to my account.

There aren't many defenses against such attacks, since I can't trust the hosts that my Internet packets transverse. Some systems defend themselves with mutable passwords that change minute to minute—I have to carry a special password-generating card whenever logging in. Best defense, of course, is to avoid using remote access, which means fewer Internet services.

More often, hackers aren't technically creative. Like other thieves, they steal through lies and deception. They simply phone a corporation, claim to be from the computer department, and ask the secretary for the password. Sometimes, they reach a smart person who hangs up and reports the conversation. Other times, well, Gus Gullible answers.

Such social engineering works astonishingly well, as evidenced by the exploits of one Kevin Mitnick. In their book *Cyberpunk*, Katie Hafner and John Markoff describe how Mitnick broke into an unclassified NSA computer by phoning someone with a guest account on that government system. Pretending to be from the NSA, Mitnick convinced the guy to give out the password. Most recently, Mitnick has been accused of breaking in to telephone company computers and several software companies, using the same chutzpah.

The expansion of the networks, coupled with the difficulty of tracking someone through the maze of the Internet, presents a fertile ground for hackers. After catching a German intruder in my Berkeley computer, I set monitors to watch for hoodlums attempting to break in. I've recorded idiots trying to log in as the system manager and plenty of other well-documented security holes.

Here's one guy who spent a day trying to log into my account, trying five thousand different passwords. Another probed twelve different weak points in my operating system. A third sent e-mail threatening both my computer and my friends.

Track 'em down? Naw . . . the first time, it was research. A chance to do science, even in the limited confines of computing. The second time is just engineering. Anyways, more clever network wizards have set traps and studied how these hackers operate.

In January 1991, Bill Cheswick and Steve Bellovin noticed an outsider requesting the password file over the Internet. Bill runs a tight system at AT&T, so naturally the attack failed. But he wondered who was behind the assault, so he sent off a bogus password file.

By reviewing his logs, they realized that the attacker was coming in from Stanford. That didn't help much, since the California computer had been compromised and the trace pointed to a telephone connection.

Within five days, their false password file turned up in France—clearly the hacker was operating worldwide. With the Gulf War erupting, the intruder returned to the AT&T computer, checking to make sure that nobody was around. By now, Bill had set up a display to show the hacker's keystrokes. He watched as the intruder tried to add a new user to the system.

Imagine Bill's quandary: he doesn't want to give the hacker an account on his computer, yet he wants to let the guy think that he's in, to make sure Bill can catch him. What to do?

Bill decided to simulate a poorly administered computer. Every time the intruder entered a command, Bill typed back a reply, perfectly mirroring what Unix ought to do. Over the next month, Bill pretended to be a computer, patiently feeding his guest just what he wanted to see. With time, he built a software jail—a virtual operating system that gave the guy a place to pad around, while insulating him from the real computer.

After a month of watching and carefully baiting his trap, Bill contacted Stephen Hansen, a system operator at Stanford. Together, they traced the calls through Portugal, eventually reaching the Netherlands. At the time, there were no Dutch laws against hacking, so the trace stopped right there. Wietse Venema, a professor at Eindhoven University, telephoned the parents of the hackers, which went a long way toward ending that string of attacks.

The hackers had swallowed the entire fiction. In messages to each other, they congratulated themselves on their depths of networking knowledge. Talk about virtual reality: they actually believed that they'd controlled an important computer at AT&T and that nobody had noticed.

Password sniffers take advantage of how the Internet sends messages—packets hop from computer to computer until reaching the final destination. A hacker at any of these nodes could, with considerable effort, monitor a fraction of the e-mail going in and out of a business. Likewise, one could fish for credit card numbers or money transfers.

Could a prankster modify the front page of USA Today by tampering with the pages sent over satellite links? Or will some idiot spread a computer worm through the nets, chewing up bandwidth or cutting down access? Whatever: I quite understand why businesses hesitate to connect to public networks.

We're accustomed to handling most forms of white-collar crime —we recognize the telltale evidence. An erased word leaves a smudge mark. A forged signature can be compared to the original. A voice on the phone can be challenged. Over the networks, these are impossible without sophisticated tools like digital signatures or cryptographic keys.

Since we can't see how transactions take place, strangers don't quite trust the system. And, indeed, fraud is a constant fear for online deals. One thief on America Online sold nonexistent disk drives to three people. He cashed their checks and evaporated, never even paying his online fees.

Computer security means more than trusted network interactions. Consider how much you would lose if someone stole your computer. You might think it's just the cost of the hardware. Think again.

Last year, my friend Charlie the lawyer called: "How much is a DEC VAX worth?"

I explain how it depends on the model number, age, memory size, and he interrupts: "Can you get it to work?"

Charlie's a criminal-defense lawyer; guys that get in trouble with the law seldom have much cash. One of his clients wants to pay off his bill with a VAX 3600.

This isn't your cheapo home PC . . . probably ten or twenty thousand dollars behind that nameplate. But Charlie can't get the system to run. "After I turn it on, it asks for a password, and that's as far as I get."

"Tried a stand-alone boot?" I ask. He hasn't, because he's never come across a VAX before. Two hours later, Charlie stops by my house and drops off this whizbang computer.

It's a VAX, all right. Complete with monitor, modem, power conditioner, and external drive. Everything except serial numbers. I'm staring at a hundred-pound penguin.

"Uh, this looks stolen," I tell my lawyer friend. He's unimpressed.

"Just get it to work and tell me what it's worth, Cliff. Leave the legal details to me." With that, he takes off.

Well, I find the boot button and fire up the workstation in single-user mode, to bypass the password protection. The friendly VMS greeting welcomes me as system manager, and I start trolling the disk.

Hmmm . . . all the system files are fine. Here's the authorized user file, SYSAUF.DAT. The directory's intact, untouched since the previous Halloween. I come across lots of personal letters, word-processed lists of clients and payroll. People don't appreciate how much gets stolen when a computer is ripped off.

All the documents have the same return address: a consultant across the bay in Marin County. I call Charlie to tell him the news about this penguin.

"Smells like this really is stolen property," I tell him. "It belongs to a company up in Sausalito."

"Damn. Well, return it to me and I'll take care of it."

"You don't understand. It's not mine, not yours, not your client's. It's stolen."

"I'll check into it," he tells me. "Do you think I can use that big monitor on my office PC? How about the modem?"

I tell him about the hardware and slowly conclude that Charlie wants to strip the useful parts from this computer and return the rest.

Huh—if this guy discovers a stolen car, he'd return everything except the tires?

From files on the disk drive, I find the phone number for the computer's owner. A phone call confirms the bad news: "Jeez, late last October someone broke into our office and stole all our equipment. We've been worried sick that our competitors have been using the information on the disk."

Losing their computer didn't bother them—they were insured. But they're a lot more sensitive about their business records.

Well, I called my local police—they picked up the workstation and returned the giant penguin . . . even the frayed cords. Sad to say, I lost a friend in the process . . . Charlie hasn't spoken to me since.

EIGHT

Comparing the Usenet to CB Radio,
Without Any Astronomy

For all its egalitarian promise, whole groups of people hardly show up on the networks. Women, blacks, elderly, and the poor are all underrepresented. This may, in part, be economic—getting on-line isn't cheap. Certainly, another part is the lack of exposure—today's teenagers, having grown up around computers, are comfortable around them.

To dabble in redundancy again, computer networks appeal to those who value techie toys over flesh-and-blood relationships. I'd like to see this reverse, as a more diverse group of people take advantage of online services, perhaps making it a happier, more tolerant environment.

For looks, gender, race, or age don't matter on bulletin boards and networks. There are no accents and all voices are equally loud. Here, of all places, the disenfranchised should thrive.

And in some places, that's exactly what's happening. I've chatted over the net with students from Gallaudet College, and only after they told me did I realize they were deaf. A woman flirted with me over e-mail; her last letter revealed that she was dying of cancer. A ten-year-old boy discussed the edge of the universe with a college professor.

The Internet began as a technical community, with convivial neighbors who'd help each other. Its friendly anarchy promised to revolutionize social interactions and transcend political boundaries. With time, it developed into something less.

In some ways, the Internet reminds me of talk radio—the land where anyone can have his say. A forum for both fringe and trivial? A place where there's plenty of talkers and few listeners?

Uh-oh . . . there's a closer analogue. It reminds me of CB radio.

Remember citizens band radio? It grew out of a wish for cheap, simple radio communications for everyman. In the early sixties, single-channel rigs were used by taxis, delivery vans, and scout troops. Later, during the oil crises of the seventies, police enforced stringent speed limits, and truckers warned each other on CB. Others joined in, and pretty soon, the forty channels were filled with profanity and vilification. I'm not the first to compare its evolution to that of the Usenet.

Strangely, CB fulfills many of the goals of the emerging National Information Infrastructure. It supports cheap universal access, with neither censorship nor restraint of communications. It supports both commercial and private applications. Heavily used, too.

Yet what a barren landscape. Conversations are strangely vacant of substance. Over the citizens band, I hear long rambling monologues interspersed with short, vicious attacks. Requests from lost drivers are sometimes met with wrong directions.

Like CB, much of the banter on the net news and chat lines is stylized to the occasion. Tune to the truckers and you'll hear Smokey reports and incessant ten-fours. Watch an online dialogue and you'll see plenty of zany aliases, smiley faces, LOL, and ROTFL. Yet for all the symbolic smiling, laughing out loud, and rolling on the floor laughing, it's a singularly mirthless amusement, devoid of joy.

And like CB, a relatively small number of people on the Internet can ruin things for others. Vitriolic flamefests that spill over into other newsgroups have the same effect as the good ol' boys who broadcast racist epithets using illegal kilowatt amplifiers. Grudges develop into radio jamming. This sludge sure isn't the same as the disciplined communications of ham radio.

Aah, amateur radio! I'm a teenager in Buffalo in 1964. Dad's showing me how to solder—we've just fixed an old Philco radio that picks up shortwave stations. Through the static and whistles, you can hear Radio Moscow, Voice of America, and the BBC. Sandwiched between them, ham-radio stations beeping in Morse code.

Nifty: the world's right behind my tuning dial, brought to life by a dozen vacuum tubes glowing in the dark.

"Learn Morse code and you can get on the air," my dad, who was truly a nice guy, tells me. He grew up in the Depression; knowing a skill meant having a job.

I study my dots and dashes, and eventually those beeps on the radio start making sense. Meanwhile, I'm learning enough electronics to draw the schematic of a Colpitts crystal oscillator, the one with the tapped capacitors between grid, cathode, and ground. Built it, too—using vacuum tubes and transformers salvaged from an old RCA television. With ten watts, that home-brew transmitter drew less power than a lightbulb.

After an interminable six-week wait, my radio license arrives in the mail. Late on a Saturday night, I'm wearing black headphones and nervously tuning across the 80-meter ham band. Through static and whistles, I hear a Canadian ham testing his rig. I tap out a call and—hot damn—he answers me. We exchange signal reports, a few comments on the weather, and then a galumphingly powerful station blots him out. The whole exchange couldn't have lasted more than five minutes.

Yowsa—talking through a telegraph key at five words a minute, I've reached a ham a hundred miles away. Nothing more than air between us.

Over the next years, those vacuum tubes resonated around the globe. I came to appreciate the terse messages telegraphed with rhythms like iambic poetry. Dad watched over my shoulder as I'd zero-beat a DX station from Kanazawa, Japan; he'd smile as I'd scribble out call signs from around the world.

Today, well, why bother with amateur radio? You can call Taiwan from your telephone. Attach a modem to your PC and exchange e-mail with a student in Afghanistan. Or aim a satellite dish at the Galaxy-5 transponder and tune in Cable News Network. But then, you'll never feel the tingle of a chirping Morse-code signal warbling in across Lake Erie.

Not exactly the same thrill when I first hooked onto the Arpanet. After plowing through the Internet packet protocol, I kludged together a program that sent my first packets across the continent. They reached a file server, and back came my reply.

Nifty, yes, but I'd only followed rules—anyone who reads the Internet packet protocol gets the same result. As the Arpanet evolved into the Internet, those thrills disappeared, leaving a useful tool in their absence. And that useful tool, so widely promoted, feels like it's evolving into a glorified citizens band radio.

Words have consequence, whether sent in mail or posted to global newsgroups. And publicly posted insults, alongside racist or sexist remarks and extremist polemics, are hardly the hallmark of a friendly community. Consideration, kindness, and chosen words go far, whether on the air, online, or in person.

NINE

On Classrooms, With and Without
Computers; Some Basic Astrophysics
for the Intrepid

Remember those goofy cartoons where you had to find all the things wrong in a picture? There'd be a six-legged dog, a duck flying upside down, a kid with two heads. Every now and then, I see something so weird that I ask myself, "What's wrong with this picture?"

All of us want children to experience warmth, human interaction, the thrill of discovery, and solid grounding in essentials: reading, getting along with others, training in civic values.

Only a teacher, live in the classroom, can bring about this inspiration. This can't happen over a speaker, a television, or a computer screen. Yet everywhere, I hear parents and principals clamoring for interactive computer instruction.

What's wrong with this picture?

The state of North Carolina spent seven million dollars to tie sixteen high schools with a fiber-optic network. It's one of those high-visibility experiments that attracts politicians and professional education consultants.

This interactive video system lets Professor Maria Domoto teach Japanese to four high schools. She can see her students and interact with them over a split television screen, even fax exams to them. But the class size still can't exceed thirty: "Beyond twenty to thirty, you lose any personal contact," she says. "I want to see the students I'm teaching."

She makes an important point: even with electronic links, teachers can't handle much more than two dozen students. It was that way for our grandparents, it will be that way for our grandchildren. Television, radio, and computers can bring great teachers into our lives. But no teacher can listen to everyone at the same time.

Professor Domoto's classes began with twenty-six students. By year's end, over half had failed or dropped out. Hardly surprising when they didn't meet their teacher in person. How can she correct a student's writing posture, or show the way to hold a brush-pen or chopsticks?

Anyways, Japanese isn't a snap course. Students won't complete it unless they're committed—the very thing that television and computers can't inspire.

Left unanswered in the North Carolina high school experiment: how to handle discipline problems. It's difficult enough in a live classroom—ask any teacher. Or perhaps discipline becomes a moot issue in the electronic classroom. With no live teacher, who cares?

Wait a second. They spent seven million dollars so their students can watch television in school. I'm wondering how many teachers they could hire and how many books they could buy for seven million dollars. What's wrong with this picture?

Chris Whittle spent far more, piping commercial educational television into schools. His Channel 1 television network folded, having promised—and failed—to make schools a better place.

In the past, schools tried instructional filmstrips, movies, and television; some are still in use, but think of your own experience: name three multimedia programs that actually inspired you. Now name three teachers that made a difference in your life.

I do remember that whenever I saw an educational film in high school, it meant fun for everyone. The teacher got time off, we were entertained, and nobody had to learn anything. Computers and the Internet do the same—they make it easy for everyone, but damn little teaching happens.

What's most important in school? Working with good teachers

who can convey method as well as content. Except to the extent that students are involved with a caring teacher, schooling is limited to teaching facts and techniques. In this sense, network access is irrelevant to schooling—it can only prevent this type of interaction.

The computer is a barrier to close teaching relationships. When students receive assignments through e-mail and send in homework over the network, they miss out on chances to discuss things with their prof. They don't visit her office and catch the latest news. They're learning at arm's length.

It's not good for the teachers either. Dr. Dave Cudaback, a senior lecturer at the University of California, Berkeley, teaches a great astronomy class. But he dreads receiving e-mail from students around the world. "I have barely enough time to spend with my own students. How can I possibly find time to answer questions from hundreds of others?"

I guess what I'm trying to say is this: students deserve personal contact with instructors—interactive videos and remote broadcasts are no substitute for studying under a fired-up teacher who's there in person.

Professor Tomasko can write integral equations on the chalkboard without taking his eyes off the class. One of those great teachers who won't let students goof off.

I'm studying radiative transfer, along with Jon Gradie, Guy Consolmagno, and five other grad students. Somehow, sunlight gets from the top of every atmosphere to the bottom, turns into heat, and then escapes. Professor Tomasko's showing us how. I'm lost, hiding in the back, which isn't easy when there are only seven people in the class. A computer monitor sure would be handy here.

"And thus we see the dependence of infrared radiation on both local temperature and thermal emissivity."

I scribble down the equation, oblivious to its meaning. The others probably know what he's talking about; I'll find out later.

"For a parcel of air in LTE, adiabatic convection is expected if and only if a driving force is present, usually a temperature or pressure differential. Actual lapse rates, of course, are governed by composition, i.e., RH." Jeez. This guy talks like an astrophysicist. In my notes, I keep a glossary of his acronyms: LTE . . . local thermodynamic equilibrium. RH . . . relative humidity.

Back in the peanut gallery, Jon Gradie and I mumble to each other. "Is that squiggle a zeta?" I ask him. "Looks like a chi to me," Jon replies.

Guy whispers that it's a gamma. The prof interrupts.

"So tell me, Mr. Stoll, is this room in local thermodynamic equilibrium?"

Gawk. What's equilibrium? "Well, the entire room's at the same temperature, so I guess so."

"Really?" Dr. Tomasko raises one eyebrow.

"Uh, it's a little warmer at the ceiling . . ."

"OK, assume the room's isothermal. But are we in LTE?"

I blew it. I'm flailing around. "Uh . . ."

"Well, what do you see out the window?"

"Outside, there's trees. And, uh, buildings." What am I doing in grad school when I could be a plumber?

"And?"

"Clouds, sky . . ."

"And what color is the sky?"

Huh? "Blue, of course," I say, still not getting it.

"What temperature do you need to get blue light?"

Oooh—a glimmer of understanding. "You need to heat something to ten or twenty thousand degrees to make it blue-hot. So the blue sky has a radiation temperature of twenty thousand degrees."

"Go ahead . . ."

"And this room's only seventy degrees. So the radiation temperature of the light isn't the same as the room temperature."

"Now, Mr. Consolmagno, could you turn off the lights?" Guy, the genius from MIT, flips the switch.

"Thank you. This room is now filled with natural sunlight coming through the window. But we are not at sixty-three hundred degrees, any more than the temperature of the sky is twenty-thousand K. Any comments?"

Jon Gradie's turn. His T-shirt sports the planet Saturn and he's a little woozy for having spent the previous night on the mountaintop, observing. Still, he answers without standing up. "We're at ordinary room temperature, but the light's coming from a much hotter source."

"Precisely. This room's mechanical temperature doesn't match its radiative temperature. Which means, Mr. Stoll . . ."

". . . that we aren't in thermodynamic equilibrium," I finish his sentence.

I stare at my notes, humbled again by a page of math. A simple concept like room temperature turns out to be unstable and contradictory. Only consolation: the prof doesn't hold my waffling against me. Six months later, he would agree to be my dissertation adviser.

I go home, turn out the light, crawl into bed, and pull the covers up over my head. Local thermodynamic equilibrium.

Since then, I've seen plenty of computer programs that calculate radiative transfer. Heck, I've written some of 'em. But not one piece of software taught me as effectively as goofing off in Professor Marty Tomasko's class did.

I'm not convinced that network access improves most college courses. At the trivial end, it's used for class assignments. Yet generations of students have managed such things by hand—there's no need to pass these over the wires. When you receive your assignments over the network, there's no place for marginal notes or a smiling "Well done" in the corner.

Nor is a computer network needed to collaborate—cooperative projects go easier when everyone's in the same room. College students live and study near each other; of all people, they don't need networks to work together. And if teaching cooperation is important, colleges should require that students work in the same room, so that they recognize and resolve conflicts.

Computers themselves aren't necessary for most college studies. They have nothing to do with athletics and fine arts. They're only incidental to the humanities, whether philosophy, history, or literature. A good term paper will shine, whether hand-lettered or laser-printed.

Judging from the courses I've attended, computers aren't essential to beginning engineering classes, although professors like to assign problems with them. Concepts like stress tensors, Gauss's law, and conservation of momentum can be illustrated, but not taught, by software. Every electrical engineer knows Ohm's law and the right-hand rule . . . I doubt that anyone learned these from a computer.

One afternoon, you sit at a round table with four others. In front of each diner, there's a plate and a single chopstick. In the middle of the table sits a big dish of rice. Without two chopsticks, none of you can eat. How do you share your chopsticks so everyone's satisfied?

Computer scientists recognize this problem as the dining philosophers problem. It has important implications in building operating systems—how do you equitably distribute resources among competing processes? How can you bypass a bottleneck? How do people share?

Strangely, computer scientists don't study this problem using computers. Instead, they use the ordinary tools of symbolic mathematics and logic. Major advances in computing often come from understanding data structures, and from sympathetically studying how people use computers. Even in computer science, the actual computer is often incidental.

OK, so I'm not an authority in engineering, humanities, or fine arts. But I've paid my dues in physics and astronomy, and in those basic sciences, computers have nothing to do with learning.

No computer can help someone understand the meaning of a wave function, angular momentum, or the relativistic-twins paradox. Software can simulate these on a glass screen, but these simplifications depend on someone else's understanding, which may be quite limited.

Up and down the line, computer programs feed us someone else's logic, instead of encouraging us to develop our own. When confronted by a quandary, we're fed someone else's rubric rather than creating our own assaults on the problem.

After all, what's a computer program except a construct of someone else's mind? If you're satisfied with that, well, go right ahead.

But to me, real learning means inventing my own ways of solving problems . . . ways that might not fit into prearranged software.

Think of the dining philosophers for a moment. Some edutainment program might let you explore different algorithms for sharing chopsticks, perhaps letting each philosopher take one gulp, then passing a pair of chopsticks over to the next guy. It's someone else's idea.

But that computer program won't give you the option of breaking all the chopsticks in half, thus allowing all five philosophers to eat with short chopsticks. Nor does it allow you to create forks or to tell the philosophers to eat with their fingers.

How about writing your own software? Now that's a different story. When you write your own macros or programs to solve problems, you explore both the process and possible answers. You invent the machine that solves the problem. It's closer to creating, farther from mere duplicating.

Under pressure to come up with ways to use computers in college, profs hand out homework that has little to do with coursework and everything to do with learning computers. Instead of creating problem sets where the science shines through and the math works out easily, they increasingly give problems that can only be solved with an assigned program. As a result, students learn how to use a set of programs, but remain hazy about the fundamental science.

In return, students interpret this emphasis on computers as meaning they must get the numerically right answer. They don't show their work—they can't, since everything's hidden in software. Instead, they're judged on whether they've uncovered that magic right answer. And it's easy to cheat—copy someone else's work, either by disk or over the network.

My sister Jeannie told me about high school kids that would save their corrected compositions and term papers. The next year, their kid brothers and sisters would recycle 'em. This had been going on for years, and no one had ever been caught.

Inspired by her story, I moseyed around the Internet to see if homework assignments are being electronically pooled. A quick search with the Gopher tool produced long lists of homework assignments and answers, from around the world. Seems that professors assign problem sets over the network and, a few weeks later, post the answers. Both assignment and answer get archived.

I heard of an introductory astronomy class that had students transforming coordinates—a useful exercise. In the past, you'd go up to the roof and pick a couple of stars about 30 degrees apart. This made the geometry simple. You'd then measure positions with a protractor, and calculate distances and angles.

But today's class provides students with a floppy disk of software to show them how to pick stars and rotate coordinates. The pupils see pretty star charts on their screens, along with lists of positions. Enter the right command, and the program measures angles. They never have to go outside.

I won't say anything about teaching astronomy without looking at the sky. However, I'm damned worried that these students spend most of their time learning tools, rather than concepts. Science is knowing about our environment, not being able to manipulate a computer program.

What's the capital of North Dakota? Where's the industrial section of Germany? On what lake do you find Kyoto?

These are ordinary questions of geography. You'll find the answers in an atlas or encyclopedia. Or look 'em up faster using the Internet—the World Wide Web will do it for you, as will key-word searches. On a Unix computer connected to the Internet, enter *gopher,* choose *Veronica,* then search until you find a likely title.

During the day it might take ten minutes, but if the network is lightly loaded, you might get a reply within a minute. The answers are Bismarck, the Ruhr Valley, and Biwa. Why don't these replies satisfy?

Because those factoids are simple and boring. Geography is far deeper than names and places. Consider more flavorful questions. What political compromises caused Bismarck to become the capital of North Dakota? Why isn't Kyoto the capital of today's Japan? What's the history of the Ruhr Valley, and what are the implications of its new Eastern European competition?

Snaggy questions like these branch off into history, politics, economics, and geology. They don't have simple, one-line replies. Their answers are charged with controversy, and they change from year to year, as our understanding of geography evolves. These questions require thinking—their importance isn't in the answers, but in what turns up during the research.

Online databases reply readily to the first type of question—simple, direct answers, the kind that show up on multiple-choice exams. It's a black-and-white view of the world, one well-suited to a digital network.

Alas, but our world has no such simplicity. The good questions have no easy answers; likely they have no answers at all. But it's the quest that beckons so seductively! Search the Internet for the pathway to world peace and justice. Find a database telling how to settle the thousand-year-old cross-cultural hatreds in Serbo-Croatia. Create a spreadsheet that balances the federal budget.

That's the problem. Answers are less important than the process of discovery. What else did I uncover in the search? Could I recast my question and run off in a different direction? What are the fallacies in my original assumptions?

The World Wide Web will tell me the volume of water behind Egypt's Aswan Dam—a fact. Far more useful is to know how to calculate this number—a skill. Sure, it's a kick to search out this fact on the Internet, but I find more satisfaction from calculating it myself.

Computer networks return answers—often the right ones—but they emphasize the product over the process. When I'm online, I sense the vast ocean of information available to me. But I'm alone, without a tutor or librarian.

Lisa Kadonaga has spent plenty of hours in the library. To understand climatic change, she studies historical weather data. This is the kind of simple database that ought to be available over computer networks.

And, at first, she found plenty of temperature records from weather stations across North America. These records went back a decade, and covered all the major cities.

But studying global warming means culling through long-term trends, going back centuries. Nobody has ever keyed that data into a computer.

Lisa's research soon took her to stacks in the back of libraries. Turned out that the database isn't simple: weather stations move, urban sprawl changes microclimates, thermometers get recalibrated. News of these crucial alterations doesn't make it onto computer databases—use those numbers at your own risk.

"A student asked me if I used my network account a lot for my thesis work," Lisa said. "Well, I get messages from researchers and from my professors, but most of the notes I send are to friends. Even now, plenty of people in our department are doing just fine without accounts. Who relies on the Internet for all their data? Even if you do find a source, there's no guarantee you'll be able to use it."

Casual users and serious researchers place their trust in the accuracy and completeness of data on the network. They're relying upon information of unknown pedigree and dubious quality, since little on the Internet has been refereed or reviewed.

Computer searches are incomplete—they can't tell us what's not yet online. One research group may post their results to the net, another may publish in a journal. The online researcher has thousands of blind spots.

All these factors are hidden from the researcher who relies on the simple string of numbers reported over the Internet. If you're satisfied with clean facts, numeric answers, and institutional reports, then look 'em up on the Internet.

I suspect that most schoolteachers know that there's little value in just getting on the net and retrieving stuff. You might as well walk into a library and randomly pick books off the shelf. A much better educational experience is to gather local data and cooperate with others in analyzing it.

I watched a group of kids measuring how weather patterns move through their town. When a rainstorm blew through, they wrote down when the first raindrops struck their homes. Later, the students compared their data and plotted how the rain clouds traveled.

These high school kids were doing real science—no weather fore-caster works at this level of detail. Sure, a network might have helped, but the science came through without the computers. Central to this project were the teachers and students, rather than the technology.

Computers emphasize test scores, rather than accomplishment. Getting the right answer doesn't mean someone has achieved much, nor does messing up an exam mean someone is stupid. These trials measure how well someone can take tests . . . hardly a useful life skill.

Remember sweating through those tired multiple-choice exams? The number-two pencils and electronically graded answer sheets? Computers can't handle anything else.

And the scores from these standardized exams—they have the nerve to report three digits of precision, when their test doesn't justify it. There's no difference between a score of 527 and 523, yet this empty precision hoodwinks the gullible into thinking that one student is smarter than another. It's as if I stuck my hand in a lake and announced that the water is 37.4 degrees.

Every year, the Scholastic Aptitude Test asks graduating high school students, "Which of these sentences is wrong?" They don't ask them to write an essay explaining how the European parliamentary form of government differs from the American congressional system or the Canadian parliamentary.

No, that problem has no right or wrong answer. It measures how well a student knows the subject. Gives her a forum to express an opinion or tell a story. Tells about her ability to cogently express herself. The testing computers can't even read these answers, let alone score them.

But you can. I can. A good teacher can.

How well does our new technology fit into the classroom?

Our schools face serious problems, including overcrowded classrooms, teacher incompetence, and lack of security. Local education budgets hardly cover salaries, books, and paper.

Computers address none of these problems. They're expensive, quickly become obsolete, and drain scarce capital budgets. Yet school administrators want them desperately. What's wrong with this picture?

Unlike books, pencils, paper, and chalk, computers have street value. Result: they're routinely stolen from schools, which are notoriously difficult places to secure. Would you leave your thousand-dollar laptop in a high school locker? Computers aren't as cheap or as lightweight as books—and the value of portable computers makes the pupil vulnerable to bullies and thieves.

A few years ago, Apple donated thirty computers to the Oakland Unified School District. Today, perhaps five are still working. Why? All that were not locked down were ripped off. Someone stole the cables and keyboards to systems that were locked to desks. And those remaining are used for nothing more advanced than teaching touch-typing.

Computers break down in ways that neither teacher nor student can fix on the spot. Try rebooting from a cooked hard disk in front of thirty impatient sixth-graders. Or install a complex piece of software during the ten minutes between classes. This preparation and overhead isn't considered by advocates for the high-tech classroom.

And when the computers do work, they're tough to teach with. Stand before a classroom and everyone looks at you. You can tell when their attention wanders, when you've made a good point, and when it's time to pack it in. You can scribble a diagram on the chalkboard, walk around the classroom, or question an individual.

But try speaking to a group that has computers on their desks. First, you can't see everyone, because those monitors get in the way. The keyboards and screens compete for the students' attention. And you can't point to the screen so everyone can follow along. If someone's lost or can't find the control key, you must squeeze behind a row of students and point to the right place.

Students in these classes have an easier time—they can hide behind the monitors and avoid the teacher's gaze. They have a perfect excuse for not taking notes—there's a keyboard and monitor where their notebooks oughtta sit.

Incidentally, try taking notes with a computer someday. For a fast typist, it works OK, though you can't draw diagrams or doodle in the margins. I feel self-conscious, worried that my typing annoys those around me.

With the exception of well-funded, privileged schools, classrooms lack the most fundamental infrastructure for computing. They're missing telephone lines and often have but a single AC power outlet.

Wiring classrooms isn't cheap. The California Department of Education estimates that it would cost almost a half billion dollars to provide telecommunications into every classroom in the state. And that doesn't include adding power outlets. Moreover, today's standard connections, Ethernet and coaxial cable, will be obsolete within a decade.

Schools have few phones, and those they have, teachers are loath to use. Typically, there's zero budget for long-distance telephone calls or online fees. Jack Crawford, active in children's networking, observed that if there are any charges at all, most teachers will avoid the system entirely. A few will use it sparingly, but the only group that will stay online are those who can charge the expense to someone else.

This hits rural school districts especially hard: few of the major communications suppliers have dial-up modems outside of the cities. On top of the online fees, such schools must pay long-distance access charges. In addition, school hours are during the daytime, so phone charges and online fees are highest when classes are in session.

To try to get around these limitations, Jack helped organize the K12net, a low-cost network that uses cheap bulletin boards rather than high-speed Internet links. They begin by assuming that schools have no money, and that individual schools will develop in different ways. They use Fidonet, a slow, unreliable, but utterly cheap way to send messages.

While the Internet is connecting professional computers together, Fidonet is strictly for the hobbyist. It uses ordinary telephone connections between bulletin boards: late at night, modems automatically dial each other, shake hands, and pass the day's messages across. Since mail is compressed and bundled, the system cuts down on long-distance phone charges.

Fidonet offers no guarantees. It might take a week for a message to get across the continent. Addresses may change without notice. Some mail falls through the cracks. If you need essential communications, pick some other pathway.

For tight-budget operations that don't mind slower responses, Fidonet works great and costs a fraction of the Internet. Schools, bulletin boards, and rural community centers are latching on. It's one of those grass-roots systems that works.

Aside from the mechanical problems of using computers in classrooms, I wonder how this digital wizardry will affect the content of schoolwork.

Certainly, college-bound students should know basic computing: enough word-processing skills to write a paper, the ability to use and modify a spreadsheet, and a familiarity with database programs. Remember, though, that plenty of profs still accept handwritten term papers.

Should computer dexterity be taught at the expense of other skills? Hard to say, especially in a time when driver's education is disappearing from many high schools.*

Maybe computing should be integrated with other classroom activities? Sounds tempting—combine computing with math, physics, or history. In a sense, we teach students to become information hunter-gatherers. Tell them how to access online resources and make sure they're comfortable finding their way around the networks.

This assumes that most everything is available online and that networks use simple, standardized tools. It also assumes that primary source material isn't messy and that students will know how to use the data presented to them. I doubt that any of these assumptions are valid.

There's a deeper assumption: that gathering information is im-

. . . .

* *"An amusing complaint from a guy who owns five computers but no car," says my editor.*

portant. These teaching projects magnify the computing side, while making the learning experience seem trivial.

In a well-publicized classroom experiment, a group of fifth-graders from Washington State conducted an online survey. As a geography project, they asked the price of a twelve-inch pizza. Using the networks, they found highs of twelve dollars in Alaska to a low of four dollars in Ohio.

A most appealing project: these students were learning geography, handling the tools of economic research, and meeting others over the Internet. All this from their online classroom.

But hold on. That pizza data could just as readily have been acquired by telephone or letter or fax. There's nothing inherent to the Internet here—it's just the data-transmission vehicle.

More damning: they were learning the wrong-most thing about geography—that data collection is an end in itself. It's usually the easy part of research, and the part requiring the least thought.

Better to hear how the fifth-graders worked with the data further, coming up with hypotheses explaining the trends in pizza prices. Is there more competition in Ohio's pizza market than in Alaska's? Are ingredients cheaper? Are these prices associated with unemployment?

Why not study Spanish, trace the flow of Pacific Rim forest products, or perform a class play? None of these have the same glamour or technological appeal as a class project over the Internet. Yet they're likely to be far more important to the students' future than a survey of pizza prices.

At the 1993 Computer-Using Educators Conference in Santa Clara, California, David Thornburg, director of the Thornburg Center of Professional Development, hooked his computer into the White House section of America Online. From there, he downloaded a dozen press releases, a presidential speech, several proposals to Congress, and hundreds of pages of governmental reports. He turned to the audience and said, "Look at all this research material that these kids now have."

In the back of the room, one teacher quietly remarked, "OK, what's next? I've got one computer and thirty kids. What can they do with this raw data? I'd have to print out a hundred pages, review what's there, then generate a lesson. As it sits, this material is worthless in a real classroom."

What do we mean by *computer literacy?* Along with buzzwords like *information superhighway, interactive multimedia,* and *paradigm,* it's a fuzzy term without fixed meaning. Defining these is like trying to nail Jell-O to the wall.*

To one person, computer literacy means that a student can type on a keyboard. Another sees it as the ability to use standard tools to send, copy, or delete files. A third expects students to be able to write a simple program in BASIC. One teacher showed me an exam where a student had to describe the functions of different pieces of hardware.

But what does computer literacy mean to a child who can't read at grade level and can't interpret what she reads? What does it mean to a teenager who can't write grammatically, not to mention analytically?

If a child doesn't have a questioning mind, what good does all this networked technology do?

Have we ever spoken of automobile literacy or microwave-oven literacy? Each of these is important today; yet high schools are shedding their driver's education programs and home economics classes. There's far more need for cooks, drivers, and plumbers than programmers, yet parents and school systems insist on teaching computer skills.

But what are these skills? Over the past decade, we've realized that programming is of little value except to those few who take it

. . . .

* *Nailing Jell-O to the wall? While a grad student at Princeton, Don Alvarez tried it. I replicated his experiment and discovered that it's not so hard.*

The obvious way is to freeze the Jell-O, but we're looking for something with a little more artistry than a tank of liquid nitrogen.

First nail the slab of Jell-O to a horizontal board with a grid of ten-penny nails, spaced an inch apart. Then tip the board up and nail it to the wall.

What won't work is to simply hold the Jell-O against the wall, then pound in nails. It sags under its own weight and tears as fast as you pound the nails. Not enough tensile strength.

up as a career. Word processing is plenty handy, but hardly requires a semester of teaching.

And just because students use computers doesn't mean they're computer-literate. How many couch potatoes know how their televisions work?

Slowly, the term *computer-literacy* is becoming passé, I'm told. In its place, educators speak of computer-aided education, networking, and technology seeding. If computer vendors seem filled with puffery, you haven't heard these people talk.

In physics, you measure the brightness of light with a photometer and voltages with a voltmeter. Bogosity—the degree to which something is bogus—is measured with a bogometer. When listening to these guys, I watch the needle of my bogometer.

It's usually administrators and consultants—not teachers—that give me the heebie-jeebies. Like when Frank Withrow, director of learning technology at the Council of Chief State School Officers, asserts that the network brings us virtual publishing; moreover, the ability to transmit information instantly has brought us to "a major crest of human development and symbolisms."*

Symbolisms? My bogometer reads midscale. Then I read David Thornburg's course materials for the fall 1994 Computer-Using Educators Conference. He says that the information age is over, replaced by some sort of communications age. He wants to reshape education because "students are going to primary source materials to research their term papers without leaving their bedrooms. The days of running through the library stacks pulling reference materials are numbered."

Not much need for books and school libraries? The bogometer needle reaches into the red zone.

Alan November, a consultant for the Glenbrook high schools in Illinois, believes that today's students are in the test-preparation business. In the May/June 1994 issue of *Electronic Learning,* he says that pupils will soon build information products that can be used by

. . . .

* *At Multiple Media: The Next Step, a conference in Atlanta, Georgia, on February 16, 1994. Mr. Withrow was keynote speaker.*

clients around the world. Teachers, in turn, will become brokers "connecting our students to others across the nets who will help them create and add to their knowledge." That one pegged my bogometer.

I'd discount such high-tech mumbo jumbo except that there are so many believers. Parents walk away from schools satisfied if they merely see computers in the classroom. Principals plead for budgets large enough to bring interactive media into their schools. Many teachers are cowed by consultants sporting fancy degrees. School board members apply for grants to bring networks into local districts. Lost in this promotion are students.

Not every kid wants to spend hours at a keyboard. Some bump into the same kind of frustrations that adults feel. Others are just bored by the experience.

Then there are the kids who can't get enough time behind the screen. At first, I figured this was great . . . a lot better than television and a chance to learn useful skills. I remember spending a month learning how to solve simultaneous equations algebraically. It would have been much more fun to play with a computer instead.

"Just because children do something willingly, even eagerly, is not a sufficient reason to believe it engages their minds," writes Dr. Lillian Katz, a specialist in early education and author of *Engaging Children's Minds*. "Remember that enjoyment, per se, is not an appropriate goal for education."

You know, there are plenty of things that I'd love to do all day long that simply aren't good for me. Offhand, I'd include reading net news and eating Mars bars. Not that those chocolate bars aren't good, mind you.

Seems to me that most learning grows out of childhood curiosity, for which there is no readily installed software package. Curiosity usually begins with our physical world, not some glowing phosphorescent abstraction. Kids need to mess around with concrete materials . . . erector sets and crayons do more than filmstrips and videos.

If schools encourage inquisitiveness, exploration, and a lust for knowledge, kids won't be afraid of learning computers. They won't have a hard time with literature, science, and history, either.

But when schools pressure kids to know computers inside and out, naturally some students will fail. Others will become automatons, memorizing instructions without engaging their minds.

Suppose that I accept that students should spend a lot of time behind computers. What's the limit? If computers, online networks, and interactive video are so important to modern classrooms, why not eliminate the classroom entirely? Students of all levels could sit behind their computers at home, and receive quality instruction from the finest teachers. Electronic correspondence courses.

A silly proposal, reminiscent of the matchbook covers that told us to enroll in their home-study course and "get a good education and step up to higher pay." Home-study dropout rates often exceed 60 percent; it's hard to believe that an electronic version would do much better, despite the gimmickry.

The Internet can probably deliver all the information taught in a university, as can a good encyclopedia. So why go to college?

Because isolated facts don't make an education. Meaning doesn't come from data alone. Creative problem solving depends on context, interrelationships, and experience. The surrounding matrix may be more important than the individual lumps of information. And only human beings can teach the connections between things.

How do we tell a kid that not everything the computer says is right? Most of us know better, but we still have a long-standing trust in computers—they don't make mistakes, they don't have biases, they don't lie or cheat.

Later, I'll talk about how the authority of the magic medium seems to override our intellectual habits of skepticism. For now, though, realize that we readily slap a seal of approval onto whatever crosses our computer screens without reviewing the content. And if adults are easily seduced, what about kids?

Yet school boards seldom review software to make sure it's appropriate and accurate—unlike textbooks, encyclopedias, and library materials. Nor do educators check the content of network feeds.

There's little to prevent students from spending their study periods scanning postings on rec.arts.erotica.

Unlike broadcasting, there's no regulation of online content. I've already seen a virtual-reality ad for Absolut Vodka. How long before kids download animations of dancing cigarettes? For that matter, who'll be responsible when some twelve-year-old tries out the explosives recipes found in rec.pyrotechnics and blows off his arm?

But hold on—everyone sees liquor and cigarette ads in magazines and billboards. Am I some kind of Big Brother, trying to filter what's acceptable?

Ouch. It sure sounds that way. Let me back off: once we provide students with network access, we have little choice but to trust that they'll use the nets wisely. The best way is to help them along, let them explore, and learn on their own. There'll be lots of wasted time, plenty of sidetracks, and an occasional eureka.

There'll be slouches, hacks, charlatans, and child molesters as well. Donald Deatherage, under the name Headshaver, struck up an e-mail conversation with a fourteen-year-old boy over America Online, then began explicit conversations that led to sexual assault. This reptile will spend four years in prison. William Steen uploaded pornography to several dozen children; he was arrested after offering an undercover policeman two thousand dollars to kill a twelve-year-old boy. He got six years.

Howard Rheingold, author of *Virtual Communities,* writes that we must teach our children to be politely but firmly skeptical about anything they see or hear on the network. That they should reject images or communications that repel or frighten them. That they must have a strong sense of personal boundaries. That people aren't always who they present themselves as. That predators exist on the network.

Good advice, except that we're simultaneously telling children that the network is a fountain of knowledge, a source for valuable information, and a helpful form of communication. We know how to keep kids away from red-light districts and sleazy adult shops. It's harder to keep them from downloading porn or chatting with sleazy adults.

• • • •

What are you telling a child when you set him down before a computer? One unspoken message is, "Go interact someplace else with this machine for a while." Nobody knows how kids' internal wiring works, but anyone who's directed away from social interactions has a head start on turning out weird.

Kids who walk up to my computer immediately ask what games I've got. They're uniformly disappointed to hear that I don't have any. Computer games satisfy in ways that real life can never touch. You jump over the ravine. You blow up the alien. You uncover the magic potion. You move on to the next level. You never have to deal with real frustrations—the illogic of human interactions. If you're thwarted, why, just pull the plug. The ultimate escape.

No surprise that children don't develop good response mechanisms for threatening behavior in the real world. We can't pull the plug on the bully down the street or the jerk that we have to work alongside. Computers teach us to withdraw, to retreat into the warm comfort of their false reality. Why are both drug addicts and computer aficionados both called users?

Thanks to television, huge numbers of Americans have become nocturnal zombies who spend their evenings inert before cathode-ray tubes. Computing is equally nonholistic: a motionless consumption of the mind.

Throughout the discussions of the National Information Initiative, the focus is on the network—the medium—and seldom the content. Computing itself is an essentially passive activity that seldom requires analytic thought.

Alone behind a computer, a user needn't interact with anyone in the room. Since keyboards can't be shared, social interactions increasingly take place over the wires. In turn, children feel less connection to their neighborhoods. Hardly surprising that a generation of network surfers is becoming adept at navigating the electronic backwaters, while losing touch with the world around them.

Roberta Friedman is a movie producer in New York. She hired a college student as an office assistant.

"He does everything I need on the computer," she told me.

"Fantastically computer-aware and works for hours at his desk. But there's a scary kind of narrowness about him. He can win at dozens of computer games. He'll sit at his desk and watch the screen all day. He doesn't look out the window at Central Park or talk to people. He eats his lunch at the computer.

"This guy is nineteen and his curiosity is numbed," Roberta continued, shaking her head. "He's sweet, extremely shy, and has almost no social graces. What's really sad, though, is that he's so bright, yet so limited."

As a way of bringing classrooms together, the Global School-house tries to connect elementary and high schools using the Internet. They promote live video conferences using interactive video and audio. Their literature quotes children: "I'm learning lots of things every minute I'm on the network," says Oscar, a student. "The Internet is so big and I'm only getting started," says another.

I wish this group well, and I hope they achieve their aims, but I'm dubious. I observed a different demonstration project over the Internet, which cost several thousand dollars: hooking up an eighth-grade classroom in Chicago to one in San Juan. After the cables were strung and the connections were made, I was appalled to discover the children asking astonishingly naive and uninteresting questions: "What does it feel like to live in Puerto Rico?" "Do you watch Michael Jackson?" They could have accomplished as much—and more—using postcards.

School districts want such showcases to convince us that they're innovating and solving the problems of teaching. I'm surprised at how few scoff at these glitzy and ineffective toys.

I see the same thing in school districts big and small. Vancouver Island, site of massive deforestation, is considering hooking up their elementary and middle schools to the Internet. According to the *Victoria Times-Colonist,* one consultant suggests that children in their Bayside Middle School "can learn about preserving our island's rain forests by linking electronically with a class in Louisiana studying wetlands. Each learns from the other's land-use issues. That is technology happening now."

Why not just rent a bus and drive everyone to Clayoquot Sound, over by the edge of the rain forest, to count banana slugs and thousand-year-old cedars? Or invite foresters and ecologists to the classroom to speak about their problems and worries? Reading text on a computer screen is far less memorable than any of these things.

Gary Nabhan touches on this point in his book *The Geography of Childhood: Why Children Need Wild Places.* He discovered that many children living in Arizona's Sonora Desert spend more time watching nature shows on the Discovery Channel than playing in the nature show outside. Research shows that more than half of our children learn about nature from television, a third from school, and less than 10 percent by going outdoors. To counter this trend, Nabhan wants children to "roam beyond the pavement, to gain access to vegetation and earth that allows them to tunnel, climb, and even fall."

Artificial-intelligence experts argue over what computers are able to do. This much is certain: no computer can teach what a walk through a pine forest feels like. Sensation has no substitute.

A physicist friend told me about buying a computer for his four-year-old: "Jesse spends hours behind the screen, studying whales and porpoises. He can identify sharks and seals, practically anything that swims."

Sounds nice. How long did his son study?

"Oh for the past month, he's been behind the computer every free minute," he told me. "He'd rather play computer games than watch television. It's educational software."

I bit my tongue, and chatted about his computer. Eventually, I ask whether he'd taken Jesse to see real fish. Now, we're ten miles from the ocean, and twice that from a great aquarium.

Well, no, he hadn't gotten around to taking Jesse to the aquarium. But Jesse was having a great time with the computer. Had more fun playing computer games than playing with other kids.

I find plenty of educational software that teaches factoids in arithmetic and geography, almost nothing about electricity, plumbing, or chemistry. What's there is uninspired—they work remarkably like flash cards. Many other programs just dilute minor educational messages with nifty graphics and squiggly sounds. I can't understand why students put up with such stuff.

Look at the bestselling program for teaching arithmetic, Math Blaster. The first page of the manual says, "State-of-the-art graphics and out-of-this-world sounds will hold your interest as you learn essential math facts."

A poorly animated green spaceman and little blue robot accompany a tedious drill-and-practice program. It's little more than a stack of arithmetic flash cards accompanied by bleeping sounds. Instead of teaching the meaning of numbers, the software rewards kids for answering questions like 5+4=? Kids see it as an imitation Pac-Man. Arithmetic becomes an ersatz game.

Math—even at the elementary school level—means more than memorizing addition tables. How do you make change for a five-dollar purchase? How many pies can you make from a dozen apples? Is it reasonable to buy a state lottery ticket?

"The price of bread is a strong function of wheat availability, but only weakly tied to yeast costs." Here's a mathematical statement that a computer can't handle. Every good math teacher can teach the meaning and utility of functions; the fastest Pentium processor can not.

Elementary school teachers tell you not to mix apples with oranges. High school instructors speak of getting the units right. College professors talk about solving problems by dimensional analysis. Simple, fundamental, and important.

Dimensional analysis is a potent tool of physics. Multiply three feet by seven feet to get twenty-one square feet. That unit—*square feet*—is exquisitely important. It's better to reply, "About twenty square feet" than "Exactly twenty-one." That latter answer is missing the dimension.

Real-world problems demand the correct dimensions yet tolerate approximate numeric answers. It makes little difference if the truck delivers eleven or twelve cubic yards of concrete. But what a difference between eleven pounds and eleven cubic yards. Or a million dollars and a million shares of stock.

Computers can't do it. They're great at generating numbers and digits, but they're no good at teaching fundamental concepts of mathematics like dimensional analysis.

How about teaching writing with computers? There, the main problem—the only problem—is to put ideas into sentences and paragraphs. The struggle to write is entirely in the head. A computer cannot speed up this process.

English teachers—bless their hearts—strive to teach writing against pretty tough odds. The emphasis on computers in classrooms makes their job harder, because they have to teach the mechanics of using a computer as well as how to write.

Indeed, if you don't know how to type, a computer will *slow down* your writing. Sometimes it's better to throw away text, but a word processor will tempt you to revise forever. The emphasis on writing tools—outliners, hyphenators, spell checkers, laser printers —takes the students' minds off the main task: to think. And then to write.

"Computers are lollipops that rot your teeth," says Marilyn Darch, who teaches English at Poly High School in Long Beach, California. "The kids love them. But once they get hooked, they get bored without all the whoopee stuff. It makes reading a book seem tedious. Books don't have sound effects and their brains have to do all the work."

Computers ought to help in writing, yet I find automated writing aids to be a letdown. At the bookstore, a hefty unabridged dictionary might cost a hundred dollars, and a damned good thesaurus is twenty dollars.

At the computer store, these same programs cost upwards of two hundred dollars, and they're not as good. My computer's thesaurus and dictionary—so simple to automate—are anemic. Someday, this will be cured. Today, however, the bargains are on paper, not on disk.

Don't believe me? Spend seventy dollars on an atlas at your bookstore. While you're paging through it, notice its precise colors and logical layout. Now think of the hundred dollars you've saved by avoiding those map-making CD-ROMs, with cruder resolution and no topography. Twenty years from now, you'll still read that atlas and dream of faraway places; the software will be long since obsolete and unusable.

Educational computer software replaces the written word with sounds, motions, actors, and text. David Gelernter, professor of computer science at Yale, writes, "By offering children candy-coated books, multimedia is guaranteed to sour them on unsweetened reading. It makes the printed page look even more boring than it used to." He's equally troubled by hypermedia, the latest fad in linking text with pictures: "To turn a book into hypertext is to invite readers to ignore exactly what counts—the story."

Yasmin Kafai and Elliot Soloway studied several popular educational programs; plenty of software came up short. They found lots of programs to teach kids letters, numbers, shapes, and colors, but felt that these make the least use of the computational medium. Math Blaster mentality pervades educational software: plenty of it looks like conventional drill-and-practice technology.

They gave several CD-ROM electronic books to Emma, a five-year-old. She reacted to the disconnected text and sound, as well as the painfully slow paging: "Pop, I hate this." Even more telling, Emma reads her printed books over and over, but has read each electronic book only once.

Since educational software is designed for single users, there's not much place for social interactions, like taking turns. Teamwork occasionally happens, but it's incidental to these programs.

A lot of children's software won't let kids save their own work. Such an obvious thing, yet popular programs often assume that nothing a child does is worth preserving.

Designers of children's software also often assume that kids of the same age have the same abilities and learning styles. They don't let them choose novice or advanced levels. Come to think of it, that's true for adult software as well. Wouldn't it be nice if programs started out simple, and their abilities grew as we became accustomed to them?

Try learning a language from a cassette tape—there's no teacher to show you how to shape your mouth or correct your pronunciation. Same's true with computers.

The promotions for "edutainment" sound like a yellow brick road leading to scholastic success. But there's no magic ingredient and no instant software solution to learning. Learning is not easy.

For a moment, forget the students. Think of how teachers must feel, surrounded by kids behind computers. They don't see the smile on a child's face when she suddenly understands a point. They can't tailor their classes to reach those bored students in the back. They miss the recognition from parents of having done a great job. Instead, the credit goes to an inanimate silicon chip. Still, I'll bet I know exactly where the blame falls when things go wrong.

Certainly, it's easier for a teacher to plop a fifth-grader in front of a computer than to teach elementary Spanish. The software does the work, right down to grading. Spiffy graphics and fun sounds take the place of close attention and repeating questions to students.

By contrast, classroom education without computers feels dull, requiring memorization, thinking, and quiet study. Most of all, it requires the dedication of both student and teacher.

Happily, there are teachers who think it's worth the trouble. Rather than fancy computers with modems and fiber-optic links, they need smaller classes, supportive parents, and the respect of our communities.

Doesn't the Internet provide access to learning materials, like encyclopedias? Well, yes, commercial networks let you search encyclopedias, as do school libraries. These computerized reference texts are exactly as interesting as any other electronic book, which is to say they're boring. Anyways, how often do you use an encyclopedia?

When high-bandwidth links allow every home to access animated, talking, holographic computerized encyclopedias, I can't help thinking that kids still won't use 'em. But Seymour Papert, professor of learning research at MIT, feels otherwise.

In his book, *The Children's Machine,* Dr. Papert looks forward to the Knowledge Machine, an important product of artificial intelligence. Note the capital letters—AI people often refer to Knowledge with reverence.

This device—a myth, in my opinion—will let children explore a richer world than what's in printed books. Using speech, touch, or gestures, the child "would steer the machine to the topic of interest, quickly navigating through a knowledge space much broader than the contents of any printed encyclopedia." Combining images and sounds, it will let a first-grade child watch giraffes eat, run, walk, or sleep. Indeed, Dr. Papert's Knowledge Machine will include "the very smell and touch and maybe the kinesthesia of being with the animals."

I, too, want to believe that technology will help students better understand the world. I yearn for an easy way to prepare children for a most challenging future. Experience and common sense suggest otherwise: learning is slow and difficult.

One way of thinking is simply to react to what's happening. It's how our minds work in traffic: that car's too close, I'd better slow down. A ball rolls into the street and I skid to a halt. I'm part of the action.

This kind of reactive thought is trained by experience. Pilots are great at it, as are pinball wizards and Nintendo addicts. It's what makes computer games fun; computers are great at teaching this kind of thinking.

But there's another kind of thinking, call it "headscratching" or "reflection" or "cogitation." It's where we get new ideas, create hypotheses, figure out solutions. This is harder and slower—we don't get the zowie feedback that Nintendo provides.

Computers don't help us much with this kind of thinking—at their best, they can give us a playing field for thought, but they lack insight. Reading helps, as does writing. Analytical criticism helps. Teachers help a lot.

Oh, I've met plenty of precocious computer whiz kids. Many zip way past me—one high school student built a digital planetarium using the orbital elements of the planets. Another wrote a program that predicted when the next subway train would arrive, integrating the schedule with where she was in the city.

Some kids imitate parents who are themselves computer experts. And, of course, it helps to have indulgent folks with enough money for fancy hardware and network access.

Still, there's one Macintosh programmer that I met who sticks in my mind for the elegance of his code. Straight out of high school, he had no money, came from a dysfunctional family and a tough neighborhood. One outstanding teacher showed him how to program and do it right.

Kids need to learn not to be afraid of computers, just as they shouldn't fear swimming, writing, or going to the library. At the same time, it's wrong to spend inordinate amounts of resources and attention on computers, falsely promising that they're the key to the future.

But don't we need to teach computer programming so that our kids will find high-paying, secure jobs? Well, no. Computer skills no longer guarantee employment.

In the early eighties, most video games used a specialized computer chip alongside a few K of memory. Programmers who could write tight assembly code earned six-digit salaries and drove sports cars around Silicon Valley. Today's cheap memory and object-oriented languages make yesterday's skills obsolete; those high rollers can be spotted commuting to mundane jobs around San Jose.

St. John's College in Annapolis, known as the great-books school, is debating whether to teach computer languages. Curiously, they're proposing to study an obscure and nearly obsolete language —Forth—so as to make it clear that they're remaining rooted in the humanities and not becoming an engineering school.

Today, their students learn Attic Greek, which is considerably more obsolete than anything found on punch cards. They claim that it disciplines the mind; a computer language will do the same, along with teaching the logical organization of problem solving.

Why don't I believe that computer languages have the same intellectual rigor as spoken ones? Classical Greek lent itself to the promulgation of a rich culture, indeed, to Western civilization. Computer languages bring us doorbells that chime with thirty-two tunes, alt.sex.bestiality, and Tetris clones.

OK, I'm pushing it way far. Still, it's weird to think of all the computer languages that have germinated, flowered, and died within two decades. If we're not constantly learning, we quickly fall behind.

Computer science departments report a huge number of applicants, apparently all expecting jobs when they finish school. Talk with some recent graduates and you'll hear plenty of discouraging news. Companies need to keep their systems running: this means people to answer questions on the phone, configure systems, update software. A decade ago, being able to program in C and Pascal nearly guaranteed a job. Today, classical computer programming isn't in as much demand.

Programming jobs are easily exported. Eastern Europe, India, and Korea have highly skilled mathematicians who'll work for far less than American programmers. A company faxes a copy of the functional requirements and a skeletal program to a company in Calcutta or Seoul, where it's coded by sharp systems-programmers.

Computer programming—once as all-American as waves of grain—is becoming a worldwide commodity. The Internet accelerates this process, by providing fast access to the latest updates and technical discussions. Ironically, the same infrastructure that's supposed to keep America in the forefront also gives competitors a close view of what's happening.

On the other hand, computer programs are sold abroad, with user interfaces tailored to each country. This customization is far more complex than merely translating language. German word processors require spelling changes when hyphenating certain words —the word *Bäckerei* becomes *Bäk-kerei*. The Japanese calendar starts anew should the emperor die. Taiwanese thumb their noses at the mainland Chinese character set. The French use different quotation marks for headlines and body text.

Sad to say, few American computer programmers have learned foreign languages, so most of this customization is done abroad. A friend of mine—a sharp Internet junkie—chose to study French merely because it was the easiest way to satisfy college requirements. "I want to get my degree and get a job," he wrote in e-mail. "History, englsh, and langages just get in the way." I wonder if his résumé mentions his mastery of the englsh langage.

"Sesame Street," widely acclaimed as an outstanding program for children, has been around for twenty years. Indeed, its idea of making learning relevant to all was as widely promoted in the seventies as the Internet is today.

So where's that demographic wave of creative and brilliant students now entering college? Did kids really need to learn how to watch television? Did we inflate their expectations that learning would always be colorful and fun? If they expected schooling to be easy, how many have now advanced from Big Bird to existential phenomenology or celestial mechanics?

Indeed, have the social effects of "Sesame Street" even been accurately documented and validated?

I see a parallel between the goals of "Sesame Street" and those of children's computing. Both are pervasive, expensive, and encourage children to sit still. Both display animated cartoons, gaudy numbers, and weird, random noises. Both encourage passive acceptance of a medium that will follow them for the rest of their lives. Both give the sensation that by merely watching a screen, you can acquire information without work and without discipline. And both shout the magical mantra: "Here's the no-effort, fun way to learn!"

I disagree. Learning isn't easy. It's often not fun. It takes work and discipline. Dancing numbers and singing frogs can't teach arithmetic. Glitzy computer programs can't teach children to treat others as they would have others treat themselves.

The Global Schoolhouse gives plenty of demonstrations to politicians, reporters, and school administrators, but there's darn little research to support this insistent drive for computers in the classroom.

Since well-off school districts have lots of computers, I expect someone will find a close correlation between number of computers and test scores. This, I'll bet, will be quoted as statistical evidence that computer networks in schools are a good thing. Bah.

What exactly is being taught using computers? On the surface, a student is learning how to read and type and use programs. I'll bet that they're really learning something else.

Kids learn to stare at a monitor for hours on end. How to accept what a machine says without arguing. That the world is a passive, preprogrammed place, where one click on the mouse gets the right answer. They're learning transitory and shallow relationships from instant e-mail. That discipline isn't necessary when they can zap frustrations with a keystroke. That grammar, analytic thought, and human interactions don't matter.

In these ways, computers complement television. No technological pathway—neither Muppet nor modem—leads directly to a good education.

Quick—what's the outside temperature?

Do you look at the thermometer in the window? Tune the television to the latest forecast? Dial the time-and-temperature service on the phone? Log into America Online and view a weather map? Or do you walk outside and see for yourself?

Suppose you get three answers: a stranger tells you that it's thirty degrees outside, the TV weather person reports seventy-five, and your thermometer says ninety. Since it's a hot day, you realize that the stranger is telling you Celsius, your thermometer is in Fahrenheit, and the weather channel is simply wrong. The convincing test, though, is your own experience. You stick your hand out the window and realize it's hot.

Computer networks replace that lust for the physical with a virtual reality.

Want the finest pictures of the sky ever made? Get them over the Internet, using the File Transfer Protocol: just type *ftp pubinfo.jpl.nasa.gov* and you'll be greeted by a log-in prompt. Log in in as *anonymous,* and you can then change the directory by typing *cd images.* List the files by typing *ls.* To get a terrific picture of Orion, just enter *get orion.gif,* assuming that the file hasn't been moved. There on your office workstation is a close-up photo of M42, the Great Orion Nebula, complete with false-color rendering.

But have you actually seen Orion? Right now, can you point your finger toward that constellation? During what season would you look for it? When you face the nebula, are you looking north or south?

Spend a few nights with a pair of binoculars, a constellation chart, and a compass. You may swat mosquitoes in the summer and shiver in the winter. But you'll get to know the sky. You'll be closer to the wonders of astronomy than any computer display can ever bring you. You'll be on an equal footing with the ancients.

In contrast, much of what comes across the computer screen is a surrogate for experience. It's living through an electronic extension of the nervous system—many sensations are dulled, a few amplified. Impoverished proxies take the place of real events. Which is more fun—playing a video game of basketball or playing a game of basketball?

As developers plow under Civil War battlefields and lumber companies saw down old-growth forests, the robber barons sometimes erect visitor centers to show what the territory once looked like. I've seen several of these and played with the multimedia displays. They're colorful, interactive, and come with professional narration.

These displays only mock: Glen Canyon Dam, for instance, has a breathtaking photo display of the now-submerged canyon. When I saw what the Bureau of Land Reclamation destroyed, I started to cry and had to leave.

All the whizbang high-tech can't possibly compare with a walk in an historic meadow or a quiet meditation among thousand-year-old redwoods. Computer displays only weakly imitate the sounds, sights, smells, tastes, and touches of nature.

Not all students are fooled by high-tech malarkey. Jon Leary, a senior at North Carolina's East Mecklenburg High School, took an oceanography course over a fiber-optic cable. His class watched video screens, the other class was next to the cameras. He reported that the students in the originating classroom had a much richer experience. "They'll show us an octopus over the TV so we get the visual idea," Jon said. "They tell us it's gooshy. We don't feel it's gooshy."

How can I sense the gooshiness of an octopus? How can you be certain that the ocean's salty? How can a chemistry student feel the heat of crystallization from a supersaturated potassium nitrate solution?

Simple: touch the octopus; taste the ocean water; hold the beaker. These are the very experiences denied by electronic and online teaching.

Come to think of it, they're the same experiences denied by astronomy. I can't see the craters on the planet Mercury, can't touch the volcanoes on Venus, can't feel the winds on Mars. So why are they any more real than a virtual world within a computer?

In one sense, they aren't. We have photographs of these planets, showing craters and volcanoes. Other parts of our solar system, like the inside of the moon, the core of the sun, and the atmosphere of Jupiter, well, we rely on computer models.

Much of what we understand in the universe is based on computer models, which are computational analogues to reality. Agricultural researchers build models of cotton growing—feed in variables like weather conditions and they predict crop yield. Economic forecasts depend on elaborate software programs that simulate the world's economy.

The difference between a Sim-City computer game and a scientific model is that while the scientist tries to come close to reality, the game builder isn't constrained by the laws of physics.

Still, the finest computer model is still just a simulation of the physical world. You seldom know its assumptions and limitations, or even if it's programmed right. Computer models aren't gooshy.

Plenty of computer models are just plain wrong or conflict with one another. Suppose the amount of carbon dioxide in the atmosphere doubles. What'll happen to the climate? The global-climate model developed by the Geophysical Fluid Dynamics Lab predicts Chicago summers could be seven degrees warmer and 30 percent drier. In comparison, the Goddard Institute model expects only a three-degree warming, and 5 percent wetter.

Much of the difference depends on programmers' assumptions about the complexity of global-circulation patterns or the reflectance of the ground. But you won't know which programmer was right unless you wait a hundred years. Often, computer models can't be tested.

I once created just such a world inside my computer. Today, I wonder how close I got to reality.

I'm bicycling home from school on an autumn night in Tucson. Over in Taurus, I see Jupiter, a few degrees away from the Pleiades star cluster. Tonight, I'm worrying about a dissertation topic.

The cloud belts of Jupiter. An atmosphere of hydrogen, helium, methane, and ammonia. We can see the tops of clouds, but what's happening beneath? Maybe a dissertation's hiding there. Maybe a dozen.

Professor Marty Tomasko got first crack at the data from NASA's Pioneer spacecraft. I know he's looking for help; he knows I'm shopping around for a dissertation topic.

Next morning, I park my bike outside Marty's office and ask myself in. "Have you seen our Jupiter images?" he asks, handing me a dozen pictures of Jupiter. "Just what we need to constrain Jupiter's cloud structure."

His desk is layered with printouts stacked on notebooks and journal articles. His reputation made us call him professor behind his back, but in the office he's strictly Marty.

Now, clear gas scatters blue light better than clouds—that's why our sky's blue. It polarizes light, while clouds don't. If you know the polarization in different colors, maybe you can figure out the height of Jupiter's clouds.

A lot of polarization means we're looking through plenty of gas before reaching Jupiter's clouds. Zero polarization means thick clouds all the way up.

"There's more unknowns than you might think," Professor Tomasko tells me. "In 1890, Lord Rayleigh solved the scattering of light on a clear day. The physics of clouds isn't so easy."

So simulate Jupiter's atmosphere in a computer program. Mix some clouds and clear gas. Calculate how much polarization you ought to see. Compare it to the spacecraft data and see if your program got it right. If not, tweak the computer program and try again.

It's computer modeling, the same method used by population planners, geographers, and sociologists. Measure, model, and compare.

"Nobody's looked at this before," Marty says. "You'll be the first to constrain where Jupiter's clouds form. If you're interested, I might be able to find an assistantship for you."

Far out—pay me to study Jupiter? I'd be happy to just work alongside this guy—he's willing to teach me the black magic of radiative transfer. I agree, and in a few minutes, I'm dancing a jig down the hallway, magnetic tape under one arm. A dissertation. Neatness.

Now I just have to understand what's before me. Red light bounces off Jupiter's cloud particles, blue light from the gas. OK, compare the images in two colors. Then what?

Spend three months in the library reading articles on atmospheric physics. Yow—they're full of Fourier transforms, matrix manipulations, and quadruple integrals. Plenty of math, but not much understanding.

It's four in the afternoon on a warm January day; I'm sitting on the steps near the university's red-brick planetarium, poking at a cheese enchilada and an avocado.

To the west, a boogum tree is growing in the middle of campus. Looks like a hairy green inverted carrot. I'm chewing on the last of the avocado, watching a dust mote drift through the sunlight.

One fleck of matter . . . might be dust blown up from the desert. Or a grain of a burned-up meteor, slowly drifting to earth. Not much difference—after all, the whole earth was once dust . . . our globe grew from particles of the early solar nebula.

How big's that speck of dust? A micron across maybe? A few thousand molecules? A million such grains might make a cloud.

There's the ticket. I'll start with the scattering properties of a single particle—one speck—and build up a whole cloud. Like understanding an ocean, starting from a single water molecule.

I run into Marty's office. "Give me a single crystal, and I'll generate an atmosphere," I tell him. "Just tell me how one grain of dust works, and I'll compute how a thick cloud of them will scatter light."

No surprise in his eyes. "And what if that atmosphere doesn't look like Jupiter's?"

"Then give me a different crystal."

"And if that doesn't work?"

"I'll keep hunting till I find the right one."

"You got it," Marty says, grinning. "A couple of months of work and you're home."

It didn't take a couple of months. More like a couple of years. Serious bug hunts within home-brew subroutines. Literature searches and late-night computing. Six-packs of Coke and a foam cot under my desk.

Slowly my computer models made sense. According to them, Jupiter doesn't have a solid surface—just layer after layer of clouds. Near the top, there's a thick cloud bank made of ice crystals. Above that, a clear layer. As gases rise from below, ammonia freezes, forming crystals. That's what I'd been watching. From their scattering properties, they're probably about two microns across. Above these clouds, clear gas.

Nice: from a few spacecraft images, a bit of physics, and two years of crunching numbers, I was able to measure the size of ammonia crystals on a planet halfway across the solar system. And today, on the department's library shelf, rests a hardbound study of Jupiter's atmosphere.

Yes, but do I believe it today? That question makes me squirm. Complicated computer models are sexy—researchers manipulate their views of reality to fit their favorite computer program. They become invested in their own models.

After years of modeling Jupiter's atmosphere and exploring parameter space, I'm not certain. I spent months researching what ought to go into my model, but I sure didn't include everything. I never explored all the possible cloud structures, only the most likely ones. I checked my software, but couldn't test every possible programming flaw.

In most research, you keep close track of systematic errors—how far is your answer from reality. In computer modeling, the numbers are usually perfectly correct, but a bad assumption or simple bug throws the answer out the window.

Computer models don't convince—they aren't simple and they sure aren't physical. I can list my assumptions, show you my data, and describe my program. But I hope you'll still be skeptical—there's plenty of places to goof up. Probably the only way to clinch the issue is a visit to the planet with a microscope and tweezers.

But then, the number of researchers who care about what I've just done would fit into a bus shelter. Most likely, you think the outer planets are boring bags of gas; maybe a methane/ammonia atmosphere isn't worth a second sniff. Or perhaps you hang around hoity-toity galactic astronomers who wouldn't give Jupiter a second glance.

That's all right—while you're hunting for black holes or role playing in some Internet MUD, I'll be finding out more about my pal. For better than half the year, he smiles at me from the evening sky.

TEN

*An Inquiry into Mail, an Experiment
with the Post Office, and a Comment on
Cryptography*

A hundred years ago, a farmer connected to the rest of the world by mail. Since he might be a long horse-ride from town, this link happened a few times each month at best. No surprise that the agricultural senators started to push for rural free delivery. Mail for everyone, every day.

Astonishing as it seems today, the post office opposed the idea. Delivering mail to the outback would be expensive; city folk would end up subsidizing the hicks. Anyways, weren't country folk illiterate?

The farmers won: postal carriers began to deliver letters, periodicals, and packages, if not to doorsteps, to mailboxes. From this sprang a blossoming magazine readership, a new value placed on literacy, and profitable mail-order firms—hence the heyday of the Sears catalog.

Snail mail. Stodgy, old-fashioned, inefficient, and interminably slow. How can the post office compete with electronic communications?

Easy—they deliver everywhere. Quickly. Cheaply. Reliably. Today's postal service is an impressive bargain. For less than a dollar, you can send a letter anyplace on the continent. It'll get there in a few days. Uniform service at a flat rate.

We're familiar with the mechanisms of letter delivery, so we hold the postal service to a high standard. Because few of us understand how electronic mail works, we're more forgiving.

Still, after using e-mail for a decade, I'm surprised by the pervasive complaints directed at the postal service. If one sack of mail gets burned by a disgruntled letter carrier, it makes headlines across the country. Should the university's computer crash and destroy three days of incoming mail, everyone shrugs.

A 10 percent postal-rate hike generates congressional hearings, yet when GEnie nearly doubled its online fees, I hardly heard a whimper. When postal deliveries aren't up to snuff, blue-ribbon commissions investigate. Should the Internet slow to a shuffle, well, I'm not sure who's responsible.

Like most of computing, e-mail is utterly unstandardized. Every day, I log into six different computer systems to pick up my electronic mail. Each system works differently, each has a different set of commands, each has slightly different abilities.

Over a Unix computer, I type either *mail* or *elm,* depending on which system is set up. Each of these has different commands; learning one doesn't help much with the other.

Over the GEnie network, however, I select the mail command by typing a number on a menu. Using CompuServe, it's *go mail;* I type in a number to tell which message I'll read. On America Online, I click the cursor over an envelope-shaped icon. On my local Fidonet node, the command is *M* for mail. I don't even want to think about Prodigy, Delphi, BIX, ATTmail, and MCImail.

On the Internet, connected through a Unix computer, I'm known as stoll@ocf.berkeley.edu. I tell my friends to use the letter *o* in *ocf,* and not a zero. They've got to spell Berkeley correctly. Oh, and use my last name, because if you use my first name, another Cliff will get the mail.

Mail sent to my other accounts depends on forwarding software that funnels messages into a Sun workstation in the basement of the University of California. My desktop computer logs in, picks up my mail, and flashes an icon. With so many links in the chain, there are plenty of things to go wrong. Indeed, it's a pleasant surprise when everything goes right.

What a demonic way to communicate. When it works perfectly, messages flash to their destination in a minute. But make a trivial mistake, or have the bad luck of a system failure, and the mail is lost without a trace.

Why not send a fax? It's far more universal than e-mail—we not only find fax machines everywhere, but they can all speak to one another. Moreover, they can handle diagrams, pictures, and any language—Japanese, Hindi, Cyrillic.

My propeller-head friends tell me about fax-modems; devices that let their computers do double-duty. A nice idea—send and receive faxes or e-mail on the computer. With half an hour of work, a sharp computer jock can get them to work, too. Usually.

I find it easier to just scribble a note on a plain piece of paper and send it over a fax. Or address an envelope, lick a stamp, and mail the letter.

A singular advantage of e-mail is its ability to be incorporated into other documents. An astronomer mails the orbital elements of a comet to me. I read his message and copy the critical information into my celestial-mechanics program. Less chance for error and no wasted time retyping.

Works just as well with reports. I receive e-mail, and copy the important section into my paper. Hardly a creative activity—it actually discourages me from critically reading the section. I'm not adding my own interpretation or correcting errors. What's my contribution if I'm only parroting what entered my mailbox? Can I claim any credit?

I have an archive of fifty megabytes of e-mail, spinning around forty-five hundred times a minute. I can search that disk by name, date, size, file type, or text. In a minute, I can find exactly the letter I'm seeking. Nice . . . a recording of what's passed through my mind.

Every few months, I climb the ladder through a hatch into my attic. Over near a dusty beam, I see a gray shoebox of letters. Here's a valentine from when I was ten; a postcard from my best friend. A love letter from my college sweetheart. Might take me an hour to find the letter I'm looking for, as I pause for each memory. Nice . . . letters that speak to my heart.

Network mail, even decade old e-mail, lacks warmth. The paper doesn't age, the signatures don't fade. Perhaps a future generation will save their romances on floppy disks and Internet Uniform Record Locators. Give me a shoebox of old letters.

Real mail has pretty stamps and postmarks—foreign envelopes show mysterious pictographs that tempt me to visit. There's a return address, reminding me of a friend's home that I once visited. Here's a pressed flower from some faraway summer. These letters bring back promises, memories, and smiles.

Pawing through a stack of letters, I found one with a gazelle on the stamp. Hey—it's from Guy Consolmagno, postmarked Nairobi.

"Greetings from the Peace Corps in Kenya," Guy wrote. "Africa is incredible. I've seen an annular eclipse, the Southern Cross, Venus bright enough to read a book by, the Rift Valley, old volcanoes, new volcanoes, bright red soil just like on Mars, lush green vegetation unlike Mars. I've seen Mt. Elgon and giraffes running along the side of the road. But I haven't seen any mail from you. What's new? Do you have a job? Is the Space Telescope still only two years from launch?"

After his Ph.D., Guy had nailed postdocs at Harvard and MIT. Then he joined the Peace Corps because he "couldn't justify spending any more time on the moons of Saturn when there were people starving in the world.

"And now, I have my assignment. Teaching graduate-level physics at the University of Nairobi. Relativity theory. Electricity and magnetism. Astrophysics. Apparently, they need someone to teach them about the moons of Saturn.

"Well, the graduate students I teach will go on to teach the teachers who will teach the high school kids all over the country, who'll eventually have enough skills to work as mechanics in gas stations or run the telephones and electric power generators and all the other trappings of an industrial society . . . which seems to be the only kind of society able to feed its people with any kind of regularity. So I'm doing my part to end starvation in Africa. I guess.

"So write! Write! Tell me about Jon Gradie. I'm starving for news! And chocolate."

When I received that letter, Jon Gradie had been five years out of grad school. He was doing a postdoc at Cornell—Carl Sagan's lab. Last I'd heard, he was classifying asteroids in the solar system. Might as well call him and get the latest scoop.

"Hey, I'm looking for information on asteroids . . ."

Jon's at the other end of the line, but doesn't recognize me. "Not again," he groans. "Look, I'm an astronomer, not a starfish expert."

Starfish? I try again. "Done any caving lately, Gradie?"

"Oh, it's you, Cliff. I thought it was another marine biologist," he apologizes. "A month ago, I published a paper about asteroid families. Ever since then, biologists have been calling about starfish. Turns out their Latin name is *Asteroidea* or something like that. Every time someone does a key-word search on asteroid families, they get me. I'm talking about a different kind of family."

One of the hazards of the online search: the computer doesn't filter out the false alarms. Sometimes you dig up gold nuggets, sometimes pyrite.

"So what've you been doing?" I ask him. "And what's the latest theory that some planet broke up?"

"Cliff, put that exploding planet stuff back in your comic books," Jon tells me. "The most you can say is that the S-asteroids may be broken pieces left over from larger bodies, but wherever they come from, they're uniform throughout."

S-asteroids? They're in orbit between Mars and Jupiter, a bit lighter in color than their cousins, the C-asteroids. And utterly unrelated to starfish.

In the past couple of years, Jon has discovered zones in the asteroid belt, and related each asteroid's orbit to its color. The inner asteroids—those closest to Mars—reflect more light; their colors match stony-iron meteorites. These are Jon's S-asteroids.

Asteroids in more distant orbits are darker and match the colors of the carbonaceous meteorites. "Which means they're close to the composition of the original solar system," Jon tells me. "We're seeing the leftovers from the planet-making kitchen."

Neatness. Using the big telescopes of Arizona and Hawaii, Jon has found ties between asteroid orbits and their compositions. "I've also found a connection between Arizona and Hawaii," he tells me. "There are caves on the Big Island made from lava tubes. Wanna come exploring and see if they link up with the mainland?"

Today, I run my fingers over one envelope from Kenya and think how I never receive such letters over the Internet. E-mail lacks warmth and importance.

No, that's not entirely true, and I have the message to prove it. I search my computer, and in a moment, my screen shows this plea from Aida Bajric, a sixteen-year-old teenage refugee from Bosnia, living in Croatia. Her e-mail came to me through the Croatian Academic and Research Network:

Situation here is very bad. People who had money left the hotel and went in Norway. The political situation is also terrible. People are very affraid of what will happent.

I finished the school year here but if I stay one more year it will be very hard. One reason is the school bus who will be this year very expensive, the other is that I can't see my future here. My mother can't find the job after twenty-two year of work as a professor so we don't have money for normaly living and for our school.

This village is far away from eyes of the world. I am Bosnian who stayed without her home in Banja Luka and the world confirmed it by giving my town to the people who expeled almost all my family from that teritory that has belonged to us for six hundred years.

Now we are in Croatia. The war is always dubious for the small people. In the first time Croats showed us their generosity but when their president comprehended that he can't take part in dividing Bosnia it changed.

A lot of people (Croats) still stay the same but terrible propaganda (TV, news, radio) in some way start to influence on them. Perhaps I would behave the same if I experienced it. I can't blame that people and I'll always be grateful.

The Croatian government and police are extreme. First they arrested Bosnians without refugee papers and sent them in Bosnia and Herzegovinia for exchanging with soldiers. Then they took cars from Bosnians. I am Bosnian Islamic religion and on every step you can feel hatred. They threat us that they will drive out us from hotel after first of September.

Please if you can find any program for us to came in U.S.A. If you can't find any program never mind and it is the most important that we'll still have a hope in despite of everything what happent. The better time will come and all of us will live in peace and love. I live for that moment.

Sincerely,

Aida

At first I wanted to say that e-mail lacks the passion of handwritten letters; that the two serve completely different purposes. Even as I write this, I'm having second thoughts. For a sufficiently powerful message, the medium is secondary.

Not long ago, I received a message from Guy Consolmagno announcing that he was joining the Jesuits. It's kinda dated—Guy's been a religious brother for the past five years.

You see, after Guy returned from the Peace Corps, he taught physics and astronomy for several years, and published a dozen papers on the moons of Jupiter. After several years of introspection, Guy found his vocation.

Seems that Guy had e-mailed the announcement to me at a computer that was just going out of commission. Sure, I had an account there, but I never logged in. Since then, the machine sat in a warehouse, while Guy studied in a Catholic monastery.

Guy went on to finish two years of postgraduate physics, worked on a South Dakota Indian reservation, and has written even more papers on the moons of Jupiter.

Around the time that Guy was assigned to the Vatican Observatory (yes, there really is one!), that old Unix computer was auctioned for a few hundred dollars. A nice person in Newton, Massachusetts, brought it home, fired it up, and discovered Guy's letter waiting in some file. Somehow, he found my home address and mailed the letter to me. Guy's note arrived five years late.

A circuitous route indeed. E-mail oughtta take a few minutes to reach its destination. Don't electrons travel near the speed of light?

Well, along the way, several things delay e-mail. Links may be down, so the packets get queued or rerouted. A computer might be especially slow, so it doesn't get around to forwarding the mail. Some part of an address may not fit the format of a distant machine, and so requires additional attention. Or the destination computer may not be in service.

We're accustomed to postal delivery times; despite grumbling, people accommodate slow deliveries. Just how bad is the postal service?

To find out, I asked my brother Don to mail a postcard to me every day for two months. He lives in Buffalo, New York; I'm a few thousand miles west in California. The whole experiment cost ten dollars.

I figured they'd average six or seven days, especially since my brother wrote the addresses by hand. Half the cards arrived in two days; many took three days, and one required eight days. Average delivery time, including weekends: a shade under three days.

Snail mail? Hardly—this is fast service. Reliable, too: every postcard arrived.

At the same time, I sent e-mail to myself from five different remote accounts. Most letters arrived within two hours; some took up to two days. Average delivery time: twelve minutes.

But I discovered that five messages never made it. Three of them bounced, due to network problems or crashed computers along the way. The other two? Swallowed by the electronic abyss.

After trying this experiment, I read about an ongoing study by Arthur Anderson, Inc. They've been testing the United States Postal Service as well. Checking intracity mail, they find that in virtually every city, 75 percent of first-class mail gets delivered within twenty-four hours. Many cities average over 90 percent. I wonder what they'd get by measuring e-mail over the Internet?

But don't believe me. Buy a bunch of postcards and try it yourself.

It's hard to compare costs of e-mail to those of the postal service. By far the most expensive part of sending a letter is the time it takes to write it. For many, handwriting is faster than typing; for some, it's the other way around. Ignoring this difference, let's look at the cost to send a message out over the network compared to postal mail.

Over the networks, the heavy expenses are upfront: computer, modem, software, and network links. And connect-time sure isn't free—commercial services charge five or ten cents a minute. At those rates, composing a message costs more than sending a postal letter.

So I write my letters offline, log on, and upload them. It's cheaper, since I'm connected for only a minute or two. But this adds yet another layer of complexity.

The postal service? For under fifty cents, I can send six pages of text anywhere in the country. By putting my data on floppy disks, I can ship several megabytes for a few dollars. Heck, I can unplug my gigabyte hard disk and mail it across the continent overnight for less than twenty dollars. It'd take me a week to do the same thing by modem, at a cost of over a thousand dollars.

I'm limited in what I can send over e-mail. If I'm confident that my friend has the right system, I can exchange sounds, pretty graphics, even movie clips.

More often, though, I send e-mail to someone who might not have the latest equipment and software. Then I'm stuck with simple ASCII text, which can only show upper- and lowercase characters. No spiffy graphics, no colorful letterhead.

Postal mail, of course, lets me send any arbitrary message—a photograph, a magazine clipping, a dollar bill. It might not get there as fast, but it gets there with style. A uniformed representative of the government delivers my letter in person.

Electronic mail can't handle glossy sales brochures or a perfumed love note. I can't download a box of chocolates or *ftp* my niece's finger painting. Nor would I want to. I want to see the real thing, right on my refrigerator door.

And I can't transfer money over the network. Someday, digital cash will let us exchange goods via e-mail. Complete with encryption, authentication, and zero-knowledge proofs of identity, this will let us make one-time transactions that are as good as dollars.

The system will know that we've been authorized to make the transactions, it'll confirm that the sellers are willing to sell the goods, it'll assign special codes to prevent our accounts from being debited twice, and—bong—the transactions happen. All with total digital security.

At least that's what I'm told.

No question that banks are hot to exploit such electronic money transfers. They probably plan on a 2 percent fee for every transaction they process.

But digital cash sure doesn't lend itself to the kind of simple explanation that engenders human trust. It certainly won't make inroads until it works without fraud.

Once digital cash comes online—if it ever does—the technofolks will adopt it and chatter about the wonders of technology. Meanwhile, the rest of the world will drop a check in the mail or cash on the counter. Simple, secure, direct, and trustworthy.

Unlike the brittle e-mail systems, postal mail tolerates mistakes. Letter sorters put up with misspelled names, addresses, and cities. If we don't include the zip code, our mail still gets through, albeit slower. Makes little difference if the address is typed, handwritten, or calligraphed.

Yow—you can paste a photograph of Alfred E. Neuman on an envelope and it'll get to *Mad* magazine. It's been done.

Get my home address wrong and the much-maligned postal service will take a stab at delivering it. Chances are it'll reach me. Worst case: like in the old Elvis song, it'll come back stamped, "Return to sender, address unknown."

Contrast this with e-mail. Everything in the address must be perfect—no errors. Ironic, when you consider that the Internet seems to have engendered an otherwise total lack of respect for spelling.

Get even one thing wrong in the address and e-mail breaks. If you're lucky, your mail will bounce; you'll get a reply saying the message didn't go through. Don't expect any help—the network's not smart enough to tell you the right address.

Maybe your misaddressed letter will wind up in some system manager's queue, where he'll read it and try to figure out who it belongs to. Or perhaps your chatty love letter will go to that clown down the hallway. Or your boss.

Hope that you didn't send your mail to a mailing list or list server! Your love letter will tickle the mailboxes of a hundred or more recipients around the world. Most will recognize it as junk mail and ignore it; others will giggle or flame you.

Or your e-mail may vanish into the ether, never again to be heard of. You'll never know, because Internet e-mail neither confirms delivery nor tells you of lost mail.

Worse things can happen. In May 1991, Eric Fair, the postmaster for Apple Computer, discovered one of them.

Eric was working swing shift on a Monday night, watching over the computer operations in the back rooms of Apple. One of his VAX computers curls up and dies.

The wedged computer was Apple's mail server, apple.com. Seems that several thousand Internet hosts were all trying to connect at once, each sending an error message. Two thousand copies of the same message were already queued for delivery.

Eric unraveled the disaster: a single character in one e-mail message got mangled. In turn, the Unix mail system recognized this error. Instead of repairing it or just ignoring the message, the software sent an error message to the destination, which was a list of several hundred computers.

Each of those systems recognized the fluke, and sent an error message backward, as well as one to everyone downstream. Within an hour, thousands of computers were sending the same message. This overload crashed Apple's mail server and relay machines across the continent. One system had over eleven thousand copies of the message clogging up its disk.

Whatever your complaints with the post office, there's no way that you can destroy it with a single letter.

What's the largest letter you can send? Over the Internet, anything over thirty-two thousand bytes stands a good chance of getting chopped. You'd think that's plenty long—maybe thirty pages. But one day, you'll connect several reports together, and the last third will be silently discarded.

Or try typing a line with a hundred characters. Most of the time, it'll arrive perfectly. On some systems, though, everything past the eightieth column will be lost. You won't find out until the recipient complains.

Don't forget that ordinary e-mail can't handle anything but text. Graphics, programs, and sound files require binary transfers or special handling.

Of course, experts won't hit these limits; they know that the File Transfer Protocol—FTP—can transfer big files. Or perhaps they'll work around the problem with a mail-encapsulation technique. Not for a novice, though.

Sending an important message? Want to be certain that it arrives? Send e-mail, then call your friend on the phone and confirm it. Send a fax. Maybe go to your post office and send a certified letter. Don't depend solely on the Internet.

It's hard to know who I can reach with e-mail. Politicians and movie stars have network addresses, but I doubt that they read everything that comes across their modems.

And the vast majority of citizens simply don't have computers. You can't reach them on any computer network.

On the other hand, postal mail reaches everyone, not just those with computers. This means every person on the continent, every business, and every government official. My brother Ray, who collects matchbooks. Dear Abby. Smokey the Bear. Santa Claus. Even the homeless can pick up letters at the general-delivery window. Now that's universal service!

Contrast the permanence of paper mail with e-mail. My shoe boxes of old letters attest to the longevity of ordinary mail. Who knows how long e-mail will last?

And what do we do with especially important e-mail? Why, print it out, of course. The printed word has more heft than the virtual.

Our first-class mail system is one of the wonders of the twentieth century. Yet it's slowly being dismantled, by overnight-delivery firms, bureaucratic inattention, faxes, and e-mail.

You wake up one morning to discover that your handwriting's gone. You can't sign your name. Your business has lost its letterhead, envelopes, checks, logos, and even the ink in your pens has disappeared.

You open your mouth, and no sounds come out. You can no longer shake hands, frown, snicker, or laugh out loud.

Oh, you can still communicate, using the same, uniform style imposed on everyone: ASCII text. The only difference between your messages and another's is their contents.

You spend your life developing your public appearance: it shows in your handwriting, signature, voice, clothing, and handshake. You leave all this behind when you send e-mail.

These are replaced with the uniform ASCII character set. Clear, unambiguous, and boring.

Oh, you can append crude computer graphics to the tail of your e-mail. A few systems let you choose fonts or even include sound and graphics. But you can't rely on these—only a few of your recipients have the special software that show such spiffy graphics.

A little icon blinks whenever a message arrives in my computer. On other systems, a bell may ring, a line of text may appear, or a mailbox may light up. This gives electronic mail a powerful sense of immediacy. After all, the letter may only be twenty seconds old when we're notified.

"Open me now," the message tells us. The same blinking icon announces a letter from one of my sisters, an invitation to a party, and a general announcement that time sheets are due today.

The Internet propagates a sense of urgency. Writers once gave me a week to answer a letter. Today, if I don't reply within a couple of days, they'll ping me again.

My natural reaction? Type out an answer and ship it across the ether. Yet after I hit enter, I don't get another crack. I'm sending out my first draft. Unpolished, unedited.

First drafts, like alpha-release software, are error-ridden and rough. Yet that icon won't stop blinking until my mailbox empties. My computer demands a reply.

And if I can't answer, I'll ignore the letter. Stash it in the file of messages that I'll get to tomorrow. That pile grows; tomorrow doesn't come, and my correspondents wonder if I ever got their mail.

Yet for all its immediacy, e-mail isn't taken as seriously as paper letters. When I e-mailed several friends asking for comments on a scientific paper, half of them replied. When I sent the same document in an envelope, they all answered. I'll bet I'm not the only one with a tomorrow file.

E-mail, unlike typed or handwritten letters, discourages reflection. While logged on, it's difficult to compose a message and then push it aside for review . . . it's too easy to press the send button. As a result, many letters are sent without thinking about their consequences.

It's not just a lack of reflection in how we compose our letters, but also in how we read. Instead of contemplating what's before us, we move on to the next file.

Periodically, important people such as politicians and movie stars show up to online interviews. They'll answer questions in a chat room, with dozens of onlookers reading their live replies. I'm surprised by the number of straight-out mistakes in their text. Hey—this is excusable. I'm seeing their raw comments, without correction.

Yet shouldn't we find more mistakes in typed and handwritten letters? After all, few typewriters have advanced correction features, but virtually every computer has a word processor and spell-checker. Indeed, many have grammar checkers.

Perhaps it's due to the decline of secretaries—in the past, bosses held them responsible for fixing spelling and grammar. Today, "superiors" compose their own e-mail. Perhaps they rely on those worthless grammar checkers.

But I wonder if word processing and e-mail themselves erode the craft of writing. Our new-found ability to easily correct flaws allows us to write first, think second. When I work with a pen in my hand, I must formulate a sentence in my mind before committing it to paper.

No one has ever, ever, ever accused me of being a prissy grammarian who insists on perfect spelling or carps about dangling participles, whatever they are. My e-mail correspondents tolerate my typos, just as I put up with theirs. What's bothersome is the network-wide lack of concern for effective writing.

I'm starting to think that e-mail destroys reflection at both ends of the communication channel. With the pressure to compose a letter on the fly, I don't reread my words and tailor my arguments. I don't give my messages as much attention as they deserve. In writing, as in reading, slow is better than fast.

I've sent off plenty of e-mail that I later regretted. Written letters, however, give me time to pause: I reread the note, address an envelope, and find the right stamp. I have time to reconsider. The angry letter that I write tonight can be reviewed in tomorrow's sunlight.

The reader is at fault, too. She reads the message scrolling across her screen and presses a button. In an instant, it's filed or erased. No reflection or contemplation. Instead of pondering difficult points, it's on to the next letter.

Instantaneous response without reflection. Our words carry less weight, so we value them less. We don't pack meaning into our messages.

Then too, ours is an age of hurry—we can't waste minutes. Schedules are tight. Deadlines press. No time to reflect.

Oh? Consider this message found in a bottle, washed ashore on the west coast of the Hebrides in 1856. The writer was obviously in a hurry:

On board the *Pacific* from Liverpool to NY—Ship going down. Confusion on board—Icebergs around us on every side. I know I cannot escape. I write the cause of our loss that friends may not live in suspense. The finder will please get it published. Wm. Graham.

In one paragraph, Mr. Graham summarizes a disaster, gives his farewell, asks for publication, and presages the sinking of the *Titanic.* Spells everything right, too.

My e-mail regularly crosses a dozen computers between my keyboard and my friend's. On the Internet, there's no technical reason to prevent one of these intermediaries from reading my message.

So suppose I'm worried about a wiretap . . . someone listening to my traffic as it crosses the network. I'm naked against such an attack, unless I use cryptography. Scramble my text and nobody can read it.

In addition to keeping messages secret, cryptography often provides digital signatures—numeric proof that the sender is who he claims to be. A good solution to forged mail.

Cypherpunks—the computer wizards promoting cryptography over the networks—believe that coded messages can answer many of the problems of our networks, assuring privacy, secrecy, and authenticity. I'm a scoffer—I find the problems fascinating, but the solutions way beyond my needs.

There's a half dozen ways to encrypt messages, including PGP, DES, and the government's proposed Clipper Chip. All of them provide bulletproof protection against casual wiretapping; most are invulnerable to attacks by the most determined opponent.

Modern crypto systems use public-key techniques. Your key is divided into a private part and a public part. Only you know your private key; your public key is broadcast to the world.

To encrypt a message, you fold it in with your private key and your friend's public key. Nobody else can now unravel the cryptogram . . . to the outside world, it looks like guacamole.

To decipher your letter, your friend uses your public key and her own private key. She reads your message, but never sees your private key.

This has all sorts of nifty side effects: since your key remains secure, your friend can only read messages addressed to her. She can't use the information to decrypt letters you send to others. Moreover, messages can't be forged—the system guarantees that a third party hasn't slipped in a phony message. An enemy, listening through a wiretap, is stymied.

Alas, but the weak points of the system aren't in the middle, but at each end. Once you've decrypted your message, do you store it as plain text on your disk? Have you stashed your secret key on your computer? Did your friend do the same?

The opponent of strong cryptographic protection is the United States National Security Agency. They want to read others' messages.

For fifty years, the NSA has run a monopoly on cryptography. It's been threatened by new techniques developed by commercial firms and even by amateurs. Think of it: scrambling methods so difficult to undo that even the NSA is frustrated.

The spooks are understandably upset to see others horning in on their turf, especially since new methods of encrypting data are so difficult to unscramble that foreign governments may adopt uncrackable communications. They worry that drug smugglers and international crime syndicates will get a jump on law enforcement.

The electronic sniffers will be unable to spy. They need an out.

So the NSA proposed the Clipper Chip, a system that provides secure encryption with a single known compromise: a special code lets the traffic be decrypted. These codes can only be accessed with the approval of a federal court, providing some measure of security and trust.

Civil liberties groups jumped on this proposal, saying that Big Brother was holding a backdoor key to the secrets of individual citizens. They also worry that NSA won't let American businesses export cryptographic systems, which will cut some firms out of lucrative markets.

These arguments bounce across the Usenet hourly; I suspect I'm one of the few who doesn't care. Plenty of problems confront the growing networked universe; I think that encryption ranks among the least important.

Hardly anyone encrypts messages, although public encryption software is commonplace. Partly it's because the programs are hard to use. The keys are hard to remember. The software's slow and rarely integrated into other programs.

Encryption programs certainly make it tough for wiretaps; at the same time, they add one more layer of confusion for both novice and expert users. Then, too, encrypted data is impossible to retrieve from a disk crash. Forget Norton Utilities—if even one byte gets corrupted, the entire message turns to garbage.

It's a rare criminal who wiretaps or intercepts communications. More likely, he'll bypass the security by breaking in to a networked computer and reading mail when it's stored as simple text. Or a coworker will read a screen while its owner is out of the office. The part of Internet traffic that's most sensitive to interception—passwords sent at log-in time—cannot be encrypted.

In my opinion, few messages need the protection of modern encryption. Most commercial traffic has no value beyond a few months. Why should I use a cryptosystem that can't be unraveled by an opponent's supercomputer within a thousand years?

I can't imagine an easier system to tap than the United States Postal Service, yet I've never received an encrypted letter. Yes, laws protect my mail, but there's a better defense: the sheer volume of envelopes passing through the post office. Indeed, fraud and postal theft are serious problems. Even so, the vast bulk of mail is, well, boring.

In the same way, most e-mail and electronic messages are so pedestrian that nobody would waste a week decrypting them. Even so, today's fad is to include a PGP public key signature on network postings. It makes the traffic seem important—someone's sending me a message with a seal attached.

•　•　•　•

Junk mail, too, pervades the Internet. There's no cost in adding one more name to a mailing list, so, well, we get plenty of unwanted mail.

You already know how to discard contest notices announcing that you may already be a winner. If you're in a foul mood, you'll ink out Ed's teeth, give him a mustache, wad up the paper, and hoop it into the trash can.

But you can't tell what's waiting in your electronic mailbox. Your screen merely says, "fifteen messages waiting." One or two may be from friends; the others may range from announcements of new computers to chain letters asking you to send money to some guy in Taiwan. Junk mail.

ELEVEN

Wherein the Author Considers the Future of the Library, the Myth of Free Information, and a Novel Way to Heat Bathwater

Few of society's major losses happen during sudden hurricanes or earthquakes. No, the big-time disasters creep up on us; by the time we notice something missing, it's already been wasted. Our cities weren't destroyed by atomic bombs or bubonic plague; blame that on suburban flight.

The telephone eroded the art of writing letters. Television cut into neighborhood cinemas. MTV and superstars weakened amateur musicians and hometown bands. The car destroyed urban trolley systems; interstate highways devastated passenger rail service; and airliners wiped out passenger ships. What is most at risk from wide-area networks?

Our library system.

Mind you, lots of librarians like networks and computers—most embrace the technology. Public libraries open up their online catalogs, so you can search them from home. And many libraries have supported local bulletin boards and Free-nets—public dial-in links to the Internet.

Take a simplistic view: the more information that's online, the less reason for the library. A fully online library needs neither books nor reference librarians; in their place are CD-ROMs and help files. It's a bookless library.

What's the library of the future? Marvin Minsky, MIT professor and bright light of artificial intelligence, saw himself there: "Can you imagine that they used to have libraries where the books didn't talk to each other?"

Edward Feigenbaum, Pamela McCorduck, and H. Penny Nii, all AI luminaries, write that "libraries of today are warehouses for passive objects. The books and journals sit on shelves waiting for us to use our intelligence to find them, read them, interpret them, and finally, make them divulge their stored knowledge."*

Feigenbaum's expert-system library uses knowledge servers to collect and summarize relevant information. Electronic textbooks and knowledge processors assist users in problem-solving and complex-thinking tasks. Knowledge structures are kept in knowledge storage and knowledge bases are maintained by knowledge engineers.

No books in their library. No librarians. No newspapers. Just knowledge.

Writing in *"Networks, Open Access, and Virtual Libraries: Implications for the Research Library,"* Clifford Lynch, a library-automation advocate, makes a number of predictions for 1996: "A user will discuss information needs with software on his or her workstation. The workstation will access a range of networked information resources, will handle budgeting among these resources, will synthesize information from multiple sources, will learn about new resources as they become available, and will perform an active information refining function. There will be no need to involve a local library provided system."

His library overflows with information and resources, has plenty of workstations and networks, but no books.

Let me describe my idealized library of the future. There are lots of books, a card catalog, a children's section with a story hour, a reading room with this morning's newspapers, plenty of magazines, a box of discarded paperback books (selling for a quarter each), a cork bulletin board stapled over with community announcements, a cheap

. . . .

* The Rise of the Expert Company *by Feigenbaum, McCorduck, and Nii (New York: Random House, 1988).*

photocopier, and a harried, but smiling, librarian. I'll see a couple of library volunteers reshelving volumes. Oh yes, locate this library smack in my neighborhood.

I'm worried that if Professor Minsky and company have their way, my library of the future won't exist. Theirs won't either. Here's why:

A couple of times a month, I visit the stacks of the University of California, where I hole up in a carrel and read musty old magazines from the thirties.

The cool stuff seems to predate computers. Dusty newspapers and magazines tell me where we've been. Here's a 1905 ad to "Increase your salary by learning Electricity"—for just sixty-five cents, you'll learn how to become a telegraph operator. Over in a 1949 *Life* magazine, R. J. Reynolds touts how more doctors prefer Camels than any other cigarette. Here's a photograph of young Richard Nixon, unraveling some microfilm found in a pumpkin.

None of these show up online; they've never been scanned into a computer. The researcher using online sources has a fifteen-year horizon . . . nothing's been digitized before 1980.

Well, almost nothing. At the Illinois Benedictine College, Professor Michael Hart founded Project Gutenberg with a goal of creating an entire library for online access. By the year 2001, they'll scan in ten thousand books, which will then be available for downloading or cheap publication on CD-ROM. A worthy cause, funded entirely by volunteer efforts.

After several years of text scanning, the Gutenberg library includes *Moby Dick, Paradise Lost,* the Bible, an address by George Bush, *Alice in Wonderland,* and the constitution of Peru.

This is great stuff, and I'm tickled to see it happening. There's a warm feeling of volunteers bringing literature online. Since 1971, they've digitized about two hundred books.

Still, I'm missing something. Two hundred books easily fit on five bookshelves. That's what I'm missing—about ten million volumes.

Professor Hart won't argue that Project Gutenberg's collection is small. But it's growing—ten books get scanned in every month.

Remember their goal of ten thousand digitized works by 2001; contrast that with the forty thousand books published yearly.

Who decides what makes the cut? The Magna Carta? The latest Tom Clancy thriller? An obscure paper written by Stephen Hawking? A biography of Michael Jackson? With all the great literature out there, I'm surprised to find *Terminal Compromise* by Winn Schwartau and *The Dawn of Amateur Radio in the U.K. and Greece* by Norman Joly among the first two hundred books.

Not that the Gutenberg folks don't have high aims. They expect a billion computer users within seven years. A tenth of these will get a complete set of their works. Every reader gets ten thousand files, each worth a dollar—don't ask me how they value George Bush's inaugural address at a buck. From these dubious suppositions, they claim they're producing a trillion dollars in value.

Such pie in the sky claims form the backdrop to a related fantasy: the online library.

One of the great promises of the online world is fast access to great quantities of information. Internet proponents talk of libraries without books, the time when essentially all publications will be available over the network. We'll be able to read and access any document from our workstations. Books will be distributed electronically.

I claim that this bookless library is a dream, a hallucination of online addicts, network neophytes, and library-automation insiders.

Al Gore said, "If we had the information superhighways we need, a school child could plug into the Library of Congress every afternoon and explore a universe of knowledge, jumping from one subject to another, according to the curiosity of the moment." Such a dream assumes that the library's books are all digitized and available on the computer.

They aren't. They never will be.

Today, over the Internet, I can search the catalogs of fifty major libraries. I can type *telnet locis.loc.gov* and see if a title is in the Library of Congress. Handy way to find a book.

But knowing that a book exists is a long way from paging

through that volume. The catalog search might tell me title, author, a few key words, and how many pages.

Online catalogs are like restaurant menus—they tempt, but don't satisfy. I want to read the book and understand the author's points. I need the full text—every picture and paragraph and page.

Yes, many library catalogs are online, but few books are, even if you include Project Gutenberg's ten score. Vice President Gore's schoolchild won't be very happy plugging into the Library of Congress online catalog. She'll be especially disappointed because the Library of Congress doesn't lend books.

This same breathy optimism appeared in a *Popular Science* article from 1965, "Putting a Library in a Shoebox": "How would you like to have the Library of Congress, occupying 270 miles of bookshelves, in your house? Sounds impossible? Well through a new micrographotography process, you may, one day, be able to have the entire contents of the great library in your den on film—all contained in about six filing cabinets."

The Library of Congress itself tries to convince you of its electronic availability. The Library of Congress Information System and the LC MARVEL—Machine-Assisted Realization of the Virtual Electronic Library—are supposed to "combine the vast amounts of information available about the library with easy access to diverse electronic resources over the Internet," according to a press release. During a year when the library closed reading rooms and reduced staff, they found plenty of money to spend on computers.

Watch out: library automation mercenaries are running a bait-and-switch operation. They promise access to the Library of Congress and some thirty-five million records. Instead, they deliver an electronic card catalog and a few dozen collections, like translations of Stalin's speeches and Leonard Bernstein's papers. They've brought practically no books online. Virtual electronic library, indeed.

How come I can't get the books over the Internet? Thomas Mann, a reference librarian in the Library of Congress, explains why in *Library Research Models*.

Fundamentally, human nature and copyright law torpedo this information utopia. People who write books, compose symphonies, and draw pictures want to be paid for their work. Somehow, the online library has to find a way to compensate authors. But libraries simply don't own the rights to republish or broadcast creative works.

Without a massive change in copyright law—unlikely, since it lives in international treaties—libraries can't put their collections online. It's not simply that copyright blocks bookless libraries. Rather, copyright is the solution to the more fundamental problem: we want to be paid for the use of our own work—our intellectual property.

We could bypass this problem by simply abolishing private property, specifically intellectual property rights. Copyrights and patents would disappear. All information would be liberated. Karl Marx would be delighted.

Uh, right. Mark Twain said, "A country without a patent office and good patent laws is just a crab and can't travel any way but sideways and backwards." Same's true for copyright law: eliminate copyright and you undercut the worth of writers.

Alternatively, libraries could license electronic rights. This would be one hell of a negotiation—publishers, authors, and governments will all want a share of the proceeds; few libraries have much cash for license payments.

I've heard of other solutions: Brad Templeton, of Clarinet Communications, created an online library with an all-you-can-read feature. For a few dollars a month, anyone could subscribe to his service. These fees would be divvied up among authors according to how often their works get downloaded. A nice idea.

Didn't work out so well. When he put a science fiction collection online, with a downloading fee of thirty dollars, few were interested. He sold plenty of CD-ROMs with the same information, but Brad feels the time's not yet ripe for a pay-per-read online library.

Maybe full text retrieval won't work for entertainment, but it's downloaded all the time for business and research purposes. Doctors and lawyers, mainly. Grad students in history can't afford it.

Frederick Hayes-Roth and Neil Jacobstein, authorities in artificial intelligence, feel that day is coming, though. Writing in the March 1994 *Communications of the Association for Computing Machinery,* they envision "a world in which people publish active electronic knowledge and get paid each time it is used. This will be accomplished by instrumenting knowledge systems and making them widely available on high-speed computer networks."

Lest you think that these guys are entirely on the level, you should realize that they write that "knowledge is being built into all kinds of products, from automobiles to microwave ovens to vacuum cleaners." Guess I ought to have a bit more respect for my old Hoover canister—it knows how to vacuum rugs. For that matter, I can now blame my burned sneakers on my housemate's microwave oven, which didn't know enough not to cook tennis shoes.

Even if copyright problems are solved, the process of digitizing millions of historical books would be impressively expensive. They'd have to be scanned in at a cost of fifty cents to three dollars a page. So each book would cost a hundred dollars to digitize.

Seem expensive? The problem is the 99.9 percent accuracy of today's best scanning systems. That places about two typos on each scanned page. Someone has to proofread and correct the text.* Expensive.

Because digitizing costs so much, commercial services supply full text retrieval to only a few thousand periodicals. This may sound like a lot of information, but the Library of Congress actively subscribes to some sixty-five thousand newspapers, magazines, and journals.

. . . .

* *Ever notice that the second or third time you read a book, you discover all sorts of typos and misprints? The more often you read a book, the more mistakes you find.*

These typos are read-errors: mistakes introduced by reading the text. To preserve accuracy, you should purchase a new edition each time you wish to read a book. Most of all, avoid used books, pirated editions, and books from unknown sources.

Public libraries are especially dangerous! Library books are read many times, introducing uncounted read-errors. Worse, borrowers (and some unscrupulous authors) can infect books with literary viruses (analogous to computer viruses) that can be transmitted to other readers.

You can avoid these problems by only reading from new books, and purchasing fresh shrink-wrapped volumes at your local bookstore. Hardcover editions are most resistant to typos and literary viruses; get these whenever possible.

Search time on the commercial NEXIS service runs around two hundred dollars per hour. Thomas Mann estimates that if they digitized just the incoming magazines in the Library of Congress, NEXIS would have to charge two hundred dollars per minute. God knows how much it'd cost to put their entire twenty million books online.

This isn't a problem for Brad Templeton. "Get prisoners to scan books," he suggests. "Teach them to type and scan books. They used to repair highways and make license plates."

Not exactly the image I want to create for online libraries. Kinda like teaching kids that only convicts pick up litter alongside highways.

There's another reason why I don't think libraries will ever go online. Electronic media aren't archival.

Oh, I hear my technofriends squeal. CD-ROMs have life spans of decades if not centuries. But the physical medium isn't the problem. It's the reading mechanism.

In 1979, as NASA's Pioneer spacecraft flew by Saturn, I helped record the down-linked data onto magnetic tape. To make certain that we didn't lose any of this priceless data, we saved it in four formats: 9-track magnetic tape, 7-track tape, paper tape, and punch cards. That's a lot of boxes of cards, but hey—I wear a belt and suspenders.

Fifteen years later, all those cards and tapes survive in a Tucson warehouse, guarded by iguanas and scorpions. They're in fine shape, but I can't read 'em. Punch-card and paper-tape readers just don't exist anymore. Nor do those big reel-to-reel tape recorders. If it were only a few tapes, I could send them away to be copied onto disk. But we're talking about a truckload of tapes.

Think of the many extinct formats: 78-rpm records; 2-inch quad-scan videotape; phonograph cylinders; paper tape; 80-column punch cards; 100-column punch cards; 7-track digital tape; reel-to-reel audio tape; 8-track tapes; DECTape; 8-millimeter movies; 5-inch glass lantern slides.

Then think of the formats that are disappearing today: 45- and

33-rpm vinyl records; 5¹/4-inch floppy disks; Betamax tapes; single-side, single-density diskettes; EBCDIC coding.

Even familiar ASCII text may be pushed aside for a coding system better suited to non-English languages, Unicode. Will my backup tape from last night be readable in a hundred years? I doubt it.

Today's information isn't just magnetic domains on ferric oxide or simple bumps on a glimmering plastic disk. The format of the data is essential, and makes the difference between being able to read a file or getting an error. A disk of files from extinct Visicalc programs may be perfectly readable, but today's spreadsheet programs can't interpret them. The latest Microsoft Word program can read files from version 1.0—quite a feat of compatibility—but can anyone read files from the Electric-Pencil, the first word processor for home computers?

Will files from my word processor or database program still be understood in fifty years? Will today's hypertext markup language—used throughout the World Wide Web, Mosaic, Lynx, and other Internet programs—make sense then?

At 11:59 P.M. on December 31, 1999, when someone discovers a bug within an ancient Fortran or BASIC program, will she have a compiler to patch it? Will she know where to look for the source code? Will the runtime libraries still be compatible?

All of these media are standardized, documented, and readable. But they become increasingly expensive to read, as equipment becomes expensive to maintain or simply cannot be repaired.

"Aah," you're saying, "just replicate the digital information onto a more modern format." A good solution, though quite expensive. Every twenty or thirty years, an entire collection will have to be duplicated.

But an archival medium shouldn't depend on duplication for preservation. Except when dealing with volumes printed on acidic paper, libraries don't have to copy books every few decades. Librarians don't have the money or the expertise to constantly replicate their collections.

File formats are often tough to replicate. You can copy a database from disk to CD-ROM, but unless your program is modified to recognize this change, you're up a tree.

Furthermore, there's a concealed proposition here: that you can take information, change the format, and still have the same thing. That's true for data. Not true for information.

When you change formats, you alter the way you access the information. A videotape isn't the same as a film, even if you ignore the different frame rate, screen shape, and color resolution. The way you access them is different.

A recipe on the computer screen has the same data as a recipe on a three-by-five-inch card. One of them is easy to use in the kitchen, when you have greasy fingers and can't find the vanilla bottle.

A city street-map is different from a database, even though the two contain the same data and describe the same area. The formats are different, and the ways we access them are different: one works great with census data, the other's at home in a glove compartment.

In the same way, an online book isn't the same as a book on paper. The format is different.

Not only do format changes affect how we get to the information, they often modify the content. You expect to hear scratches on a 78-rpm recording of Alexander's Ragtime Band; listen to the same piece on a compact disc, and the very same scratches seem joltingly out of place. Sheet music for "Brother Can You Spare a Dime" includes more than just the notes and lyrics. On the front cover, over in the corner, is a blue eagle, the symbol of the National Reconstruction Act—one attempt to alleviate the Great Depression.

Another reason why book-based libraries won't disappear: it's confusing to do serious research over the network. I get lost in hyperspace—or is it menuspace? After a few searches and lateral jumps, I'm not sure what data I'm looking at.

The Internet Gopher is classic: it's easy to hop from university to library to archive to catalog. Each of these provides a dozen options: shall I scan for a key word or download a file or choose from a numbered menu? Or do I use the hypertext in Mosaic, where I double-click on a word to jump to another document? Even the most dedicated explorer tosses in the towel, befuddled. Sometimes, it's hard to figure out even how to give up—does logging out disconnect all those virtual links?

Information servers may tell us titles of files. But in order to see if the file's actually useful, we have to download the whole thing. So we fire up FTP and transfer the file to the computer. Then, as every network user discovers, files whose titles seemed interesting actually aren't what we wanted. We end up throwing out most of what we download. It's like buying a book mail-order just to assess whether it's the volume we need.

Then there's the problem of commercial and no-cost information services. Brad Templeton feels that we can't have a free electronic library alongside one that charges. In his opinion, as the networks grow, commercial sources will blossom, and the free lending library will wither. They won't entirely disappear—Brad thinks they'll archive whatever isn't in digital format, help with information searches, and provide terminals for the poor.

Now listen to library-automation advocate Dr. Clifford Lynch in *Networks, Open Access, and Virtual Libraries:* "Many smaller public libraries will be reduced to lending current novels and will be unable to fill other information needs for their user communities," he writes. "They will have neither the funding nor the expertise to operate as intermediaries to electronic information."

What will the electronic book look like? Some sort of miniature laptop computer, I'd guess. We'll download selections and page through them electronically. I've tried reading electronic books. They're awful. What a great way to drive patrons away from libraries.

There's yet another reason why online libraries won't work. Or maybe it's a reason why they'll thrive. Thomas Mann of the Library of Congress calls it the principle of least effort. According to him, most researchers, even serious scholars, will choose easily available information sources, even when they are low-quality. Researchers are usually satisfied with whatever can be easily found rather than expending more effort to dig up better sources.

George Zipf, one of the pioneers in information science, put it a different way. Confronted with a variety of pathways to an answer, people choose the one that requires the least amount of work.

After surveying a thousand researchers and policy makers in rural mental-health services, John Salison and Toby Cedar concluded, "Information sources tend to be chosen on the basis of perceived ease of use, rather than on the basis of the amount of information expected from the source."

Mann writes, "If a system makes only some sources easily available—especially if those sources are very superficial or of poor quality—then it can do real damage to the quality of research, for it will encourage users simply to make do with whatever sources are readily retrievable, regardless of their quality or completeness."

In other words, people are lazy. Ease of use is more important than content. Put something online—anything—and researchers will love it, whether or not it's right.

This is a driving force behind the move for online libraries, and indeed, the Internet itself. There's a feeling that any answer is better than none. It might be the wrong answer, an incomplete or misleading answer. But it's better than nothing. Instead of plowing through lots of books, get Professor Feigenbaum's knowledge processor to do my work and tell me the answer.

If I can discover the single concrete fact that solves a problem, I'm home free. All it takes is an online library, an expert system, network access, and speedy, fifth-generation computers.

Oh, if only the world worked that way! I've long sought a simple solution to my research. Just log in, ask the right question, search the right key words, turn the crank, and—zot—there's my answer.

I don't believe in magic. Good research, like good art, good cooking, good teaching, and good whatever, requires patience, creativity, multiple approaches, time, and work. Lots of work.

The easy, boring questions have simple answers. How far is it to the sun? I can look that up over the Internet, though with more difficulty than you'd expect.

But how do we know the distance to the sun? How accurate is this measurement? How do we know the accuracy? These are a bit tougher.

How does the sun's distance change from century to century? How does this affect climate? These are nifty questions—you won't find clean answers anywhere.

The dream of a universal fountain of information, free for all comers, will ever remain that: a dream. If this were simply an illusion, I'd shrug. But the rush to computerize libraries has several nasty side effects. One is how libraries spend their limited money.

Money spent on electronic gizmos and network access fees comes from the same source that buys books and pays librarians. Frankly, I'd rather visit a library stocked with lots of books and a competent librarian than one with online catalogs, CD-ROMs, terminals, and fewer books.

That's why I fear Minsky's, Feigenbaum's, and Lynch's library of the future. It cannot happen, for reasons of cost, copyright, and preservation. But in the rush to get there, we'll spend barbarous gobs of money on electronics, and a pittance on books and librarians.

Want another reason why networks are bad for libraries? Because they destroy the library as an archive. To which do you entrust your cultural heritage—Meade Data Central or ten thousand libraries across the continent?

Here's the plot for a John Grisham thriller: A terrorist ring is out to destroy the American legal system. So they plant a bomb in the Westlaw computer building, over in Eagan, Minnesota. Since Westlaw keeps copies of their data off-site, the terrorists make sure bogus data gets shipped there.

Come the witching hour, law libraries, attorneys, judges, and legislatures are effectively frozen. They can't get any references.

Today, that plot won't quite work. Most law libraries still subscribe to paper journals, if for no other reason than to give a backdrop of bookshelves for photographs of attorneys. But as libraries replace books with cathode-ray tubes, those paper archives will disappear.

Everywhere, library administrators want to eliminate periodicals. They know the costs of journals—the subscription fees, the handling and cataloging expenses, shelf space, and theft problems. Cheaper to just give patrons a computer terminal.

Here's the problem: with fewer subscriptions, there's nobody to pay the editorial staff, let alone the printers. The journal folds. Both writers and readers lose.

And reading an online journal is a cheat. Gone are graphs, photographs, equations, and typography. And we can't read a whole journal at a time—we get slices, perhaps one article or one author or one paragraph. Online services destroy the integrity of the journal.

You probably think that digital archives are permanent. Then consider Coffee Line. For the latest scoop on coffee beans, we'd call the Dialog system to sip information on growing, marketing, and packaging. Here's where we'd get the number of tons of Kona coffee shipped. All updated weekly.

Well, it's gone. Log into Dialog and we see this greeting: "Coffee Line is unavailable as of October 1." Why? It was uneconomical to carry.

Will the same thing happen to your favorite database? Tune in next year and see. Meanwhile, scream bloody murder when your library administrator wants to reduce journal-acquisition budgets.

Suppose you live in the Midwest, a couple of blocks from the University of Minnesota. It takes a few minutes to walk over to the campus library and browse their most recent archives. How often would you visit their library?

Good news! Thanks to the Gopher information service, you can save your steps and search their archive any time of day. The complete information archives of hundreds of universities are tied together over the Internet.

Just log into most any Internet host, ask for a gopher server, and connect to the mother gopher, the University of Minnesota. They've put most of their archives online, and you can read the latest copy of the *Minnesota Daily* or scrabble through their phone book. If you want information from another university, navigate to that server, or try a Veronica database search.

Here, you'll find telephone directories to several universities, a list of upcoming seminars on Zernike's orthogonal polynomials, and posturing statements on the Law of the Sea.

Such an electronic search is a long way from Feigenbaum's knowledge server. It's a long way from a real library, too. I won't be surprised if you never access this archive. Some people, however, desperately want it.

I get an emergency message from one guy who needs help doing research. He's writing a master's paper on the social implications of applied science. Most of the year's gone by and he's against a deadline.

Naturally, I point him toward the library, where there are plenty of books on the subject. But that's not what he wants to hear. "I'm in a hurry," he tells me. "I've got a meeting with my adviser next week and I've got to show progress big-time."

All the more reason to head to the library. But he wants it faster. "Can you get me information from the Internet?"

Well, sure, but it won't be of much use. I point him to Veronica, and show him how to do key-word searches. Most of the network servers are busy, so we try again and wait. And wait. While we're twiddling our thumbs, I mention that our search will only cover the past few years.

"That's OK," he replies. "I only need the most recent reports. The outdated stuff isn't important."

Ouch! Anything that isn't online isn't important. If he can't get it instantly—not even in a day, but in a few minutes—it has no value.

How can I tell him that essentially nothing that he turns up will have much value. A computer search might turn up references to some books and a few reports. What's not there? Virtually everything in print. Simply by going to a computer, he's tunneling his vision. His research will be shallow to the point of nonexistence.

He doesn't accept this explanation. "Isn't there some way to get the computer to do my research for me?" he asks. "Once I get the printouts, I'll write the report."

Yowsa—this guy is a believer. He thinks Marvin Minsky's dream is reality. For him, research simply means collecting data; writing the report will be easy.

You might think he was just a lazy SOB who deserved to be roasted by his adviser. Well, it was his professor who told him to get the information over the computer. Professional researchers don't appreciate the limitations of computer-based searches. They just think about the money they can save by avoiding the library's outrageously exorbitant photocopy fees of twenty-five cents a page.

Wouldn't you be suspicious of a research paper that listed no source prior to 1990? Ideas just don't pop out of the air like that. Likewise, I respect those who dig deeper and find out that Charles Darwin was only one of several scientists developing theories of evolution, that Carl Sagan wasn't the first to write about nuclear winter, or that Thomas Edison should share credit for the light bulb with Sir Joseph Swan.

In the end, the Internet answered his needs in exactly the right way. For half an hour, all the Veronica database servers responded with "Too many connections, try again later." Up against a pressing deadline, this guy gave up on the Internet and walked over to the library. I wonder what he concluded about the nature of computerized research.

The latest online mirage is video-on-demand. Cable companies, Hollywood studios, and telephone monopolies have all been hypnotized into thinking that we will one day key in the movie we want and zing—it'll pop up on our TV.

It's a surprisingly tough engineering problem, keeping a thousand movies ready for instant retrieval. These can't be on videotapes, since most viewers will request the same popular films. Imagine having ten thousand copies of Jurassic Park, each starting at a different time.

What if this challenge is met? Will consumers forgo trips to local video shops? The first trials say no. AT&T, TCI, and US West built a video-on-demand system for Littleton, Colorado. After a year of promotion, families requested just two or three movies a month. Despite a colder than usual winter, most preferred to visit the corner video store.

The ubiquitous videotape, so simple to use, is a wonder indeed, holding upwards of four gigabytes of data. If it takes you twenty minutes to walk to the store and back, you've created a three-megabyte-per-second communications circuit.

I'll bet the denizens of Littleton chose their mom-and-pop video stores over video-on-demand for the same reasons that people pick real libraries over online databases: they're intuitive and easy to use. You browse through a logically cataloged system. You know exactly what you're getting. If something's already checked out, you can wait for a few days.

Video-on-demand, that killer application of communications, will remain a dream.

Learn some arcane commands, tunnel though layers of pointers, and you can perform electronic searches. Often, you'll turn up the trivial, mundane, and obvious. You don't know if you've traversed a complete search or only scratched the surface. Nor can you easily control the costs. Speaking of scratching, a MEDLINE search for parasites told me that most dogs have fleas. Cost: twenty-five dollars.

How do you learn to search for answers on the Internet? There are lots of Internet lectures and information-superhighway seminars, but surprisingly little training. It's hard to learn to navigate the ocean of data without a terminal.

My favorite way to learn the Internet happens on the first of each month—that's when you'll find me enmeshed in the great Internet Hunt.

Instead of crawling around the caves south of Tucson, Rick Gates of the University of Arizona creates a monthly list of questions. He posts them to the net, and competitors from around the world try to answer 'em. It's a free-for-all, spanning archives, net news, information servers, and Knowbots, whatever they are.

The Internet Hunt picks from a potpourri of trivia, all available online. Some questions are simple: what's the president's e-mail address? Others take a bit more digging: where was the most recent Canadian earthquake? What's the official advice for travelers going to Belize? How many animals show up in Lewis Carroll's *Alice's Adventures in Wonderland?*

When the quiz master asked how much it costs to join the fencing club at the University of Tasmania, one guy used the gopher system in Pisa, Italy, to find a pointer into an Australian information service that returned the result: twelve dollars for students, forty-five for nonstudents.

Here's the cool thing: you get points for describing your Internet tools and search strategy, but zero points for the correct answer. Kinda like stashing a dollar bill in a library book and giving clues to your students. All voluntary, entirely unfunded. Write to rgates@locust.cic.net for more info.

So don't bother me on the first of the month. From the moon-drenched shores of San Francisco Bay, I'll be sniffing out answers, matching wits with the huntmeisters of the Internet.

You don't own something unless you can find it. Accordingly, information isn't yours unless you can retrieve it. An online library without a catalog isn't much good—it may take a day to find the book you want. And if you don't remember the author or title, the book might as well be stashed in a vault on Jupiter's third moon, for all your chances of discovering it.

There's a shortcut around cataloging problems: go browse the stacks. You walk to the right area of the library and eyeball the shelves. It's everyone's favorite way to find books, and it's the one method denied to us by computer searches. When you browse, you create your own searching technique.

Sure, every computerized library system has a browse feature, one that's supposed to let you list books with similar subjects or other books by the same author. It ain't the same as settling in next to a shelf of books.*

It's serendipity, an important part of research. Walk to a bookshelf and browse. You're likely to find a book close to what you need; there's a good chance that one will have a bibliography to point out other sources. It's not random chance—libraries are built to encourage just this delightful discovery.

Now don't confuse the technology of books with the methods of searching. The guy that invented the bookshelf didn't make libraries useful. Credit that to Mr. Dewey and the generations of librarians that developed and refined the cataloging systems.

There are thousands of information services available on the Internet, ranging from cardiology data to the phone books of the University of Tasmania. Yet I know of no good retrieval system—one that's easy to learn, runs on all systems, covers a wide area, responds quickly, and is available all the time. When I do find it, it'll be out of date in three years and I'll have to relearn all the commands.

How much information can we send across a communications line? What's the fastest modem that we can attach to our computers? 14,400 baud? 28,800? 56,000? Is there a limit?

You'll find the answers in the July 1948 *Bell System Technical Journal:* "The Mathematical Theory of Communication." With neither computer nor Usenet, Claude Shannon invented communications theory.

Written in a subdued tone, this is one of the most important reports of the century. Here's where the word *bit* first appeared meaning binary digit. Every modem, disk-compression program, and fiber-optic line owes its existence to this paper. Just reading his refer-

. . . .

* Even if your library is equipped with those dirty-trick time-toggle switches at the end of each stack. You know, the ones that shut off the lights right when you finally find the missing puzzle piece or long-lost volume. They're like screen savers that shut off your monitor just when you're about to work. Or, just as bad, rolling bookshelves that prevent browsing. Called Spacesavers, they're mechanical analogs to data compression: they slow access while reducing reliability and convenience.

ences sends a shiver down my spine: Nyquist, Pierce, von Neumann, Tukey, Hartley, Wiener, even the great astronomer Chandrasekhar shows up here.

He told us that information is contained in messages. "Frequently the messages have meaning; that is, they refer to . . . some system with certain physical or conceptual entities. These semantic aspects of communication are irrelevant to the engineering problem." Shannon was warning us not to confuse messages with meaning.

Consider the following thirty-eight-byte messages:

- Bet $12 on Bonny the Horse in the 7th.

- Thrice welcome, darling of the spring!

- pnqidMrybgsakApw894kvmdsjW$eifkslekfj.

To a computer, all three messages have equal amounts of information—thirty-eight bytes. A communications theorist might say that the last one holds the most information, since it has the most randomness and is most difficult to compress—that is, it has the highest entropy.

Common sense says otherwise. One of these messages may win a hundred dollars, another is from a poem, the third is a waste of time.

The data hucksters illegitimately apply Shannon's definition of information to our common-sense idea of information.

There's a vast amount of data available over computer networks —far beyond megabytes, gigabytes, or terabytes, it's well into the petabyte region.

Yet how much common-sense information is this? Data isn't information, any more than fifty tons of cement is a skyscraper. A string of bits might represent a draft treaty between two nations, a slice from a rock video, a thousand digits of π, or random noise. Data is just bits and bytes . . . grains of sand without a concrete aggregate. Information has utility. It has meaning.

Most important: information is not knowledge. Back to my central thesis: my computer can access the Swiss molecular-biology archive, yet I still know squat about DNA transcription. Everyone has access to quotes from the New York Stock Exchange, yet who can predict what'll happen tomorrow? And having the latest Jupiter images sure doesn't mean you understand planetary atmospheres. Professor Tomasko, my dissertation adviser, would single me out as living proof.

There's a relationship between data, information, knowledge, understanding, and wisdom.

Our networks are awash in data. A little of it's information. A smidgen* of this shows up as knowledge. Combined with ideas, some of that is actually useful. Mix in experience, context, compassion, discipline, humor, tolerance, and humility, and perhaps knowledge becomes wisdom.

Minds think with ideas, not information. No amount of data, bandwidth, or processing power can substitute for inspired thought.

Dazzled by computers and communications theory, we've been misled into thinking that experience can be broken down into bits and bytes. Those with the most information have the most power.

This is patently false. The Internet, that great digital dumpster, confers not power, not prosperity, not perspicacity.

Vice President Al Gore warned that we must not "divide our society into information haves and have nots." I'm not worried a bit: information is everywhere. You can take as much as you want.

Doesn't worry Charles Osgood, of CBS News, either. "Not all information is good information," he says. "We're already getting so much information, so fast, that it's more than our brains can process, digest, and evaluate."

Will tomorrow's library resemble today's Internet? Without librarians, I find utter disorganization: right next to photographs from the Hubble Space Telescope, I find economic statistics from the state of Maryland.

. . . .

* *1 smidgen = 7.25 trifles.*

Network resources are chaotically scattered; some files are cataloged, others aren't, still others are mislabeled.

Instead of the Dewey decimal system or Library of Congress cataloging, there's an informal reference system called Uniform Record Locators. For example, the Internet poetry archive, maintained by the University of North Carolina, is at http://sunsite.unc.edu/dykki/poetry/milosz/milcov.html.

Works fine until some Tarheel sysop reorganizes their disks. You're left holding a dangling pointer—your file exists somewhere, but good luck finding it. And online information is constantly being moved and reorganized, so few pointers stay valid for long. I started my own personal catalog of useful Uniform Record Locators; after one year, only half still worked. But the poetry section of my neighborhood library? They don't shuffle books around but once a decade.

How should a book's bibliography reference this location? When the record locator changes, the printed reference becomes meaningless. Even if the archive stays put, someone may update the files, confusing anyone looking for the original work.

Libraries have a nifty system for storing books; it's the same one that I use to look 'em up. I'll bet librarians have an instruction list or some kind of cheat sheet. There's a place for every book.

The Internet, however, has no such organization—files are made available at random locations. To search through this chaos, we need smart tools, programs that find resources for us. These tools work after the fact: something's posted to an archive, then an automated cataloging tool discovers it and adds it to a catalog.

These programs don't do a good job of searching, partly because they pay a lot of attention to titles and ignore a file's contents. Then, too, computer tools are great at finding strings of characters. It's much harder to search for meaningful information.

A few months ago, I read an article about the nuttiness of running a day-care center as a business. Where do I turn when I want to dig it up today?

Well, try the Internet. Searching with Veronica for child-care centers turned up plenty, but not the article I needed. Reading postings from misc.kids turned up lots of messages about breast feeding, sex after childbirth, and bad names to give kids (Barbara White won't name her daughter Snow). Still I found no direct reference. After six hours searching for instant gratification, I gave up and biked to my library.

My librarian pointed me to the *Reader's Guide to Periodical Literature.* Bingo. *The Wall Street Journal,* July 21, 1994. They had back issues of the paper, and within fifteen minutes, I left grinning, even after forking over the outrageous, obscene, and usurious photocopy fee of twenty-five cents a page.

Turns out, *The Reader's Guide* is available online. But I have to pay for access—for some reason, the concept that all information should be free hasn't yet reached them.

Hasn't reached the Telebase system either. Glance through their catalog of services for the IQuest reference services. There are maybe eight hundred databases to search, including *Who's Who, Consumer Reports, Magill Survey of Cinema,* and the *Los Angeles Times.* Handy, but expensive: five dollars to scan for one piece of information. It's easy to drop a hundred dollars inside an hour. Public libraries will go under if they offer this service.

In Montgomery County, Maryland, community activists fought hard to restore library hours after a decade of shrinking schedules. Most of them blamed stingy taxpayers.

Allen Hengst, a librarian at the Bethesda Regional Library, is grateful for the activists' support, but sees another villain: the library promoters themselves.

Their "complicity in promoting costly technological fixes—like CD-ROMs—siphons off precious dollars, literally bleeding the libraries dry," Mr Hengst writes in a letter to the editor of the *Washington Post.*

His library spends four thousand dollars for each multimedia PC workstation. "This initial outlay does not cover maintenance costs," he adds. "The operating system for the CD-ROM computer at Bethesda Library was inadvertently deleted this month by a user who pushed the wrong button."

You'll find this librarian answering questions at the information desk, not behind some computer terminal. He wonders whether public library materials will be available in a fair and equitable manner. After a year of watching patrons use the CD-ROM system: "I've yet to witness this resource being used by the poor and deprived for whose benefit we're told it must be made available."

My librarian friends tell me that some of the most popular books are those in Vietnamese, Chinese, Spanish, and Korean. For example, in San Jose's public library, Vietnamese fiction books have been read so often—one more than 120 times—that their covers are falling apart. CD-ROMs and online databases don't address the needs of these people. Librarians do. Longer hours do. More books do.

Indeed, despite the vast resources available on the Internet, I feel quite alone on it. Ask a stupid question of a librarian and she courteously points me to a reference book. Ask the same question on the Usenet and I get flamed.

Searching for obscure information? Dig through the global resources of the network. Find a link to NEXIS or MEDLINE to scan the latest documents (but don't forget to pay!). Run a gopher search and hope that you don't get messages like "bad article number."

If you've got a Mosaic or Lynx browser, you have access to a hypertext system—one that lets you read a document, select a word, and jump to an associated page that uses that word. Hooked into the World Wide Web, you hop from one file to another. You click on the word *Constitution* to see the text of that document. Pick the cute soccer ball graphic to list the latest World Cup scores. Choose a flashing tickertape icon to get a listing of the Dow Jones Industrials.

It turns research into a kind of computer game. But like all computer games, you can only go where the programmer intends— maybe you don't want the text to the American Constitution, but rather that of Peru. And, like automated voice-mail systems, which give you a dozen choices at every level, these systems are impressively frustrating. Sometimes you reach dead ends, other times you traverse circles.

It's easy to make fancy home pages on the World Wide Web. But jumping from one document to another baffles me even more than watching someone channel surf. I'm never certain of my location in a twisty maze of cross-references.

These hypertext documents lack unity: one page may be dense with information, another may be a vacuum. Its advocates speak of nonlinear text—you don't read a straight line of text, but can jump around as you wish. As a result, the author's logic, structure, and reasoning disappear. You get random facts.

The World Wide Web seems well tuned for automated key-word searches. Your computer combs through files, picking out words in titles or text. It feels like you're riding atop the world's finest index. You're not.

Key-word-in-context lists are weak substitutes for a genuine index. Such searches profane the whole idea of research. In their facile expediency, they deliver information too effortlessly to be trustworthy. I know neither the depth nor breadth of the search: what databases did I miss? Would I get different results if I'd capitalized the name?

And real reading is processing the assembled information; getting there is the fun part. Absorbing one highlighted nugget about spherical aberration isn't the same as chugging through a whole page on mirror testing, which tells you a lot less about the design debacle of the Hubble Space Telescope than an entire chapter.

Come to think of it, that's another distasteful thing about computer manuals. They usually have terrible indexes. Tech writers, believers in technology, think that a computer-generated index is good enough. Yep, their programs will flag every occurrence of each important word, but can't tell whether a word shows up as a main point or an aside. Jumbo the Pachyderm won't get indexed under "elephant."

Still frustrated with your information search? I repeat: go to a library. You'll meet a live person who may even help you find an answer. Information from a library is just as free as the online stuff. Except for those outlandish, heinous, and ghastly photocopy fees.

Five months before the comet was due to crash into Jupiter, I began my literature search. I didn't start out with a string of book titles; no, I began with a list of subjects. Jupiter. Comets. Atmospheric physics. Radiative transfer.

I headed over to the University of California in Berkeley and walked into the reference room, the one with the astonishing gold-leafed ceilings and carved-wood murals. Notebook under my arm, I strolled over to the card catalog to do a subject search. Something was missing.

Someone stole the card catalog.

A quick inquiry told me that librarians had conspired to steal my card catalog. They'd replaced it with an invisible database. Instead of fifty beautiful wooden cabinets, I now find two dozen computer terminals. My most important reference tool had disappeared. *Aieeee!*

The reference librarian hushed me. "Don't scream in the library. Besides, everything you need is right here on the computer."

As the blood returned to my face, I listened to her talk about the day of the changeover. Most of the librarians celebrated with a party —no more filing and no more missing cards.

Other libraries, including Harvard, the University of Maryland, and Cornell University, have thrown out their card catalogs, usually with festive celebrations. Novelist Nicholson Baker surveyed hundreds of libraries and told how one shot a gun at their catalog, another talked of a bonfire. By the time you read this, most American card catalogs will have been steamrollered by modernization.

One librarian told me of the morning she spilled a drawer of cards on the floor—took the rest of the day to rearrange. Another spoke of how each special book needed additional information handwritten on its card.

"B-b-b-but that's no reason to destroy the whole card catalog," I stuttered. "My card catalog gives me more guidance than any electronic system."

The reference librarian realized that she had a weirdie on her hands, so she patiently showed me how to use the computer. "It's really quite easy," she said in the same condescending tones that I hear over software help lines. "Just follow the on-screen menu."

Computers are the best way to find out if a book is in the library.

They're terrific for looking up a single book, whether by author or title. Before I head over to the library, I dial in to make sure they've got what I need.

But now I'm doing research on comets and planets and atmospheres. I don't know the titles or authors of these books. For my work, I need subject cross-references. I need the professional guidance that's embedded in a good card catalog. I need the intuitive searching mechanisms of the cards.

As I talked with the librarians, I learned that a few faces were missing from Berkeley's end-of-the-card-catalog party. Some librarians complained of the loss of information—not everything on the cards made it into the computer. Others recognized that computerized searches might not be the best way to do research. They know the value of serendipity—those cards tell you things that no computer can.

For, as the old timers knew all too well, one or two missing cards will mean incomplete searches. Outsiders don't realize that entire missing card catalogs make for vastly less complete research.

After strident objections, Berkeley's card catalog was saved—but not by much. Today, the automation promoters will tell you that you need an appointment to visit it in a warehouse, five miles off campus.

Why would anyone be unhappy with online catalogs? Librarians will tell you that when the library changes from cards to computer, they meticulously scan in all the information, so that nothing's missed. The computer has everything from the card catalog, as well as immediate access. All the information's now in a system that's much more efficient and easier to use.

Not so! Computerized library catalogs don't perform the same function as card catalogs. They're really listings of what's on the bookshelves—an inventory of books by title and author.

If you walk into a library already knowing the book title, you're hunky-dory. Looking for *The Astronomical Scrapbook?* Want the latest murder mystery by Sue Grafton? Head right for that computer terminal, buddy.

Things aren't so sweet for those unsure of exactly what book they want. Many people research whole topics, like the Pullman Strike of

1894, or Robert Moog's first music synthesizer. They need subject listings and cross-references. Computer catalogs are especially stingy here—each book gets only a few subject listings. And those subjects aren't cross-indexed—you can't jump from book to book, like you could with a card catalog.

Others walk into a library with a broad idea of where they're headed, but need to narrow their searches. Suppose you're working on Victorian architecture but haven't decided which area. The computer will overflow—there are way too many entries on that subject. Browse the card catalog, though, and you may settle on Victorian chimney decorations. Again, because the electronic catalog points to individual books, rather than whole concepts, the computer lets you down.

Then, for some researchers, browsing and shelf gleaning work far better than directed computerized searches. I'm one of those primitives; I paw through the index cards to get a feel for what's in the collection and to point me in new directions. For inspiration.

I know that a card catalog isn't sexy—it doesn't have a nifty name like Gladis or Melvyl or Hollis. Nor does it emblematically show the world that this library is poised on the cutting edge of technology (sounds painful, doesn't it?). Rather, the card catalog is the mute legacy of generations of competent librarians who cared about their local collections.

Professor Beverly Lynch of UCLA and past president of the American Library Association reminds me that the central concept of library science was the selection of materials for the local collection. After automation came along, *resource sharing* became the watchword.

In other words, you should no longer expect to find a collection tailored to the needs of your area. Instead, computers turn every library into a piece of a giant puzzle. You can buy wallpaper with book patterns—row after row of bookbindings. Television studios use it to create the illusion that they have lots of reference books. Maybe libraries ought to buy wallpaper with patterns of computer terminals, so that visitors will think they're high-tech.

Computerized card catalogs don't behave the way I expect. I ask for a listing of books about comets and Jupiter, and get the reply

"622 records retrieved by your search." I want a few books, not a truckload.

Without Boolean commands, computerized subject searches can't discriminate between Saturn the planet, Saturn the god, and Saturn the car. So researchers learn a logic system to express their needs—library patrons become computer programmers.

On the green screen, I see only a listing, one book at a time. It's linear, without the possibility of a chance discovery. There's nothing to touch. No inspiration. That three-by-five card is concrete. Or at least paper.

Compare the computer screen to the card catalog's beautiful wooden cabinetry. Perfect cubbyholes and little drawers that smell like oak, not like plastic and ozone. All those little drawers . . . they make me want to store socks in 'em. Better yet, make one whole wall of my bedroom into a card catalog, with a pair of socks in each drawer.

With all those socks in those little drawers, how would I search the stacks? Guess I'd have to dial in over the computer. No question —the computer's the right way to see if a book's in the library. Works any time of day or night, too.

But for inspiration, for serendipity, for feeling connected to other researchers, I'll take the cards. If you ever hear of a library about to burn a card catalog, give 'em hell.

While you're at the library, search for professional commentary on computerized card catalogs. Sure enough, you'll find plenty of technical reports praising the wizard machines. None of the library journals warn against tossing out the catalogs. The big-name librarians are all on board; inevitably, they're administrators who never meet library patrons at the main desk.

With a Ph.D. in computer science, Clifford Lynch is the director of library automation for the University of California, Berkeley. His department replaces card catalogs with computers.

"There's a lot of foolishness written about online catalogs," Dr. Lynch wrote to me. "Some of it comes down to sentimental arguments about the joys of card catalogs."

Guess I am sentimental. And I do find joy in card catalogs, too.

I'm not the only one. Nicholson Baker, writing in *The New Yorker,* recognizes the card catalog as an important research tool, being discarded by libraries across the country. According to him, throwing away these catalogs is a paroxysm of shortsightedness and anti-intellectualism.

He's damned right. I'd add cheapness too: online systems are always cited as a cost savings for libraries. However, that money goes into terminals and programmers instead of books, cabinets, and librarians.

Electronic catalogs won't let you do reasonable things. If you ask to browse through the subject looking for books on folklore, the computer responds, "Peak Load Restriction: Your search consists of a common word which would slow down the system. During peak load periods, your search cannot be completed."

No card catalog ever spoke to me this way. As Mr. Baker points out, this request is utterly reasonable, especially from novice users. Yet the system is designed to help only the advanced—those who can speak the language of the online catalog system.

Next time you're in Chicago, check out their public library's computerized catalog system. If a book isn't owned by a branch library, the damn computer won't tell you the call number. This means you can't walk over to the shelf where it *would* be and see if there's a nearby book covering a similar topic. *Grrr.*

Even though I constantly use computers, I still have to figure out how to look up a book. I forget the commands between library visits. Every library has a different online system; my own library has three, all mutually incompatible. Their terminals have sticky keys. At the very moment I need the command menu, it's scrolled off the top of the screen. I need help.

So do kids. Leslie Edmonds of the Downers Grove Public Library in Illinois asked fourth-, sixth-, and eighth-graders to look up things like *Fire Stations, Insects—Poetry, Octopus Pie,* and *The Curse of the Blue Figurine.* She found that two thirds of children's card-catalog searches were successful, but only 18 percent of their online searches were. None of the fourth-graders used the computerized system successfully.

I can't blame 'em. Computer jocks can't figure out these systems.

Libraries, strapped for cash, have spent many millions of dollars developing and maintaining computerized card catalogs. They claim it's efficient—after all, librarians no longer have to add new cards to those little filing cabinets. I'll bet that on the whole, libraries have lost money on the deal. And with fewer books on the shelves, they'll slowly lose the support of their patrons.

Still, someone out there thinks it's important that children have online access to the computerized catalog of the Library of Congress. Never mind that they'd have to visit Washington to read the books.

At the same time that librarians are throwing out card catalogs and replacing them with computerized shelf lists, libraries are canceling evening hours. What's wrong with this picture?

It's July 19, 1994. Comet Shoemaker-Levy 9 has just splattered into Jupiter, and every planetary scientist is watching. The Hubble Space Telescope, recently repaired, is beaming down images that make me salivate. Twenty major observatories have aimed electronic detectors at the planet. I'm watching all this from behind my workstation.

Me, I'm still modeling the atmosphere of Jupiter. I wonder how quickly energy dissipates from the impact. With a mathematical description of Jupiter's atmosphere in my computer, I'm set to calculate the effects of the comet. By knowing how much energy is emitted in the infrared and visible, I may be able to furthur constrain the planet's cloud structure.

A nice piece of work—give me some pictures of the comet's impact, and I'll start turning the crank. There's a bit of time pressure . . . a dozen other theoretical astronomers are playing with the same problem. I'd like to win the race. All I need are those images.

I log on and *ftp* to the file server at the Space Telescope Science Institute. Within ten seconds, it oughtta respond with its usual cheery greeting: "Login please." I'll type anonymous, and it'll give me limited privileges to download files.

A minute passes. Not a peep from my trusty network. Maybe the computer's down. I back out of *ftp* and check the computer with *ping*.

Ping is a nifty Unix utility to check for a slow network. It sends a small packet across the net, and the distant computer bounces it back. The packet itself has a time stamp—when it returns, my computer calculates the round-trip delay. In short, I'm timing echoes across an electronic chasm.

> ping ftp.stsci.edu	*I start sending packets*
PING MARVEL.STSCI.EDU: 56 data bytes	*Here goes the first one*
64 bytes from 130.167.1.125: time=964 ms	*reply took almost a second*
Timed out waiting for echo reply	*that packet was lost*
64 bytes from 130.167.1.125: time=583 ms	*half a second reply*
Timed out waiting for echo reply	*another lost packet*
Timed out waiting for echo reply	*another gone to the wind*
64 bytes from 130.167.1.125: time=617 ms	*a bit over a half second*
64 bytes from 130.167.1.125: time=994 ms	*almost a second delay*

Uh-oh. Long delays here. Packets ought to take a tenth of a second to cross the net. I'm seeing five or ten times that long. Lost packets as well. Other servers are corked up too: Jet Propulsion Labs, Center for Astrophysics, NASA's Goddard Spaceflight Center.

Because everyone and his pet Pekinese wants those pictures. There's only a few thousand astronomers in the world, yet the publicity surrounding this event invites a hundred thousand file transfers. Making things worse, each picture is b-i-i-i-g-g-g. A quarter megabyte or more.

While I'm waiting for the astronomy data to percolate through clogged arteries, I reach into my jar of chocolate-chip cookies and wonder: how come I can't get those images now? What needs to be overhauled?

Word travels fast when there's good stuff on the astronomy

archive or the MTV file server. The network is designed to handle average loads; when everyone wants files from one place, well, everything slows down.

Solution: add more bandwidth to the backbone. Install faster fiber-optic links. Build more file servers. Double the bandwidth, and files zip twice as fast. A nice technical patch.

That's what computer jocks are proposing. David Wasley, director of network services at the University of California at Berkeley, says, "Congestion is going to happen, and there's no way to avoid it. We simply have to find ways of adding capacity as needed."

This will cure the Internet bandwidth problem in exactly the same way that building more highways will solve traffic congestion. The number of bytes or cars traveling across the continent increases.

Have we learned nothing from the past five decades of highway construction? Every roadway has been built explicitly to lessen traffic, yet today's traffic jams are worse than ever.

Highway construction draws more cars onto the road. It also promotes a gasoline-intensive world that makes living in the burbs a viable lifestyle and commuting to work an honorable time-sink. Arguably, it's responsible for devastating our railroads, trolleys, and cities, not to mention the meadows and forests that end up under asphalt. It has forced us to rely on foreign oil, virtually eliminated blacksmithing as a profession, caused lots more litter, and resulted in the blossoming and later eradication of Burma-Shave signs. Oops, I meant to just say that making more roads brings more cars onto them.

In the same way, I doubt that adding bandwidth to the Internet will solve future bandwidth crunches. Indeed, we'll only find more people trolling the net, trucking larger files across the wires.

It's a curiosity of the Internet that congestion causes delays. A differently designed system might let the data through quickly, but degrade the quality. We'd get fast data, but it'd have mistakes.

The secret is that the Internet is a connectionless network. There are no end-to-end circuits. Your message is broken into packets, and each one finds its own path to the destination, routed by switches along the way.

It feels like there's a pipeline between your computer and mine, but each packet might take twenty or thirty hops. Indeed, different packets from one file transfer might take different paths.

This is dynamic routing; a message goes out as many packets, and each of them finds the best pathway. If an intermediate computer crashes, the message will still get through, because the originating computer will eventually resend the packet.

Packets from lots of people can share a single cable. To send a message to England, I don't need to rent a cable from Berkeley to London.

And this all works fine until the system gets crowded.

When the network is overloaded, there's little that can be done. The network can delay packets, which makes it seem slow. Or switches can simply drop packets, which cause computers to resend them. Either way, the Internet feels slow.

It's the tragedy of the commons. When there's only a few villagers setting their cows out to pasture, everything works fine, and the community thrives. With free grazing, each individual naturally puts out plenty of cows. Eventually, the pasture turns to overgrazed mud, and everyone loses.

Same thing happened to the cod fisheries off the coast of Newfoundland and the clear air of Los Angeles. No one individual is at fault; rather, it's that we're not charged for how much we use a limited resource.

Adding more bandwidth, just like expanding the village commons, won't solve the problem. Big scientific problems, like volume visualization and hydrodynamics modeling, can eat gigabytes per second. Even simple stuff, like showing moving images and voices over the Internet, can swallow many megabytes per second.

And there are limits to how fast you can move data. Even if you create superfast links, the speeds of the trunk lines will exceed the speeds of the switches. A computer must read the destination address of every packet whenever it reaches a node. With a dozen or more nodes between me and you, this switching delay limits how fast data travels. We're accustomed to communication links being the bottleneck; soon it will be the switching system itself. In the next decade, network traffic jams will be caused as much by the interchanges as by the thoroughfares.

If every user expects the kind of service that's being touted by today's Internet hustlers, a gigabyte per second bandwidth won't be enough.

After all, information is free on the Internet. There's no cost involved in sending e-mail, searching for data, or transferring files.

Hogwash. Information isn't free. Never was. Somebody paid for that magazine at my front door. And it's not just the cost of the paper—those writers, editors, and printers didn't work for free.

And information over the Internet isn't free, either. Somebody paid for that green Ethernet cable running up my wall, the high-speed packet router, the fiber-optic links, and the gigabytes of disk space.

Today's Internet conveys the illusion of a zero-cost network. I pay nothing to transfer a file during the middle of the night. Same price during the middle of the day. Same price to send a paragraph of e-mail or a book-length dissertation. Same price to send a message across town or across the ocean. Without a working accounting system, Internet messages cost about the same as air.

This inverted economics discourages efficient network use. The fanciest programs, like Mosaic, consume lots of bandwidth simply to show pretty background pictures. Interactive Telnet sessions require that a full packet be sent across the net with every key tapped. Samples of rock music consume far more community resources than a twenty-word e-mail message.

I contend that as long as network pricing doesn't reflect costs, the Internet will be abused. There's plenty of ways to charge for service. Most commercial services simply charge for online time. I pay the same cost whether I'm logged in and reading rec.humor.funny's joke of the day, or if I'm transferring a huge Photoshop file.

Because people aren't charged for transferring files across the Internet, computer jocks download images from network servers like alt.binaries.pictures.erotica. These files are big, and moving them around costs money. It would be far cheaper to just buy a pornographic magazine—except that users aren't billed for Internet use.

Why not charge by the number of bytes sent or the distance of the connection? New Zealand and Chile already have some kind of usage-based billing, but the Internet fundamentally wasn't designed to handle this kind of bookkeeping. It'll require a serious change in how the network is run.

Jeffrey MacKie-Mason and Hal Varian of the University of Michigan propose auctioning resources: when you send a message, you include the price you're willing to pay to get a fast response. The network routers compare your bid against those of others, and route the highest bidder's traffic first.

But none of these billing proposals is popular among net surfers. When services cost money, they feel boxed in. They don't want to pay to use information.

Maybe I've got it wrong . . . perhaps it's OK to charge to *distribute* information, but not for the information itself.

Well, information over the phone isn't free, even ignoring the cost of the connection. Someone gives of their time and expertise. Five minutes with an attorney costs money, even though legal libraries are open to the public.

A dozen programmers create a word processor . . . they sweat for a year, recasting functions and chasing bugs. The castle they've built of bits is just a single file. This is information, too . . . hardly free.

Who owns that information, anyways? Simply because you own a book or a CD-ROM doesn't mean that you have the right to duplicate it or republish it.

Yet I've listened to the Free Software Foundation argue that programs are fundamentally different from books, because you read and enjoy the latter, the former is only used. They say that copyrights harm society by preventing the free flow of information.

Information should be free. I hear this argument from those who duplicate software or break into computers. It's techno-Marxism—abolish private property and we'll all be happy.

Perhaps in some dreamworld, all information—books, programs, databases, videotapes, recordings, tomorrow's newspaper—will be freely distributed to everyone. We won't have to pay anyone to catalog this info-utopia, either. When you want something, just ask for it, and an expert system will deliver it.

I'm still chewing on chocolate-chip cookies when I realize that an hour's passed by, and I still can't get my images of Jupiter. Strange: I don't really taste food while online. My keyboard gets greasy but I'm not sure how many cookies I've consumed. The computer's stolen the best part of eating.

For ten years, White Sands Missile Range ran the most important archive on the Internet: the SIMTEL software library. This library stored gigabytes of public-domain programs for mainframes, personal computers, and everything in between. When I needed a program, I'd first scan SIMTEL.

Keeping this organized, pruned, and indexed took three full-time staff members. Archiving information isn't passive and trivial —they needed to continually scan for viruses, duplicates, and obsolete programs. They had to store documentation alongside programs and make catalogs of program descriptions. Some of this they automated, the rest, well, it took some sharp archivists.

These guys wrote no code, received no thanks, and constantly had to justify their work to bigwig ignorami. They worked for the good of the community, as does every librarian, whether checking books or cataloging software.

Came the budget crunch, and White Sands felt the squeeze. The SIMTEL archive contributed zilch to the missile base; no, it was for the general good of the community. Three petition drives over the Internet, phone calls and e-mail to the Pentagon, all failed to save this library. Today, if you're looking for an obscure piece of software, well, I'm sorry to tell you that the Internet's finest archive is now just a memory.

But SIMTEL is not why I can't get those Jupiter images tonight. I'm down to my penultimate cookie when the cursor on my screen flashes. It's not just a slow network: my home computer's been disconnected for ten minutes. After waiting two hours without hearing me type, my Berkeley computer logged me off.

The advancement of astrophysics won't be hurt by a two-hour delay—it'll take, oh, a couple of months to analyze the Jupiter data. But there you have it—the Internet during a crunch. Not a good sign for a system that's touted as an emergency service to get the word out during natural disasters.

The last San Francisco earthquake, in 1989, showed the Internet working just peachy in passing traffic. But then, most homes didn't lose electricity. And the local phone system kept working, so network messages made it through, albeit slowly. That's because the Internet routes packets around faults. The system can't guarantee delivery, but it tries its best.

But I'm not so sure about the next disaster. Few Internet computers have emergency power supplies to keep them running for hours—nobody requires that service providers have backup generators.

Then, too, data flows along the same routes as telephone traffic— if one's cut, the other will be dead, too, although the Internet has the advantage of more robust rerouting capabilities.

Wait a second. During an earthquake or flood, my home computer will be worthless. Electricity's the first utility to fail, followed quickly by the telephone. I'd need a laptop computer linked over a cellular phone modem. Cell phones will probably be clogged, too.

Anyways, most emergencies require motion and muscle, not electronic cogitation. When the Hayward fault slips and my side of Berkeley slides into San Francisco Bay, the essential communications will happen over walkie-talkies and ham radio, not the net.

But then, what's essential? My astronomy research isn't. That SIMTEL software archive wasn't. Maybe libraries aren't.

Visit your local library and then tell me why libraries are desperate for funding. I can't understand it—these are our number one community institutions for information. Since we keep hearing that this is the information age, wouldn't you think they'd be a political top-priority—the center of every neighborhood, where people go for the latest news?

And that's just what's happening. Libraries are becoming the place for online access. In Cleveland, Los Angeles, and Victoria, British Columbia, local libraries already provide free public Internet links. Yowsa—these Free-net systems reach into real neighborhoods.

Still other libraries have developed local bulletin boards, where real community issues get aired. National issues fade into the background next to arguments over speed bumps, garbage pickup, and parking meters. Here's where electronic communities merge with real neighborhoods—a mix of libraries, amateur computerists, and backyard politics. Naturally, they're underfunded; but one day, the people funding information superhighways will realize that the real action's in the alleys and backroads.

And if there's one thing librarians do know how to do, it's catalog things. They've got centuries of experience in dealing with books about weird topics. So answer me this: how come they're not consulted right in the beginning of the design of most databases?

The global Usenet is a good example of the confusion that happens in the absence of librarians. It's the weirdest way to organize information.

Unlike Gaul, the Usenet is divided into eight main parts: computing, science, recreation, news, society, talk, miscellaneous, and alternative. The first three network groups are easy—you'll find comp.graphics.animation or rec.sport.rugby. The news section is about the Usenet itself: topics for news administration, policy issues, and statistical listings.

That divides the rest of the world into four groups: society, talk, miscellaneous, and alternative. The society newsgroups concentrate on cultural and religious arguments—fights between the Armenians and Turks or the Taiwanese and Chinese. Here too is soc.singles, where people post messages about singles get-togethers. The talk newsgroups are for political, religious, and philosophical spoutings. The alternative area is wide open for anyone to create forums to discuss any subject.

A curious way to divide the entire range of human interaction. One that works well, so long as most users are interested in computing science, engineering, and recreation. While there are thousands of newsgroups devoted to computing, there's surprisingly few aimed at the humanities. Pick a topic, and it's unlikely that it's covered on the Usenet. Want to discuss the business of growing bananas? Well, it doesn't belong in any of the groups, except miscellaneous.

I mention this only because it's obvious that no librarian would ever develop such a freaky, byzantine system. I'll bet some computer jock wrote down a list of things he considered important while riding the bus. He created this system that afternoon, and, well, that's what we'll have to live with for the next hundred years. Banana growers find themselves in the same category as the disabled, home-owners, and real estate investors: miscellaneous.

New Internet users often blame themselves for not being able to find information: "Oh it must be my limited understanding. If only I thought in a more connected way, I'd be able to find what I'm looking for." They don't realize the disorganization of the network is the root of their troubles.

As computers invade libraries, librarians spend a lot of time learning how to operate them. Next time you need your library card renewed and you wonder where the librarian is hiding, check to see if he's taking a class in how to access some database.

Pause for a moment to remember Eratosthenes. You probably remember him as the Greek astronomer who first surveyed the earth's size. Around 200 B.C., on the first day of summer, he noticed that the noon sun fell straight down a well in Syene, Egypt, yet came down at 7 degrees from the vertical in Alexandria. From this ratio, and the distance between the cities, he measured the size of the earth.

He was also the mathematician who invented a way to search for prime numbers by simply counting. Write down the odd numbers from three upward, then strike every third number after three, every fifth after five, every seventh after seven, and so on. What's left are the primes. The Sieve of Eratosthenes finds primes without division or factoring.

Wonderful experiments carried out with neither computer nor network. But he had a far more powerful tool at his disposal. Eratosthenes was the chief librarian of the library of Alexandria.

This city was home to the great lighthouse at Pharos, one of the seven wonders of the ancient world. Oh, but think of the library—it's the real monument that shone through the centuries.

King Ptolemy the First sent messages to all the sovereigns and governors of the known world asking for works by anyone—"poets and prose-writers, and all the others too." Any books on board ships passing through the harbor would be confiscated and copied, the copies going back on board.

This collection of five hundred thousand scrolls marked the apogee of Hellenic Greece. Ptolemy Philadelphus would hold symposia, where he quizzed the greatest sages of the day: "How can the kingdom be preserved?" "In legal proceedings, how can one win the assent of people who fail to see the truth?" "How can one stay on good terms with one's wife?" and "How should one employ one's leisure?"

A Jewish scholar, unaware that his questioner owned all the books in the world, answered this last query: "Above all, you should read."

Now this hasn't much to do with computers or networks, except for what happened nine hundred years later. When Amrou ibn al-As raised the flag of Mohammed above the walls of Alexandria, he asked the Caliph Omar what to do with the Library. Sadly, the response read: "If the books are in accordance with the book of Allah, we may do without them, for the book of Allah more than suffices. If they are not in accordance, then there is no need to preserve them."

They took six months to burn those books, using them to heat water for the public baths.

Imagine you could go back in time and save the library of Alexandria. Let's say there's a half-million volumes. They're cylindrical scrolls, so they don't pack tightly. Maybe you could fit a couple thousand into a big yellow moving truck.

So you phone Ryder Truck Rental, round up three hundred vehicles, and drive them through a time warp to the Nile Delta, 50 B.C. The convoy loads up with books and escapes into the desert, spiriting the books away before any mob can reach the doors of the library, well in advance of Julius Caesar or Caliph Omar.

Here, two millennia later, knowledge that would otherwise be destroyed becomes a treasure for today's scholars and historians. We could understand the background of Aristotle's thought, re-create the details of daily life in Mesopotamia, or read sequels to Homeric epics *(The Iliad Part III: Revenge of the Trojan Horse)*. And amazingly enough, we'd still be able to read them. If only the same were true for my old eight-inch CP/M floppies.

But this is missing the most important part: the books' real value is as a part of a functioning library at the heart of the ancient world. Those scrolls belong in Alexandria—along with the librarians —ready to instruct and inspire everyone who came in to read.

The missing scrolls should teach us a lesson today: when we don't protect our treasures, the loss echoes for ages.

But that's not how our public libraries will end.

No, I don't worry about the bookless library, an efficient, money-saving edifice that's utterly empty, housing only shiny banks of modems, disk drives, and books that talk to each other. A place without visitors, children's story hours, or librarians.

Nor will our books end up warming our bathwater or carefully scanned into a six-inch cubic monolithium-fluoride crystal.

Instead, I suspect computers will deviously chew away at libraries from the inside. They'll eat up book budgets and require librarians that are more comfortable with computers than with children and scholars. Libraries will become adept at supplying the public with fast, low-quality information.

The result won't be a library without books—it'll be a library without value.

TWELVE

*Where the Author Considers Bulletin
Boards, User Groups, and Reexamines
His Modem Settings*

Want to set up your own bulletin board? Likely, you already have everything you need. A small bulletin board uses the same computer, modem, and phone line that you use to call into a network. Get a copy of the right software, publicize your phone number, and you're off.

Friends program their computers to dial your phone, the two modems shake hands, and they start conversations, upload messages, and exchange shareware. A wonderfully simple way to spread the good word, organize for a cause, or pick up a few rumors. An electronic watering hole.

Or maybe you're tired of reading the same old newsgroups over the Usenet. To start a new group, you'd have to get the approval of a hundred or more others—a tough hurdle. So you compile a few friends' e-mail addresses and start a mailing list. Whenever someone sends mail to you, your computer forwards it to everyone on the list. At once, you're an information source, a conference center, a publisher, and a junk mailer.

There are still other ways to get the word out. Put your message in a file server, so others can download it from the Internet or a commercial service. Send data from your modem to a friend's. Drop a disk into the mail. Or just pick up the telephone.

There's an Internet mailing list to swap crochet designs. At another site, I found a program to help with pattern making. On the newsgroup alt.sewing, I followed a discussion of restoring treadle sewing machines. And several users on rec.crafts.quilting regularly organize block exchanges. The Usenet rec.pets.cats provides a forum for cat lovers. There's even a mailing list that will warn you against going caving with flashlights or crawling through abandoned grain elevators. Great stuff here. I always check in, right after I do something stupid.

From San Juan, Puerto Rico, Sharon Castellanos moderates an online prayer group over CompuServe. Rabbi Kalman Packouz sends a weekly Shabbat Shalom fax to several thousand Jews over the Internet. Jazakallah Khairun and Nauman Mysorewala moderate the soc.religion.islam newsgroup.

At their best, these and other forums give a place to learn about other religions, meet fellow believers, and discuss differing interpretations. At their worst, well, there's plenty of righteous fanaticism and intolerance.

Joe's bulletin board system with a few dial-in ports and a link to the Internet, forms an entity that's never been seen before. Joe lets anyone use his BBS without taking sides. He's only interested in meeting people, catching rumors, or perhaps collecting online connection fees.

Joe's a common carrier, like the telephone company or a trucking firm. His services are available to anyone who'll pay his fees. Like the phone company, Joe doesn't regulate what you say: he doesn't read your mail or filter your comments.

Or does he? Sysops weed out messages they don't approve of—inflammatory insults, profanity, commercial ads. In fact, one of the major headaches in running a bulletin board is scanning uploads for viruses and commercial software.

In addition, common carriers are inevitably taxed, licensed, and strictly regulated—hardly the métier of the kid down the block.

So a bulletin board system isn't really a common carrier: the operators have to watch the content of what they carry.

Then maybe Joe's a publisher—like a newspaper, his bulletin board is a place to post facts and opinions. Authors write articles and Joe distributes them for the public to read. He's an editor, printer, and distributor, all in his spare time. On the edge of the free press, he keeps us informed.

Well, maybe not. Publishers stand behind every story they print. Inaccurate reporting leads to libel lawsuits, so reporters, editors, and authors must submit accurate work. Mistakes show up in court.

Not so for bulletin board operators. They're not held responsible for what goes out over their modem ports—indeed, with hundreds of messages a day, sysops can barely skim what's posted, let alone consider them in light of libel law. Sure, most will cull the obviously inflammatory messages, but, because of sheer volume, they can't possibly check every note. Moreover, a lot of bulletin boards are run by amateurs with no visible means of support. Holding these guys to the standards of publishing would quickly freeze the whole system.

Small-time bulletin boards need both the freedom to publish and protection from lawsuits. It's uncharted legal territory, though courts so far don't appear to hold system operators responsible for what others post to their systems.

There are other ways to look at a bulletin board system. Maybe it's an electronic soapbox—a public place to sound off without worrying about long-lasting effects. Or perhaps it's like a hotel room, where visitors temporarily check in and interact with a local community, all the while expecting a certain amount of privacy.

If a bulletin board is a publishing house, why haven't there been more libel suits? Just glance at the insults and flames posted to the nets—surely someone takes umbrage. And many of the users send and receive these messages from work, often high-tech outfits with deep pockets.

People get away with things on the Usenet that they'd never be able to pull off on the street. Throw a punch during a heated argument and you could get arrested or sued; it's not even necessary to make physical contact. Continually shout abuse at someone and you'll be sued for slander. Write it down and it's libel.

So, with written streams of calumny pouring back and forth across the Usenet for all to see, why aren't more people getting slapped with injunctions and lawsuits?

Maybe most people aren't that sensitive. Some who get flamed simply turn away. Others see the medium as being so unimportant that it's not worth a lawsuit.

I suspect the main reason why we see so few lawsuits is that the network provides an ideal forum for a rebuttal. Whatever someone says against you online, you can reply to within hours, with the same distribution, and to the same audience.

And unlike a newspaper, where a back-page correction lacks the impact of a front-page headline, every Usenet posting carries the same weight. Responses get about the same audience as original comments. There's no need to appeal to a higher court—we're judged by the strengths of our arguments.

Yet lawsuits will come. As long as people can figure out the source, they can go after the guy who posted the message.

But what do we do about anonymous messages? Anyone can post them from some commercial services, like America Online, from amateur bulletin boards, or through special Internet remailers that strip off identifying information.

One solution is to require bulletin boards to be responsible for anonymous users. If you're libeled from an unknown person, go sue the electronic publisher. Should the service require identification, however, the bulletin board would be absolved of liability.

Seems to be a reasonable compromise, though it'll sure discourage anonymous bulletin boards—they'd lose the protection against lawsuits. Probably it won't happen—compromises aren't popular on the Internet.

Electrical engineers speak of signal-to-noise ratio—it's a measure of quality in a communications channel. Compact discs have better s/n than phonograph records; FM radio is better than AM broadcasts.

No place better illustrates this principle than on the Usenet. With its thousands of newsgroups, I have to plow through a vast number of postings before stumbling on one worthwhile notice. I'm shoveling massive amounts of ore in search of a nugget.

As more people post messages to this network, the general noise level increases. In turn, those with something worthwhile to say no longer visit. Gresham's law again: babble drives out dialogue.

Moderated Usenet conferences do quite a bit better, but it's hard to find someone who's willing to put in an hour a day simply to filter out chaff.

Since there are so many postings to the Usenet, and they're so nicely categorized, you'd expect to find answers to well-posed questions.

Rather, it's more like drinking from a firehose. You get plenty wet, but still walk away thirsty. Every day, well over a hundred megabytes of postings flow by—far too much to even skim, let alone read. So you pick and choose.

It's best to follow the entire thread of a conversation before contributing, lest you step on someone's toes. For this reason, you'll find students spending hours a day reading Usenet postings—they're keeping up with a hundred simultaneous conversations. If they don't follow continuously, they may miss a bon mot.

While skimming these messages, you're aware of the vast amount of information passing before your eyes. Charles Kuralt, retired CBS News correspondent, said, "Thanks to the interstate highway system, it's possible to travel across the country without seeing anything. I wonder if the information superhighway will offer a corollary—a dulling impact on our cerebral cortex."

Yes, I get glassy-eyed from reading innumerable postings that have nothing to say—a vast echo canyon, endlessly repeating calls from people who want to hear their own voices.

A question sent yesterday may be answered today and discussed for the rest of the week. Yet in a month, someone else will ask the same question again, and the cycle will repeat.

Suppose only one person in a hundred is crazy. With a million people on the Internet, you can expect to find thousands of nuts. Most of them will leave you in peace. That leaves only a few thousand who want to throw monkey wrenches into the machinery.

These are the morons who post racist and anti-Semitic messages to newsgroups. They're the idiots who spam the net with thousands of identical bulletins. They're the reptiles who infect software with viruses and upload it to an archive. Cloaked by the anonymity of online services, other reprobates harass women on chat lines and e-mail.

In real life, we know how to avoid these creeps. On the network, well, there's no way. They're literally in your face. Writing in *The New Yorker,* John Seabrook told of his shock at reading his first insulting letter. Having received hundreds in my mailbox, my skin's become a bit thicker.

School-yard bullies, now behind keyboards, will attack you for holding an opinion contrary to theirs. Rude individuals take out their aggressions on newcomers, flaming them for minor goofs. It's reminiscent of the intense hostility of drivers in a traffic jam, though even more public.

Still others do their best to vandalize discussions by intentionally posting provocative messages. Pranksters will ask, "Can someone send me that amazing file on how to get the IRS to pay you millions of dollars?" They'll then laugh as dozens of newbies ask for copies and scores of replies pop up saying that there is no such thing. The virtual community is hardly a tolerant and accepting neighborhood.

Post a simple, direct question: "How do I rid my yard of raccoons?" Within a day, you'll get the obvious replies: "With an electric fence." "Use a trap." "Squirt 'em with a hose."

Then comes a next wave of rebuttals: "Electric fences hurt animals." "Raccoons are too smart for traps." "Hoses waste water." Another set of counter-rebuttals becomes more personal: "How can you think of hurting innocent furry creatures?" "How dare you accuse me of wasting water!" "Just stuff the damn thing." And so on.

Within a few days, a flame war has broken out, with a few people personally attacking each other, and others sitting on the side scratching their heads.

The first few dozen times, I smiled, watching arguments over trivia. After a few months, I began wondering whether I was actually learning anything.

Eventually, I got a headache from this virtual cacophony. It's like reading transcripts of a call-in radio show. Today, I've become a Usenet lurker—occasionally reading newsgroups, seldom posting.

These virtual communities seem so alluring because the real ones have pretty much disappeared. But what a weak substitute for a dinner with my neighbors or a caving trip with Jon Gradie.

Where will you find the far end of my modem today? More and more, it's connected to local bulletin boards, an arm's length from the Internet. Often, only a few dozen users meet there—small, friendly get-togethers where I don't mind asking questions. These systems, almost always run by amateurs, specialize in local interests or hobbies. A great place to meet neighbors, get help with a recalcitrant program, or find out what's happening around town. The fun happens here.

Since these bulletin boards are a few miles from home, there are no long-distance phone charges. No user fees, either. And I can meet the gang face-to-face, over coffee or ice cream.

Local bulletin boards fill the void left behind when television and suburbanization killed the neighborhood pubs and cafés. Instead of pretzels and chips, sysops provide shareware to download. Smart operators have learned that a warm welcome guarantees that friends will return.

There's more to your local bulletin board than an electronic watering hole. Over in Berkeley, the Berkeley Macintosh User's Group was formed to compare notes, back when the Mac was just introduced.

Today, BMUG's bulletin board is a place to pick up gossip and compare notes—and not only about computers. There are plenty of local happenings posted, including seminars, street fairs, and picnics.

And user-group meetings . . . aah! A huge computer conference may draw ten thousand attendees; a user-group meeting may have only fifty. But here's the place to get questions answered, meet friends, and listen to rumors of the latest releases. When a vendor stops by to give a talk, or some member chats about how to manage

3-D spreadsheets, I can speak up with questions instead of passively listening.

User groups and bulletin boards, libraries and schools. Every community has 'em—they're a part of every neighborhood. These are the palettes of local color that generate community identity.

Sure, local bulletin boards lack the mystery and status of the global Internet, as well as the awesome volume of data provided by international archives. And some bulletin boards are plenty shady— little more than pirate outposts, places to exchange stolen software or pornography.

Yet, hardy as any weed that can never be completely paved over, novel ideas continue to blossom over bulletin boards. As diverse individuals discover this new medium, I smile to see the uses it's put to. For all my kvetching, I'm all grins to see people pressing the limits and finding new ways to express themselves.

12½

An Embarrassing and Self-referential
Addendum to Chapter 12, Included
Because the Author's Sister Said She'd
Beat Him up if He Didn't

Some of the weirdest discussions take place on the Well. This computer's located in Sausalito, California, and is heavily influenced by the folks who brought you The *Whole Earth Catalog*. People log in from all over, though mostly from around San Francisco.

For some reason, the Well's discussions are a cut above the more pedestrian Usenet. I can't figure out why—its interface is primitive and difficult to navigate. It's not a free service, nor is there universal access. Maybe these serve as crude filters: only the dedicated stay online.

Unlike the Usenet, there's no anonymous posting—everyone's identified. Moreover, the Well places a "host" in charge of each group—they'd never be called censors or cops. When things get out of hand, the hosts pour oil on the virtual waters. In short, the Well is a place of relative tolerance in the networked world.

Here's an extract from an atypical thread on the Well, the Whole Earth 'Lectronic Link. It's about a subject that I know quite well. Notice both the friendly banter, topic drift, and occasional flame. It began on October 17, 1992, in the books conference . . .

> *Topic 484: Ghostwriters and Their Works*
> *By: Kathleen Johnston*
> I finally read The Cuckoo's Egg and found it thoroughly satisfying

as a mystery novel. A beautiful job of writing. Then I realized that Cliff is unlikely to have turned out such a masterpiece on his first and only try.

Who wrote this book? What other ghostwriters have I missed?

17:22 Bryan Higgins:

Just because Cuckoo's Egg is good doesn't mean that Stoll couldn't have written it as his first book. I think the ability to write has more to do with an innate talent than something that's learned by publishing previous books. And who knows how much nonpublished writing he's done. I think your question's a little insulting.

17:46 Kathleen Johnston:

Bryan Higgins, if you can get beyond the insult, please consider what a brilliant formula novel this is. And the two people in the credits who probably ghost for a living.

Perhaps this was heavily edited. But turning the story of a hacker at a monitor into a gripping thriller is beyond the ability of a dedicated astronomer.

17:52 William Calvin:

Yes, but this was a Berkeley astronomer . . .

17:57 Mike Godwin:

Kathleen Cuckoo's Egg was not ghosted. It was edited, of course. But I read Cliff Stoll's unedited prose on a fairly regular basis, and I can attest that (a) he writes well enough to have produced this book, and (b) it's in his writing style.

Since Cliff is himself a WELLbeing, I think it would be nice if you apologized to him.

18:08 Katherine Hardy:

I thought that was quite a jump to a questionable conclusion.

18:19 Kathleen Johnston:

Yup. It was a jump. And it got a terrifically prompt answer to a question that has been nagging me. I certainly won't apologize: I already have heaped praise on him. Marvelous writer. I assume that the structure was edited into a gripping narrative.

It reminds me of Watson's The Double Helix. A first-rate writer turned into a one-time mystery formula.

What is the boundary between ghosting and editing?

19:27 Bryan Higgins:

Why does being an astronomer mean you can't write well? I'm a computer programmer—how well can I write?

19:29 Bryan Higgins:

And I think it was a thriller because that's how Stoll saw it at the time rather than an artifice of the writing. Of course, it's well-written, too.

19:41 Alan Eshleman:

It never once occurred to me that The Cuckoo's Egg was ghosted. Cliff certainly writes entertaining e-mail. Seems to me that he (1) had a great story (2) found his voice, and (3) trusted his editors.

19:46 Kathleen Johnston:

Yes, he trusted his editors. And yes, non-English majors can write. But to get to that level, you need practice. Or good editors. But we probably will never know. Cliff? We're all eyes.

21:02 Kim Serkes:

I must question the assumption that Stoll couldn't possibly have written the book by himself. I can't see any evidence on which to base such an assertion. And who knows what Stoll has "in his trunk," other unpublished manuscripts.

21:50 Kathleen Johnston:

I don't have a problem with ghostwriting or heavy editing. So I'm not making any big judgments about him. I have, however, made a major judgment about the quality of his work.

23:44 Bob Rossney:

Yes, you've judged that it's too good for him to have written. Which is pretty darned insulting.

23:47 Jeanne Devoto:

Good God, Kathleen. You accuse the man of publishing work under his own name that he hasn't written, imply that your conclusion follows because as an astronomer, he can't possibly be a good writer, and you don't understand why perhaps such a statement, with no scintilla of support, let alone proof, might call for an apology? Just perhaps, if one happens to be the anal-retentive type who takes accusations of false authorship seriously?

23:57 Mark Theodoropoulos:

Gads, we'd better get to work finding out who's behind the improbable prose of Isaac Newton and Harlow Shapley.

Sun, Oct. 18, '92 00:10 Bob Rossney:

And that Darwin. Those biologists are notorious nerds.

01:00 Earl Crabb:

So, is there really a Kathleen Johnston, and, if so, who's writing this stuff under her name? Someone really ought to tell her, before this gets out of hand.

09:58 Calton Bolick:

I'm sorry, but I don't think that this elitist nonsense should go unchallenged. As a big fan of The Cuckoo's Egg, I was utterly appalled by Kathleen Johnston's charges. On what did she base her immediate assumption that the book was ghostwritten? The fact that, after all, Stoll is only an astronomer and not a professional writer. Why? Are science nerds automatically assumed incapable of coherent prose and organized narrative? Are only members of the Writers Priesthood allowed that? This reminds me of the old idiotic argument of some scholars that Bacon must have written those plays attributed to Shakespeare, since a commoner like Bill was obviously incapable of such fineness of feeling . . . I think you do owe Cliff an apology. "It's a great book, but Stoll is too dumb to have been the writer" is not what I'd call a compliment, and your fallback ("Okay, he can write sentences but he's obviously incapable of putting them in the proper order") isn't much of an improvement.

10:12 Scott Marley:

I think perhaps Kathleen meant her comment merely to be amusingly catty, not knowing that she was taking aim, not at a total stranger, but at a most respected friend or acquaintance of many of us on the WELL. Perhaps she'll give permission for the hosts to kill this topic, which is giving us all no pleasure and considerable embarrassment.

10:21 William Calvin:

Whoa! Kathleen was complimenting him, in case you didn't notice. I agree with her that the mystery-story adventure quality of Cuckoo's Egg is very good, not the sort of thing that most scientists who write nonfiction books can pull off (including me). Plenty of scientists have, however, done it, especially if they've gotten some good advice or editing. There are rules of fiction that simply are not apparent to most writers of nonfiction, and Cliff seems to have discovered them. Kathleen noticed that, and I certainly did (I'm envious).

10:30 Katherine Hardy:

To me, there's a big difference between criticism of someone's work and saying that a book is too good to have been written by the "purported" author.

11:05 Stewart Brand:

Many people over-imagine what editors do these days. Mostly all they do is make deals. The days of great author/editor partnerships are almost entirely over. Many writers now hire their own editor on the side, since they'll get so little time or talent from their publisher's editor. On The Media Lab I got more good advice on the text from my agent, John Brockman, than from my editor, Dan Frank at Viking, and Dan's one of the good ones.

13:23 Sharon Fisher:

I suppose people think he buys his cookies at Mrs. Field's, too.

13:25 Mike Godwin:

His cookies are so good—an astronomer couldn't possibly have made them.

18:41 Scott Marley:

Kathleen complimented the book. Of Mr. Stoll she said that he couldn't have written it. If that's a compliment, remind me never to ask you what you think of my new shirts.

18:59 Mike Godwin:

Scott, your new shirts made quite an impression.

19:10 Kathleen Johnston:

It appears that there aren't a lot of people who want to talk about ghostwriting here.

It also appears that Scott refuses to read the clarifications of my statements that I have posted elsewhere.

And it appears that the angriest people here insist on ventilating in public, rather than clarifying by e-mail.

By the eighth posting there were no more issues of fact, as far as I can see. And the only person who would have a personal issue with me has not been heard from.

So get real people. What's so upsetting about ghostwriting?

19:25 William Calvin:

What's so upsetting about ghostwriting?

Depends on whether the person is promoting himself/herself with the book, and whether the quality of the writing would misrepresent the intellectual or professional capacities of the person. A ghostwritten book about a screenwriter would trouble me. Ghostwritten books, purporting to be the thoughts of a political candidate, are unethical, in my humble opinion. But most nonfiction books really don't fall into that category, and ghosting there doesn't bother me, especially if it makes the book more readable, more accessible to a wide audience. Ghosting speeches for executives to give at banquets are somewhat misleading, but hardly unethical.

19:47 Scott Underwood:

I am interested in this topic, and it's unfortunate that it got sidetracked. I read Cuckoo's Egg, but I do not know Mr. Stoll and so I found it utterly believable that a popular book was ghosted. In a related vein, finding out that William Safire (I believe) wrote "nattering nabobs of negativism" and that Bush's "thousand points of light" and "kinder, gentler" possibly were grabbed from Dylan Thomas by his speechwriter makes me believe almost anything about writing in general.

What is the dividing line between ghosting and editing? And why are writers the only artists who are microscopically examined before their work is released? Help me with this . . . restore my faith in literature!

Up to now, I'd been unaware of this thread—I may spend a lot of time online, but I sure don't watch every newsgroup. Kathleen Johnston sent me e-mail about this flame war; so around 3 A.M., I log in, and scan the notes. I wonder: how should I reply?

OK, put yourself in my shoes. Realize that there is no way to prove that I wrote *The Cuckoo's Egg*—not having had a chaperone present during the whole process, there's nobody who'll vouch for my authorship.

Should I flame Kathleen Johnston? She's asked for it—practically begging to be shot down. Especially her sideways comments that astronomers can't write. What about Galileo, Newton, and Sagan? A sharp, barbed comment would put her in her place, and score big points with the peanut gallery.

I wrote just such a nastygram, complete with excoriating putdowns. After printing it out, I smiled for a moment, reread the note, and tossed it. In this community, my words are sure to rebound.

Anyways, I'm not angry. Actually, the attention is flattering, and I'm warmed by the comments from friends known and unknown. Pardon me for snickering though—here's a dozen people discussing my work alongside Shakespeare. Yowsa!

How about answering Kathleen's question by telling a story? There's the ticket . . . prove that I wrote the book by my own words. Here's my reply:

> Zooks! Cool problem in authentication.
>
> First, no insult taken (whether intended or not). Several people have asked me if Cuckoo's Egg was ghosted. It isn't. Wasn't heavily edited, either.
>
> Go back to early 1988. Rich Muller, a Berkeley astronomer, suggested that I write a book. "I can't write a book," I told him. "I don't know how to write."
>
> "It's easy," he said, "Just write an outline, a sample chapter, and a bio. Send it to John Brockman. He's a book agent in New York City."
>
> Now, I'd never heard of John Brockman, but I had an extra day or two. I wrote an outline: one paragraph for every chapter. Stuff about networks, operating systems, and cryptography. Then I wrote one full chapter and sent along a paragraph about who I was. Mailed it to New York.
>
> A week later, John Brockman calls from New York. "I can't sell your book," he says. "You've got an interesting story, but you can't write."

That's all he says. No criticism, no suggestions. Oh, he suggested a ghostwriter in the Bay Area.

I call the ghostwriter. He's only interested in money—doesn't care about the story. I don't care about money, and I get the heebie-jeebies when I think about someone else telling my story.

So I return to computing and astronomy. A month goes by. Two months. Three months. A German prosecutor leaks the story. Two days later the New York Times headline reads, "Berkeley Astronomer Cracks Computer Spy Ring."

First person who calls that morning is John Brockman. "Lemme sell your book."

"John, I can't write any better today than I could three months ago."

"Makes no difference. Let me sell your book."

Well, why not? I hang up and summarize this in my diary. "How much should I write a book for?" I ask myself. I won't write it for free. OK: I'll write it for $500, but I'll grinch and moan. For $1000, I'll write it and I won't complain.

Ten hours later, John Brockman calls back. "Sold your book, Cliff. $N,000"

Gleep . . . for that kind of money, I'll write N books. I won't grinch, either.

Well, Doubleday bought the proposal. I had 7 months to finish the book. I dive in, follow my outline, and write the first 5 chapters. Show 'em to my pal, Guy Consolmagno. He's thinking about joining the Jesuits.

Guy's face drops as he reads them. "Cliff, this is terrible. It's all about computers and operating systems and cryptography."

"Exactly. That's what the outline calls for."

"Cliff, don't write about computers. Write about people."

"But it's not about people. This is a book about computers."

"I can't help you, Cliff. Your problem is that you don't know how to write."

But he did help me. Said to get a book on how to write. So I pedaled down to Cody's and looked up the classics: Fowler, Strunk and White, Sir Arthur Quiller-Couch. They were talking to accomplished writers. I couldn't understand them. They said to create memorable passages, full of style and impact. Not much help when I wasn't sure what to say.

Then I found Write to the Point by Bill Stott. What a change! It encouraged me to use the forbidden word, "I." Told me to ask questions. Gave me permission to use dialogue. And short sentences.

For the next five months, I wrote half-time while working at Lawrence Berkeley Laboratory and Harvard-Smithsonian Center for Astrophysics. Mostly, I flipped between my logbook at work and my personal diary from home. There's no embroidery, however, I did slide the dates by a few days, to remove jogs from the story.

My sister Jeannie helped edit as I scribbled. She also wrote part of one chapter (about her chasing after a high school student in Washington) and put a few paragraphs into my mouth. In short, I was loath to write any conclusion to the book. She felt that the book would be incomplete without the main character growing up. Which eventually happened, in a sad way.

My experience is much like Stewart Brand's. My editor at Doubleday, David Gernert, lightly edited the story. He bumped up the technical side of the book, while pulling together threads about life in Berkeley. Today, Rich Muller works on the automated supernova search at LBL. Jeannie just had her third daughter and lives in Oxon Hill, Maryland. And Guy Consolmagno is a Jesuit brother working at the Vatican Observatory.

06:56 Kathleen Johnston:

Thanks for showing up, Cliff. Your delightful posting whets my appetite for more storytelling, so I'll buy your next in cloth.

07:02 William Calvin:

Just natural talent. Welcome, Cliff!

10:06 Howard Rheingold:

If I didn't confess, nobody would know that the ghostwriter Cliff called—an obvious idiot—was me. And he's right. Another book about computers was the last thing I was interested in. I don't do it any more, but when I did ghostwriting, the first and main thing that interested me was the money. Why else should a writer do something like that? It's a paradox. If I had ghostwritten the book, it probably would have sunk like a stone.

10:37 Carrie Lynne Phyliky-Lay:

It was big of you to confess, Howard. It hasn't ruined your image in my eyes.

10:45 Howard Rheingold:

I confessed because I thought "what an idiot!" when Cliff described this mercenary ghostwriter who turned down the opportunity of the century, and then I realized that I happened to know this idiot very well.;-)

14:03 Sharon Fisher:

Great posting, Cliff! Who wrote it for you?

THIRTEEN

A Conclusion, Which Does Not Mention Axolotls

The popular mythos tells us that networks are powerful, global, fast, and inexpensive. It's the place to meet friends and carry on business. There, you'll find entertainment, expertise, and education. In short, it's important to be online.

It ain't necessarily so.

Our networks can be frustrating, expensive, unreliable connections that get in the way of useful work. It is an overpromoted, hollow world, devoid of warmth and human kindness.

The heavily promoted information infrastructure addresses few social needs or business concerns. At the same time, it directly threatens precious parts of our society, including schools, libraries, and social institutions.

No birds sing.

For all the promises of virtual communities, it's more important to live a real life in a real neighborhood.

I began this meditation with a perplexed ambivalence toward computers, networks, and the culture that enshrines them.

At first, I wanted to think about technical issues. But I found myself returning to the same themes: real life and authentic experience mean much more than anything the modem can deliver. The culture of information isn't knowledge. Electronic networks erode important parts of our community.

Computer networks, like cars and televisions, confer a most seductive freedom, the "freedom to." As I step back from the insistent messages beckoning from across my computer, I'm beginning to wonder about a different kind of freedom—call it a "freedom from."

Certainly, few will toss out their computers or back away from their keyboards. Our networks are far too useful, and there's so much available over the modem.

Oh?

It's late on an October evening in Oakland; I smell popcorn in the kitchen.

I'm done meditating.

How do different tools affect writing style? I was curious, so I tried an experiment: to compose this book, I used a pen and paper, a Sears typewriter, and a word processor. The following substitution cryptogram tells which sections I wrote with which tools.

```
5      40 9 62 7 2      7 19 2      56 7 62 9

5 2 56      3 63 62 33 7      7 19 2      17 3

118 2,      9 3 5 24 9 62 3 14      17 3 9 7,

3 4 14      4 3 4 61 5 4 30      5 4      24

62 4 30 19 3 4 14.      7 19 2      24 5 63

9 3 9 21      3 4 14      63 62 30 62 1 2 7

2 9      56 2 17 7 5 62 4 56      17 3 1 2

32 9 62 1      1 21      7 21 67 2 40 9 5 7

2 9.      7 19 2      9 2 56 7      40 3 56

40 62 9 14      67 9 62 17 2 56 56 2 14.


7 62 14 3 21      5 56      19 3 24 24 62 40

2 2 4,      3 4 14      7 19 2      30 9 3 17

208 24 2      56 1 5 24 2 56      3 7      7

19 2      24 62 62 4.
```

Appendix: Not Quite A Bibliography

Remember the race between John Henry and the steam-powered spike driver? Well, here's your chance to prove me wrong. How many of these books can you get on the Internet? How many at your library? Your bookstore? Your computer?

Who Owns Information? by Anne Branscomb. Does your phone number belong to you, the phone company, or the public? What about your address? Your medical records?

The Vanished Library by Luciano Canfora. I cried as I read of the destruction of the library of Alexandria.

The Experts Speak by Christopher Cerf and Victor Navasky. Listen to important people predict the future. All wrong.

Firewalls and Internet Security: Repelling the Wily Hacker by William R. Cheswick and Steven M. Bellovin. An outstanding computer-security book telling lessons learned from trapping a hacker in a computer.

The Internet Guide for New Users by Daniel Dern. A detailed nuts-and-bolts book to bring you on the net. Friendly advice on virtually all aspects of the Internet.

What Computers Still Can't Do: A Critique of Artificial Reason by Hubert L. Dreyfus. The artificial-intelligence cult hates this book. Dreyfus shows how their naive optimism leads to dead ends. Not an easy read.

The Rise of the Expert Company: How Visionary Companies Are Using Artificial Intelligence to Achieve Higher Productivity and Profits by Edward Feigenbaum, Pamela McCorduck, and H. Penny Nii. Big companies will make gobs of money by harnessing expert systems. The Japanese will make a super-fast computer that will leave the rest of the world behind. Uh, sure. Read this book alongside *The Experts Speak.*

Unix Hater's Handbook by Simson Garfinkel, Daniel Weise, and Steven Strassmann. Title says it all.

Endangered Minds by Jane Healy. Think that "Sesame Street" is out to educate? Think again.

Zen and the Art of the Internet by Brendan Kehoe. A delightful tour of the network.

Four Arguments for the Elimination of Television by Jerry Mander. Much of what he says about television applies to computing: it mediates experience, replaces human images with artificial ones, and works against sensory experience. Before flaming me, read this book.

Library Research Models by Thomas Mann. Here's a librarian who knows computers. He'll tell you what you miss when you only rely on the online god. He's paid his dues looking up the most obvious and obscure—in ways that no online system can do.

Plain Magazine, published in Chesterhill, Ohio. About leading a simple, direct life. A refreshing alternative to *Wired, Mondo 2000,* and dozens of other computer journals. No gushing praise for technology here: hand-printed covers on newsprint.

The Cult of Information by Theodore Roszak. A well thought-out treatise pointing out fallacies in information-age thinking.

Acknowledgments

This book grew from scribbled notes on the back of an envelope following a Mexican dinner with Don Alvarez. Thanks to him for ideas and encouragement, not to mention some great enchiladas.

Here's my deep appreciation and warm thoughts to Lisa Kadonaga, friend, geographer, and editor. Despite a most perplexing time juggling graduate school and a heavy teaching load, my pal helped create, organize, and tailor this work.

For services above and beyond the call of duty, I owe my sister Jeannie three cheers, two salutes, and a yellow yo-yo. Her common sense, zany ideas, and editorial insight kept my feet on the ground and pencil to the paper.

I appreciate the generosity of Don Woods, who, in addition to helping create the game of Adventure, kindly allowed me to use an extract of his work. Thanks also to the participants of the Books Conference on The Well, who happily gave me permission to quote them.

For putting me up and putting up with me, I owe thanks to Louis D'Agostino, Janet Alvarez, Karen Anderson, Reva Basch, Gloria Clements, Guy Consolmagno, S.J., Caroline Earhart, Chris Frank, Roberta Friedman, Mike Godwin, Pat Haber, Beverly Lynch, Garry Preneta, Cecilia Preston, John Ramsey, Mendel Sachs, Dan Sack, Stephan Stoll, Jim Thomas, Susan Wolfe, and my family. To each, I also owe a jar of plum jam.

Thanks also to John Brockman as well as the good folks who

swim with the Doubleday Dolphin: David Gernert, Ellen Archer, Janet Hill, Chris Pavone, Kathy Trager, Amy Williams, Renée Zuckerbrot, and Sylvia Coates.

And a burlap sack of thanks to Pat Cregan for warm support, constant patience, gentle suggestions, and a contemplative garden. May her roses bloom as our rose flourishes.

Index